CHARTER OF THE HUDSON'S BAY COMPANY 1783–
IZATION OF THE NORTH WEST COMPANY IN MONTR
NWC BUILDS FORT GIBRALTAR 1811: SELKIRK ACQUI
OF ASSINIBOIA FROM THE HBC JUN 1812: AMERIC
S EN ROUTE TO ATTACK MONTREAL CUT NOR'WEST'S S
NE SEPT 4 1812: MACDONELL FORMALLY PROCLAIMS PO
AS SITE OF RED RIVER SETTLEMENT MID-OCT 1812: SI
ISTS REACH THE FORKS 1813: THE HBC BUILDS FORT DO
AY 1813: COLONISTS RETURN FROM FORT DAER TO PO
AS JAN 8 1814: MACDONELL ISSUES PEMMICAN PR
TION JUN 21–AUG 1814: STROMNESS COLONISTS ARR
FORKS JUN 18 1814: TEMPORARY TRUCE NEGOTIA
EN NWC AND HBC JUN 19 1814: CHIEF GRANDES OREIL
SAULTEAUX ADDRESSES NWC JUL 14 1814: MACDON
NCES PROHIBITION ON THE RUNNING OF BUFFALO W
S JUL 1814: THE NWC'S AGM AT FORT WILLIAM DISCU
EGY VIS A VIS THE SELKIRK COLONY FALL 1814: N
R CAMERON APPOINTS GRANT AND 3 OTHERS CAPTA
E MÉTIS OCT 1814: CAMERON REPUDIATES THE J
OMISE; MACDONELL ORDERS NOR'WESTERS TO QUIT F
LTAR SPRING 1815: GRANT AT FORT GIBRALTAR RAL
ÉTIS JUN 1815: CAMERON SENDS FOR MÉTIS AND FR
O ATTACK COLONY JUN 11 1815: COLONY IS DESTROY
NELL SURRENDERS, COLONISTS LEAVE FOR UPPER CAN
1815: ARTICLES OF AGREEMENT ENTERED INTO BETW
AND HBC RE. DISPERSAL OF COLONY OCT 13 1815: CH
VISITS SETTLEMENT MAR 1816: CAMERON NAMES GR
N-GENERAL OF ALL THE HALF-BREEDS MAR 17 1816:
N SEIZES FORT GIBRALTAR APR 1816: SETTL
ORT DAER; METIS GATHER AT FOR
'S COMMAND MAY 8 1816: GRAN
OF THE HBC AND SEIZES CARGO JU
NY CAPTURE BRANDON HOUSE AN
JUN 11 1816: SEMPLE DESTROYS F GIBRALTAR
6: MÉTIS FORCES REACH PORTAGE LA PRAIRIE JUN
BATTLE OF SEVEN OAKS JUN 20 1816: SURVIVING
ABANDON COLONY FOR JACK RIVER AUG 13 1816: SELK
TS NOR'WESTERS AT FORT WILLIAM JUL 1 1817: SELK
5 SAULTEAUX AND CREE CHIEFS INCLUDING PEGUIS
Y JUN 30 1818: COLTMAN SUBMITS HIS REPORT OCTO
TRIALS RELATING TO CHARGES AGAINST BOTH SELK
HE NWC OPEN MAR 26 1821: HBC AND NWC MER

THE SEVEN OAKS READER

the

SEVEN OAKS

READER

Myrna Kostash

Foreword by Heather Devine

NeWest Press

Library and Archives Canada Cataloguing in Publication

The Seven Oaks reader / edited and with a preface by Myrna Kostash.

Issued in print and electronic formats.
ISBN 978-1-926455-53-2 (paperback).
ISBN 978-1-926455-54-9 (epub).
ISBN 978-1-926455-55-6 (mobi)

1. Seven Oaks, Battle of, Man., 1816.
2. Fur trade — Manitoba — History.
3. Manitoba — History — 19th century.
I. Kostash, Myrna, editor, writer of preface

FC3212.4.S48 2015   971.27'4301   C2015-906615-8
                                               C2015-906616-6

Editor: Don Kerr
Index: Judy Dunlop
Book design: Natalie Olsen, Kisscut Design
Author photo: Arete Edmunds, ArtLine Photography

NeWest Press acknowledges the support of the Canada Council for the Arts the Alberta Foundation for the Arts, and the Edmonton Arts Council for support of our publishing program. This project is funded in part by the Government of Canada.

#201, 8540 – 109 Street
Edmonton, Alberta T6G 1E6
780.432.9427
NEWEST PRESS   www.newestpress.com

No bison were harmed in the making of this book.
Printed and bound in Canada
1 2 3 4 5   18 17 16

CONTENTS

FOREWORD

The Battle of Seven Oaks . . . or, How My Ancestral Uncle Got Arrested, and How My 5th Great Grandfather Lied on the Witness Stand to Get Him Out of Trouble

As a descendant of some of the participants in this notorious event, *and* as a professional historian of Canadian Native history, I ask myself what approach I should take to welcoming the reader to this most recent, and truly unique, narrative of the Seven Oaks saga.

One of my ancestral fifth – great – grandfathers was a Canadien freeman named Antoine Peltier dit Assiniboine. Apparently in the service of the North West Company during the Seven Oaks crisis, he married a Native woman, Marguerite Sauteaux, *à la façon du pays*. Her son, Pierre "Bostonnais" Pangman, grew to be one of the Métis 'chefs' at Red River, and was arrested for his activities against the Hudson's Bay Company. His stepfather Antoine Peltier dit Assiniboine was called as a witness in the Selkirk Trials, and I have read the trial transcripts prompting me to carry out a more detailed contextual study of the Battle of Seven Oaks, with particular emphasis on the familial links among the participants.

What Myrna Kostash has accomplished in *The Frog Lake Reader* and *The Seven Oaks Reader* is not merely a reinterpretation of historical facts. Instead she has deconstructed, reordered, and supplemented the existing historical narratives in order to permit "an examination of the meaning of how historical events get interpreted and re-interpreted over the years." She has forced readers to interrogate the relative validity of the existing versions of the Seven Oaks story by breaking apart each separate narrative into discrete snippets of information, not unlike pieces of a storyboard. She then sorts these isolated narrative remnants into groups according to elements of the 'plot' that each piece of information represents. The elements are then combined into a new chronology of events that presents *all* of the differing perspectives, side by side, for the reader to compare and contrast. Some additional, contemporary commentary is also provided as a chorus that gives the reader some insights into the modern-day impact of this important event.

The contemporary commentary is one of the most compelling reasons to read this book. Few historiographical analyses reflect on the long-term, modern-day, consequences of historical events except in an abstract and general fashion. But the *Seven Oaks Reader* is also about private family tragedy and community decline, and the oral stories and songs shared and preserved by Métis people in the confines of their communities. One discovers, very quickly, that the memories — and the wounds — of this event are still fresh.

Some readers will no doubt be surprised and even angry to learn a few details about Seven Oaks that seem to have been overlooked by their teachers and professors in the past. Others will appreciate being exposed to the significant elements of a large body of historical information without having to hunt through libraries and websites to find each article and book.

But, as one learns quickly after even a cursory examination of the extensive historiography of this conflict, just about everyone – the participants, the contemporary observers resident in Red River, the partisans of both the Hudson's Bay and North West companies, and the descendants of the Métis and AngloScots combatants – has strong opinions on the subject. The modern-day professional historians who have sifted through those surviving accounts, and written their own assessments of Seven Oaks over the last two hundred years, also have convincing and intense perspectives on these events. These scholarly writings feature numerous facts that have been dutifully unearthed, carefully analyzed, and logically presented. But they are re-constructions of historical events. And they have their own implicit biases. Scholars are as shaped by regional, class, and racial biases as other writers might be, except that they are possibly more adept at obscuring their partisanship by the methodological tools at their disposal. If historians privilege the written eyewitness accounts of non-Indigenous men over those of Métis and First Nations participants, and denigrate (or ignore entirely) the oral accounts of these events that continue to be passed down through generations of Red River residents, they are guilty of producing incomplete and inaccurate histories. And these scholarly histories are as much opinion pieces – in their own academic way – as anything that John Halkett, Samuel Wilcocke, or 'Mercator' penned in order to move public opinion in the cities of the Canadas and Britain. They can also be as emotionally manipulative as any ballad by Pierre Falcon, or any *mise en scène* painted by C.W. Jeffries.

What I like about Kostash's approach is that it is fundamentally egalitarian — democratic, if you like. Myrna does not privilege the different pieces of information, according to source or perspective. Instead, she puts it all out there, and lets the reader evaluate the bits for themselves. In doing so, the reader is forced to reflect on how the event has been shaped, and how the shaping of this history has impacted Western Canadians today.

Heather Devine
University of Calgary
October 2015

PREFACE

Modelled after my *Frog Lake Reader* (NeWest Press, 2009), *The Seven Oaks Reader* gathers together a wide diversity of texts with differing perspectives to narrate a controversial historic event, in this case the "battle" between armed settlers and armed Métis buffalo hunters on 19 June 1816 at The Forks of the Red and Assiniboine Rivers in what is now Winnipeg. The death of twenty-one settlers and one Métis led to no conclusive judicial outcome but has reverberated down through the generations of descendents of both communities as a formative event in their history in western Canada. As a born and bred western Canadian who has lived most of her life in Alberta, I was nevertheless ignorant of this "legacy" incident and so I set out to find as many sources for its telling as I could.

An initial treatment of these materials was broadcast in 2011 as *Incident at Seven Oaks* on the CBC Radio "Ideas" program (produced by Kathleen Flaherty), and it is from that program that I have used excerpts of interviews with Jack Bumsted, Ron Bourgeault, and Lyle Dick.

More than a textbook or anthology of voices, the *Reader* works as a drama of interplaying, sometimes contradictory, contrapuntal narratives. Given that some of the narrative dates to 1816 and that the historians themselves began publishing histories of Manitoba as far back as the 1850s, it is unsurprising that, from an editorial point of view, there are inconsistencies and even infelicities of word usage and spelling. So, one reads of both the Hudson Bay Company and the Hudson's Bay Company, of North-Westers and Nor'Westers (agents and employees of the North West Company), of Bois Brules and Bois-Brûlés, of mixed bloods and Mixed Bloods, of Metis and Métis, of Miles Macdonell and Miles MacDonnell. There are discrepancies among accounts of dates, numbers, and place names. Certain words and characterizations, now found offensive, were in common circulation as male Euro-Canadian voices long dominated the telling of this tale. But the last half-century has introduced a welcome chorus of new voices from among Aboriginal and female narrators.

The *Reader* is published in the wake of the Report from the Truth and Reconciliation Commission. It is my and the publisher's hope that it will find favour among Canadian readers generally and educators specifically who are called upon by the Commission to "build student capacity for intercultural understanding, empathy, and mutual respect." It is in that spirit that it is offered to the public.

ACKNOWLEDGEMENTS

I owe a debt of thanks to the indefatigable and ingenious labours of editorial assistant Lauren Cross who edited the Works Cited and Further Reading pages and composed the Author Biographies. Her "reader's notes" on the next-to-final draft were a felicitous commentary that helped me produce the final draft. I am thankful to NeWest Press's substantive support throughout the process of producing the *Reader*, from Douglas Barbour, President of the editorial board and Don Kerr, Board member, who guided me through the first drafts, to the Press's staff, Paul Matwychuk, General Manager, Tiiu Vuorensola, Office Administrator, and Matt Bowes, Marketing & Production Coordinator. A timely grant from the Alberta foundation for the arts allowed me to complete the final draft. I am thankful for this support.

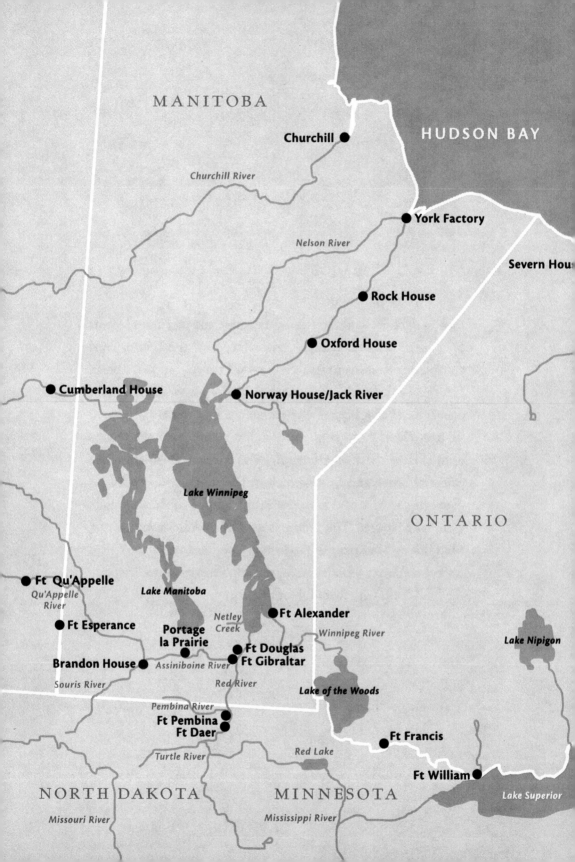

MANITOBA

HUDSON BAY

Churchill

Churchill River

York Factory

Nelson River

Severn Hou

Rock House

Oxford House

Cumberland House

Norway House/Jack River

Lake Winnipeg

ONTARIO

Ft Qu'Appelle

Qu'Appelle River

Lake Manitoba

Netley Creek

Ft Alexander

Lake Nipigon

Ft Esperance

Portage la Prairie

Winnipeg River

Brandon House

Assiniboine River

Ft Douglas
Ft Gibraltar

Souris River

Red River

Lake of the Woods

Pembina River

Ft Pembina
Ft Daer

Ft Francis

Turtle River

Red Lake

Ft William

NORTH DAKOTA

MINNESOTA

Lake Superior

Missouri River

Mississippi River

CAST OF CHARACTERS

Individuals mentioned in cited texts.

William Auld (c. 1770–c. 1830): surgeon and trader for the HBC at Fort Churchill.

Henry Bathurst 3rd Earl Bathurst (1762–1834): British politician; Secretary of State for War and the Colonies (1812–1827).

Francois Firmin Boucher: NWC clerk; Cuthbert Grant's lieutenant at Seven Oaks; acquitted of the murder of Robert Semple.

D'arcy Boulton (1759–1834): lawyer, judge, and political figure in Upper Canada.

Duncan Cameron (1764–1848): partner in the NWC who, together with Alexander Greenfield Macdonell, was placed in charge of the Red River department at Fort Gibraltar in 1814. From there he challenged the HBC colony of Red River, which was established two years before by Lord Selkirk and governed by Miles Macdonell during the period known as the Pemmican War.

Chief Peguis (c. 1774–1864): Saulteaux Indian chief at Netley Creek; aided and defended Red River settlers; one of five Saulteaux and Cree chiefs who signed a land treaty with Lord Selkirk in 1817.

William B. Coltman (?–1826): merchant and justice of the peace; with jp John Fletcher, given a special commission to investigate the fur-trade war in the West and the Battle of Seven Oaks; issued Report 1818.

Peter Fidler (1769–1822): surveyor, map-maker, chief fur trader, explorer, and long-time employee of the HBC.

Samuel Gale (1783–1865): lawyer and judge; defended Lord Selkirk's interests in Canada.

Cuthbert Grant (1793–1854): fur trader, Métis leader, farmer, office holder, justice of the peace, and politician; son of an NWC partner and a Métis mother; in 1812, at the age of 19, he entered the service of the NWC and travelled to the northwest where he was posted to Fort Espérance (Sask.) on the Qu'Appelle River. As Métis captain, he led the North West Company forces at the Battle of Seven Oaks in 1816. In 1828, the Hudson's Bay Co. named him Warden of the Plains. He retired from the HBC in 1824.

John (Wedderburn) Halkett (1768–1852): HBC director; married sister of Lord Selkirk, Lady Katherine Douglas; main British defender of Selkirk's efforts in North America.

Owen Keveny (?–1816): HBC employee; recruited colonists for Lord Selkirk; murdered 11 Sept. 1816 on the Winnipeg River.

Jean Baptiste Lagimodiere (1778–1855): fur trader, pioneer settler; made his first trip to Red River in 1800 as an employee of the NWC; retained by Miles Macdonell as a buffalo hunter for the Selkirk colonists; married Marie Anne Gaboury, grandmother of Louis Riel.

Lord Selkirk; Thomas Douglas, Fifth Earl of Selkirk (1771–1820): Scottish philanthropist who sponsored emigration to Canada, particularly of Highlanders and Islanders to the Red River settlement at

The Forks. As majority shareholder of the H BC, he was involved in bitter competition with the N WC at their base in Fort Gibraltar on the Assiniboine River.

John Macbeth (1854–1897): Manitoba lawyer and politician; served two terms in the Manitoba Legislature; son of original 1815 Red River settler, Robert McBeth.

Alexander Greenfield Macdonell (1782–1835): brother-in-law as well as cousin of Miles Macdonell; in command of Fort Gibraltar, the N WC post on the Assiniboine River.

John Macdonell (1768–1850): militia officer, fur trader, businessman; brother of Miles Macdonell; in charge of the Upper Red River department of the N WC until 1809, then of the Athabasca department until 1812.

Miles Macdonell (c. 1767–1828): army officer and first governor of the Red River colony, 1812-1815; married to Nancy Macdonell, sister of distant cousin Alexander Greenfield Macdonell.

Sir Alexander Mackenzie (1764–1820): Scottish explorer who made the first European overland crossing of what is now Canada to the Pacific Ocean in 1793; partner in the N WC on whose behalf he also made expeditions to the Arctic Ocean.

Archibald Mcdonald (1790–1853): colonial administrator, author, fur trader; clerk and agent for the Red River settlement 1812; winter of 1814-15, served as one of Governor Miles Macdonell's principal lieutenants.

John McDonald (1771–1866): known as John McDonald of Garth; N WC partner and farmer.

John Mcleod (1788–1849): fur trader; clerk with the H BC in 1811; given charge of the H BC's operations at Red River in 1814-15.

Simon McGillivray (c. 1785–9 June 1840): nephew of Simon McTavish; London-based partner in the NWC; along with his brother, William McGillivray, defended NWC interests in struggles with Lord Selkirk and the HBC; instrumental in the merger of the NWC and HBC in 1820.

William McGillivray (1764–1825): Montreal-based fur trader, head of the NWC, landowner, politician, and militia officer; negotiated union with the HBC in 1820.

Henry Mckenzie (1781–1832): fur trader, merchant; in charge of public relations for the NWC under pseudonym, Mercator.

Simon Mctavish (c. 1750–1804): Scottish-born fur trader and the chief founding partner of the North West Company.

Alexander Morris (1826–1889): Lieutenant-Governor of the North-West Territories 1872-1876; treaty commissioner for Treaties 3, 4, 5, and 6 and helped negotiate Treaties 1 and 2.

Pierre-Chrysologue Pambrun (1792–1841): Canadian militia officer and fur trader in the HBC (Pembina); key witness in the legal proceedings between the NWC and HBC.

Peter Bostonois Pangman Jr. (1791–1850): Freeman bison hunter in the Pembina region; together with Cuthbert Grant, William Shaw, and Bonhomme Montour, he was one of the four "Chiefs" of the Métis.

Joseph-Octave Plessis (1763–1825): Roman Catholic priest and archbishop in Quebec.

John Pritchard (1777–1856): fur trader, settler, author; left NWC service in 1814 and settled at Red River; taken prisoner by the Métis in 1816; subpoenaed as a witness at the trial in York of two Nor'Westers charged with the murder of Robert Semple.

Colin Robertson (1783–1842): **Chief Factor; left N W C in 1809; seized Fort Gibraltar from the N W C, acquitted at trial; agreed to reestablish Red River colony and rebuild Fort Douglas in 1815; led an H B C expedition to the interior, 1819.**

Pierre-Guillaume Sayer (c. 1796–1849): **fur trader and farmer at Grantown.**

John Schultz (1840–1896): **physician, merchant, Lieutenant-Governor of Manitoba (1888-1895). After 1867 advocated the union of Rupert's Land with Canada; played a leading role in opposing Louis Riel's provisional government in 1869.**

Robert Semple (1777–1816): **merchant and author of travel books; governor of the Red River colony, 1815.**

George Simpson (c. 1786–1860): **governor of the H B C (1820-1860), author, and businessman.**

John Spencer (1790–1881): **hired by H B C 1806, appointed as a Councilor and Sheriff of Assiniboia under the direction of Governor Macdonell, 1814.**

John Strachan (1778–1867): **arch-Tory; first Anglican bishop of Toronto and founder of Trinity College (at the University of Toronto). Fierce opponent of Lord Selkirk's settlement projects.**

James Sutherland (c. 1777–1844): **fur trader; H B C clerk at York Factory, master at Cumberland House; a prisoner of the N W C in 1816; promoted to the rank of Chief Factor in Swan River District in 1821.**

Rev. John West (1778–1845): **Church of England missionary, teacher, and author; appointed as H B C chaplain in 1819.**

Thomas Douglas, the 5th Earl of Selkirk.
(Glenbow Archives, NA-2247-1)

ONE: BEGINNINGS

MK: In Spring of 1816, rumours swirl through Assiniboia — in today's southern Manitoba — that the Nor'Westers, men of the North West Company of fur traders, Métis hunters, Canadian *engagés* [contract employees], and clerks, are preparing for war against their commercial rivals, the Hudson's Bay Company. They face each other from their respective posts, Fort Gibraltar and Fort Douglas, near the juncture of the Red and Assiniboine Rivers known as the Forks. There are settlers a kilometre north in a loop of the Red, named Point Douglas.[1]

June 19, 1816: a group of Métis and Nor'Westers disembark from a canoe at the mouth of Catfish Creek, where it empties, swift and muddy, into the Assiniboine. They have with them large bundles of pemmican that they transfer to oxcarts for transport overland north-east across the plain. At this point, the horsemen are still well away from the Selkirk settlers on the Red, and from Fort Douglas, downstream on the Red. In fact, they are deliberately avoiding fort and settlers. Or so they will claim.

1 Point Douglas AKA 1813, Colony Gardens; 1817, 1826, Red River; 1858, Fort Garry – or Garry for short; 1873, Winnipeg.

But that evening of June 19, a watchman in Fort Douglas spots a group of the horsemen, some thirty-five of them, armed and riding in the direction of La Grenouillière or Frog Plain. They seem to be riding toward the settlement itself. The alarm is raised, Governor Robert Semple calls for volunteers, hands them muskets and ammunition, and marches out with them, some twenty-five-strong, to intercept and confront the horsemen. They meet at a bend in the river, in a grove of trees known as Seven Oaks.

What happened next has been called a battle, a skirmish, a massacre. It was over in fifteen minutes but it was long in the making, starting as early as the charter of the Hudson's Bay Company.

The Fur Trade Wars

HUDSON'S BAY COMPANY

From the Charter of the Hudson's Bay Company, 1670:

Charles the Second By the grace of God King of England Scotland France and Ireland defender of the faith &c

To All to whome these presentes shall come greeting [...]

doe make ordeyne constitute establish confirme and declare by these Presentes and that by the same name of Governor & Company of Adventurers of England Tradeing into Hudsons Bay they shall have perpetuall succession And that they and theire successors by the name of Governor and Company of Adventurers of England Tradeing into Hudsons Bay bee and at all tymes hereafter shall bee persons able and capable in Law to have purchase receive possesse enjoy and reteyne Landes Rentes priviledges libertyes Jurisdiccions Franchyses and hereditamentes of what kinde nature and quality soever they bee to them and theire Successors And

THE SEVEN OAKS READER *Myrna Kostash*

alsoe to give grant demise alien assigne and dispose Landes Tenementes and hereditamentes and to doe and execute all and singuler other thinges by the same name that to them shall or may apperteyne to doe.

MK: The "lands, rents and privileges" to which the Company of Adventurers trading into Hudson Bay were granted "perpetual succession" comprised an area as extensive as all of Europe and containing about fifty thousand inhabitants. (It was named Rupert's Land after Prince Rupert of the Rhine, the first Governor of the Company.) The mainly Indigenous population was made up of three nations: the Crees, Ojibwas, and Assiniboines. (McNeil) The Charter was as vague about territory as it was wide-reaching.

Kent McNeil, Osgoode Hall Law School, York University, Toronto: It is commonly assumed that this territory encompassed all the lands in North America that drain into Hudson Bay and Strait. I am going to challenge the assumption that the Charter actually conveyed the whole of that territory to the Company. My view is that the Company's territory included only those lands within the Hudson watershed that the Company was actually able to possess and effectively control. Even in 1869-70, when the Company surrendered Rupert's Land back to the Crown, most of the lands within the Hudson watershed were not possessed or controlled by the Company at all — they were possessed and controlled by Aboriginal nations, some of whom had inhabited the region for thousands of years.

Jack Bumsted, historian of the fur trade in Canada and its wars, interview: You have to understand this territory wasn't *anything* at this point, it didn't have a name, it was the Indian Country. In a vague sort of way it could be referred to as Rupert's Land but it didn't have that title yet either. This is *terra incognita*, it is land in which there are Aboriginals, the beginnings of a mixed-blood society, a handful of fur traders. No maps and no boundaries. Nobody has any notion of what anything is. Nobody had any rights out here. There was nothing out here. I have to keep repeating that. There is no government, there is no authority out here.

But in any case, whatever monopoly rights the HBC had under the Charter had never been legally challenged by anybody into the 19th century. The North West Company never bothered legally challenging the Charter. It could have done so, gone to court in Britain but chose not to because they figured it was too expensive and why bother when they could poach instead in HBC territory?

Marjorie Wilkins Campbell, author: By the time Wolfe and Montcalm met on the farmer's field which history knows as the Plains of Abraham, there were two routes to the northwest, routes destined to meet as surely as the blades of a pair of scissors. But not for several decades. So far, the Hudson's Bay Company had done little exploring. (Campbell, *The Nor'Westers: The Fight for the Fur Trade*, 5)

THE NORTH WEST COMPANY

MK: Under Highland Scots management, the North West Company describes a group of Montreal traders who pooled their financial resources in 1779. With the added resource of experienced French-Canadian labour, they had by the 1780s become a major force in the inland fur trade and capable of resisting the gradual advances of the HBC down from the posts on the Hudson Bay. (The surnames of some of the partners have become legendary: McTavish, Frobisher, McGill, McGillivray, Mackenzie.) The Company's annual trade was valued at about £100,000, thanks to the trapping and export of some 20,000 beaver pelts a year. By the time Alexander Mackenzie reached the Pacific by overland route, the Nor'Westers had control of more than two-thirds of the Canadian fur trade. (see Jennifer Brown, "North West Company," in *Canadian Encyclopedia*)

Bruce Sealey and Antoine Lussier, authors: Up at two a.m.; a six hour paddle; breakfast at eight; lunch at noon, which consisted of a piece of pemmican hacked off and chewed while the paddling continued; supper at nine p.m. and then a few hours sleep in the open before beginning another day; this was the accepted schedule for a voyageur.... The strenuous life led by the canoe men helps us to appreciate their vast appetites, at which modern man marvels and in his ignorance often considers as an example of Métis gluttony. The geographer and fur trader, David Thompson, noted that the daily ration for each voyageur consisted of either eight pounds of fresh meat a day or one and a half pounds of pemmican. (Sealey & Lussier, *The Metis*, 26)

Alfred Silver, author: In each canoe, *the milieus* cocked their paddles over the gunwales, the *gouvernail* propped his long steering paddle out against the stern, the *avant* leaned up and forward over the bow. Mister Henderson barked, *"Allons!"* The painters were cast off. The guide — the *avant* of the bourgeois's canoe — looked back over his brigade and swung his arm ahead. As the *milieus'* backs dipped forward in unison and the paddle blades dipped into the river, the *chanteur* — paid twice the milieus' wage for his prodigious voice and memory, sang out:

"Au près de ma blonde ..."

The rest of the brigade joined in on the response line, synchronizing their paddle-strokes to the rhythm of the song. The singing also served to drown out the wailing of the wives and mothers and children running onto the wharf as the brigade picked up momentum.

"Qu'il fait bon, fait bon, fait bon

"Au près de ma blonde, qu'il fait bon dormir." (Silver, *Red River Story*, 17)

MK: Donald G. McLean, late researcher/writer, at Gabriel Dumont Institute, described a voyageur's canoe as capable of carrying loads as heavy as 3742 kilos of cargo that could include butter, powder, rum, dry goods, tallow, and guns on its journey west from Montreal. Usually the canoes moved in brigades of three or more with crews of eight men working up to eighteen hours a day, a cheap source of labour McLean describes as "indentured" to the Company. "They paid such low wages that the voyageur often returned to Montreal indebted to the company." There was no such thing as voyageurs going on strike, because troublemakers were simply discharged, nor was compensation provided in the event the worker was injured or killed. (McLean, *Home From the Hill*, 34–5)

This is to be compared to the status of the trading post's clerks who were transported to their posts as passengers with the brigades.

Margaret A. Macleod, author, and W.L. Morton, historian: Gentlemen travelled as gentlemen in the canoe brigades, with robe, tent, travelling-desk,

THE SEVEN OAKS READER *Myrna Kostash*

preserved foods, wines, and every comfort obtainable. The canoe-men and personal servants would do all the work of travel and making camp along the rivers and lakes.... At dusk the gentle-men were carried ashore on the backs of the middlemen, and stretched their legs while the servants prepared the supper and raised their tents. Before the sun rose, they would be roused by the guide's cry of *lève! lève!* and would drowsily take their places once more, to recline, smoke, talk or write as hour by hour the sweating *voyageurs* drove the great canoes. (Macleod & Morton, *Cuthbert Grant of Grantown*, 8–9)

MK: But many of these voyageurs settled down in marriages with Indigenous women and the children born to them of these unions would become the Métis, mixed-blood and bilingual progeny who were equally at home with the culture of their mothers' people as with that of the Company men of the trading posts, connections to whom, through their fathers, gave them preferred employment around the forts, as interpreters, canoemen, fur packers, and man-ual labourers. (in McLean, 37)

Eventually, the Mixed-Bloods would also become a military presence on the plains. But first they, like the Nor'Westers, had to come to terms with the Charter claims of the HBC to a mono-poly on trade and jurisdiction in their territory.

Fred Shore, professor of Native Studies, and Lawrence J. Barkwell, historian and author: The usual practice of the Métis was to provide for their own rules while accepting certain of the Hudson's Bay Company's laws along with some First Nations' laws providing that these did not interfere with Métis law.... Seen in this light, the relationship between European law and Aboriginal law can be envisaged as co-equal and co-existing with certain areas of mutual acceptance and others of rejection. Assuming that the only law which existed was that used by the Hudson's Bay Company's is not only an extremely ethnocentric interpretation but foolish, given that the Métis were the one force in Rupert's Land capable of defending their law with a proven military force. (Shore & Barkwell, *Past Reflects the Present*, 215)

Marjorie W. Campbell: It was different on the St Lawrence.... For to Montrealers, French or English by ancestry, the northwest was both the land of potential big business and the stuff of dreams. In the northwest a man might make his fortune. (Campbell, 6) From time to time the Montrealers in the northwest met servants [employees] of the Hudson's Bay Company armed with printed leaflets threatening severe penalties against any man who dared trespass the monopolied though as yet unexplored territory of the English concern. They ignored the threats, confident that they had inherited not only the trade formerly carried on by New France but the right to the rewards of their enterprise. It mattered little to them that the servants of the Hudson's Bay Company taunted them as being pedlars while the English persuaded the natives to carry their pelts to them. (Campbell, 8)

Chester Martin, historian: So long as the Indians hunted during the winter and brought their furs five hundred miles by canoe to Hudson Bay in the summer, there was little incentive [by the HBC] to push inland, to establish winter trading-posts, or to take more than a casual interest in the enormous territory specified by the Charter.... Traders were content with a life of placid indolence. (C. Martin, *Selkirk's Work in Canada*, 28)

Joseph Tassé, author and journalist: It was the era when the Hudson's Bay Company and the North-West Company were locked in a merciless struggle — what the voyageurs called *la conteste* — in the hunting territories the exploitation of which they both laid claim to. The employees of the North-West Company, composed for the most part of our countrymen, were designated by the name of *gens du Nord-Ouest* or simply *les Canadiens* while their adversaries were called *les Anglais*, or *les gens de la baie d'Hudson* or even better, *les gens du petit Nord*. (Tassé, *Les Canadiens de l'ouest*, 339 mk trans)

MK: This was still a period of what historian Bumsted (*Sovereignty*) calls "informal competition" with both French and English fur-trading companies building trading posts in the Hudson's Bay region. Historian George F.G. Stanley described how they were each "trying to outpace the other, until they reached the extremities of the continent both in the north and the west, dotting the whole country with fur trading posts, small agglomerations of [trade] post Indians and mixed-bloods, and unsightly garbage dumps." (Stanley, *Manitoba 1870*, 6–7)

Jack Bumsted, interview: And of course the HBC itself had been very slow to move inland from the bay where it had established fur trading posts and expected the Aboriginals to come to them. That was the trading pattern through much of the 18th century, although by the end of the century it was clear to the HBC the NWC traders — who were just that, individual traders who were operating under the umbrella of a partnership — but in any case the NWC was clearly taking over the fur trade in the interior to the south of Hudson Bay. Nevertheless, by the time of the early 19th century the HBC still hadn't moved directly into the Red River area.

MK: By 1803 the competition had become intense. As Bumsted writes in *Lord Selkirk: A Life*, from the point of view of the North West Company, their de facto presence on HBC territory "deserved some recognition by their rival," monopoly or no monopoly, charter or no charter, that they were no mere interlopers on the territory but in fact controlled the bulk of the fur trade. (203)

Chester Martin: In the competition that ensued, the Hudson's Bay Company laboured under fatal disadvantages.... Too timid to venture far afield, the Hudson's Bay traders were systematically brow-beaten and bullied out of their rights by the well-trained Canadians. The Canadian trader went fearlessly among [the Indians], made lavish use of rum and spirits, and in 1811 took out by canoe to Fort William from the Hudson's Bay territories alone, more furs than that company shipped from their own ports on Hudson Bay.... The 'North-westers' looked upon their rivals with undisguised contempt. (C. Martin, 29)

MK: Fur-bearing animals had been trapped in the Red River country of the Red and Assiniboine rivers since the 1680s, but by the beginning of the nineteenth century, the resources of that region could no longer sustain a fur economy for the trappers, hunters, and traders who now sought their fortune in Athabasca country. Because the inbound and outbound journeys of the fur brigades now extended so much further west and north, it was essential that they secure a sufficient supply of food, mainly pemmican, both for their own provisions and for the trading posts deep in the interior. For this the Red River and Assiniboine country was ideal, for the bison herds — pemmican on the hoof — were still abundant and the Métis hunters around the posts practiced in the hunt. Fatal to this enterprise, however, was any suggestion that the territory, cleared of fur trappers and traders, was ripe for agricultural settlement. "Settlers brought farming, crops and livestock. They brought civilisation, laws and lawmen," as a government of Scotland website observes. They would have to be resisted. (Education Scotland)

Métis

George Bryce, clergyman, educator, historian: [The Hudson's Bay Company] were a dignified and wealthy Company, reaching back to the times of easygoing Charles 11, who gave them their charter. For a hundred years they lived in self-confidence and prudence in their forts of Churchill and York, on the shore of Hudson Bay. They were even at times so inhospitable as to deal with the Indians through an open window of the fort. This was in striking contrast to the "Nor '-Wester" who trusted the Indians and lived among them with the freest intercourse. (Bryce, *The Romantic Settlement*, 29–30)

MK: A former director of the Native Law Centre at the University of Saskatchewan, Donald Purich is the author of a communal history, *The Metis*, in which he details the HBC's protocols and regulations regarding their employees' relationships with Native women — liaisons meant imprisonment or pay loss and even in some posts whippings. If you were unlucky enough to contract a venereal disease, you were docked a month's pay. Chief factors [the most senior officers at a post] themselves were threatened with loss of salary if they admitted Native women into their posts. "Many of these rules were impossible to enforce and were openly flouted."

(23) Nevertheless, they had an inhibiting impact: far fewer Mixed-Bloods were born of HBC (Scottish)-Native unions than resulted from NWC (French)-Native relationships. In the case of the *voyageurs*, many chose to live around the posts or even join Assiniboine Indian groups where they lived in camp with them.

Alfred Campbell Garrioch, clergyman and author: **Bois Brules [Métis]** ... lived much as the thoroughbred savages, and to whom they were superior chiefly in being able to speak both Cree and French, instead of Cree only; and from whom they were distinguishable chiefly by their clearer skin and heavier build, but from whom they differed not a whit on the easy, graceful step of the moccasin-raised man or woman, while in the matter of undressiness, though the Frenchman did not quite equal his red brother, yet on special occasions there were some who were wont to adapt themselves to the unsophisticated tastes of the Indian, and to appear in a scantiness of broadcloth that left the narrowest possible margin on the side of decency. (Garrioch, *First Furrows*, 35)

MK: Both populations, however, were equally indispensible to the fur trading companies. They were invaluable go-betweens with their Indigenous relatives, spoke their languages, and had learned their wilderness skills in the woods and on the plains: they were woodsmen and horsemen and hunters. It was as buffalo hunters of the great bison herds in the Red River valley that they became involved in supplying the NWC with pemmican. The basic food of the fur trade was pemmican — and it would eventually feed the Selkirk colonists as well, and keep them from starvation until they became self-sufficient in food. So pemmican was a big business for the Métis who produced and traded it. University of

Regina sociologist Ron Bourgeault looks at the history of the fur trade in terms of economics and class struggle.

Ron Bourgeault, interview: [The Métis] occupied a certain economic, commercial position where they were encouraged to systematically harvest the buffalo as a commodity for sale to the NWC. They were encouraged to be independent commodity producers separate from Indian hunting communes on the plains. So one can say of the French-speaking Métis buffalo hunters under the NWC: they liked their position. They could systematically harvest the buffalo meat, sell it and get manufactured goods.

And they would produce the pemmican. Nothing romantic about that. It was protein, to feed people around the fur trade posts in the interior. You can only hunt around a trading post for so long and then you start to hunt it out. So there had to be another system for the mass production of protein. That's where your buffalo hunters come in. So they would sell it to the NWC. They were encouraged to do that. And the Métis who were doing that were the offspring of French labourers and local Indian women. So they have one foot into Indian society and another foot into mercantile capitalist society.

Henry Martin Robinson, author, newspaper owner, and editor: To manufacture pemmican the flesh of the buffalo is first cut up into large lumps, and then again into flakes or thick slices, and hung up in the sun or over the fire to dry. When it is thoroughly desiccated it is taken down, placed upon raw hides spread out upon the prairie, and pounded or beaten sometimes by wooden flails, again between two stones, until the meat is reduced to a thick, flaky substance or pulp.

[Pemmican] is the travelling provision used throughout the Fur Land, where ... its great facility of transportation renders it extremely valuable. There is no risk of spoiling it, as, if ordinary care can be taken to keep the bags free from mould, there is no assignable limit to the time pemmican will keep. It is estimated that, on average, the carcasses of two buffaloes are required to make one bag of pemmican — one filling the bag itself [one hundred pounds], the other supplying the wants of the wild savage engaged in hunting it down. (Robinson, *The Great Fur Land*, 135)

MK: The hunt, a semi-annual event, early summer and late fall, did indeed "supply the wants" of the hunters and their families; according to Grant Anderson, writing for the Gabriel Dumont Institute, a successful hunt could provide as much as a million pounds (454 metric tonnes) of meat, hides and bones to the community. (208-10) But it provided much more than that. By combining into their own culture the traditional knowledge of their Indigenous mothers and the "entrepreneurial spirit" of their European-Canadian fathers, the Métis eventually developed, on the basis of their hunt, a variety of military, legal and governance protocols. From these same fathers, most had been exposed to Roman Catholic religious traditions.

R.G. MacBeth, clergyman and author: The buffalo hunters had their own code. Each camp was in the hands of a headman, who had a primitive cabinet to assist him in the preservation and protection of life and property. My older brothers went periodically with the buffalo-hunters, and they claimed that amongst the camps and cavalcades there was a wonderfully well-worked out series of regulations. We find such "laws" as these: "No buffalo to be run on the Sabbath day." They were strict on this point as a matter of conscience, but they also discovered in those early days what has been proven in munition factories in war-time, namely, that a day of rest is an absolute necessity if physical, mental and moral collapse is to be prevented. "No party to fork off, lag behind or go before without permission." "No person or party to run buffalo before the general order." There was no privileged class amongst these people. (MacBeth, *The Selkirk Settlers in Real Life*, 57–8)

George Bryce: The Bois-Brulés from childhood were familiar with the Indian pony, knew all his tricks and habits, began to ride with all the skill of a desert ranger, were familiar with fire-arms, took part in the chase of the buffalo on the plains, and were already trained to make the attack as cavalry on buffalo herds, after the Indian fashion. In the famous half-circle, where they were to be so successful in their later troubles, of which we shall speak. (Bryce, *Romantic Settlement*, 28–9)

Ron Bourgeault, interview: So they were aligned with the North West Company and saw themselves as, one, loyal to the NWC and, two, as indigenous to the territory. And I'm assuming from their internal politics, that they saw the HBC as an encroachment on their territory. They had no loyalty to the HBC. But the NWC had not yet politically developed a position of declaring sovereignty over the territory. They were just operating commercially.

The Métis are born of the territory. They are nationals. It is the beginning of being indigenous nationals of the territory. That same phenomenon was going on among the emerging merchant class of the NWC who did not see themselves as being strictly British or as British transplants into the territory. They start to see themselves as indigenous to the territory. It's a phenomenon. But don't confuse or cloud the issue by saying the Métis saw themselves as having early forms of Aboriginal rights. That is not the case. It's the case that they are indigenous, they are born in the territory, they see themselves as nationals of the territory. It's the *beginning* if you like of nationalism against the colonial rule.

Lord Selkirk and his Settlement

Alexander Ross, fur trader, historian: Red River Settlement ... is an isolated spot in the wilds of North America, distant 700 miles from the nearest sea-port, and that port [York Factory] blockaded by solid ice for ten months in the year. Our history dates from the grant of this wilderness to Lord Selkirk, when it was marked by no human footprint but that of the wandering savage or unscrupulous trader; a land inhabited only by the bear, the wolf, and the buffalo, where the bleating of sheep and the lowing of oxen were as unknown as the sound of the church-going bell and the whirr of the grindstone. (Ross, *Settlement*, v)

Manitoba Historic Resources Branch: Several thousand years before the arrival of European immigrants, many Native nations in North America had developed sophisticated farming methods. Four centuries before Europeans settled beside the Red River, Native people were agricultural pioneers in the valley. Recent archaeological digs reveal a thriving Native farming site on the river's east bank at Lockport, 15 kilometres north of present-day Winnipeg. The origin and identity of this farming people are unknown.

It made sense to locate farm gardens near the river. Water for

THE SEVEN OAKS READER *Myrna Kostash*

crop irrigation and the presence of fish to balance the diet were two obvious advantages. An added benefit of the Lockport site was the nutrient-rich layer of new soil left behind by receding flood waters each spring.

Clearing the land of tall, prairie grasses, trees, and brush required the quarrying and fashioning of stone knives and axes. Wooden digging sticks were used to break up the soil. Hoes made of wood and the shoulder blade of the bison were used to till the soil. Corn was planted in small hillocks and arranged in rows one metre apart. Beans, squash, and flowers may also have been grown. A meal comprised of corn and beans would have provided Native families with the same complete protein as one containing meat.

By 2,000 years ago, corn was being grown as far east as the Atlantic seaboard and as far west as the Rocky Mountains. The Native farmers at Lockport developed a strain of corn that could mature in the typical 100-day growing season near the present-day Canadian border with the United States Midwest. The adaptation of corn to the long-day, short-season environment of the Red River Valley — from the plant's original short-day, long-season climate in Central America — testifies to the selective plant breeding skills of these first farmers.

George Bryce: Inasmuch as this tale is chiefly one of Scottish and of Colonial life, the story of the movement from Old Kildonan, on the German Ocean [North Sea], to New Kildonan, on the Western Prairies — we may be very sure that it did not take place without irritation and opposition and conflict. The Scottish race, while possessing intense earnestness and energy, often gains its ends by the most thoroughgoing animosity. In this great emigration movement, there were great new world interests involved, and champions of the rival parties concerned were two stalwart chieftains of Scotland's best blood, both with great powers of leadership and both backed up with abundant means and strongest influence. It was a duel — indeed a fight, as old Sir Walter Scott would say, "a l'outrance" — to the bitter end. That the struggle was between two chieftains — one a Lowlander [Selkirk], the other a Highlander [Alexander Mackenzie], did not count for much, for the Lowlander spoke the Gaelic tongue — and he was championing the interest of the Highland men. (Bryce, *Romantic Settlement*, 33)

Sir Alexander Mackenzie, explorer, NWC partner: The Red River runs in a Southern [actually northern] direction to [from] near the headwaters of the Mississippi. The country on either side is but partially supplied with wood, and consists of plains, covered with Buffalo and Elk, especially on the Western side. On the Eastern side are lakes and rivers, and the whole country is well wooded, level, abounding in Beaver, Bears, Mouse Deer, Fallow Deer etc. ... There is not, perhaps, a finer country in the world for the residence of uncivilized man, than that which occupies the space between this river and Lake Superior. It abounds in every thing necessary to the wants and comforts of such a people. Fish, venison, and fowl, with wild rice, are in great plenty, while at the same time, their subsistence requires that bodily exercise so necessary to health and vigour. (in Colby, *Mackenzie, Alexander*, 68–9)

MK: Selkirk had been so moved and aroused by Alexander Mackenzie's account of his explorations, which were described in *Voyages from Montreal Through the Continent of North America to the Frozen and Pacific Oceans in 1789 and 1793*, that he made use of Mackenzie's own words to impress the Colonial Office with the prospects of a Red River colony.

At the western extremity of Canada, upon the waters [Red River] which fall into Lake Winnipeck … is a Country which the Indian traders represent as fertile & of a Climate far more temperate than the Shores of the Atlantic of the same parallel & not more severe than that of Germany and Poland. Here, therefore, the colonists may, with a moderate expenditure of industry, be certain of a comfortable subsistence and they may also raise some valuable objects of exportation. (in Kelsey, *Red River*, 72)

MK: The Scottish Lowlander, Lord Selkirk, had a vision: to resettle dispossessed Scots and Irish to colonies in North America. Nor did he overlook the plight of the Indigenous people whose "farther progress" to a civilized life was thwarted by "the vices" of European settlers in their vicinity: how much more salutary would be their contact in the territories of the Hudson's Bay Company with hardy settlers from his homeland. The Indians, wrote Selkirk, were "prepared for a further progress in civilization. Nothing, however, has been done to facilitate their improvement." (Selkirk, *On the Civilization of the Indians*, 6) His vision of a settlement of farmers on the Red River was just such a preparation.

In 1792, Lord Selkirk took an extensive tour through the Highlands "to explore many of its remotest and most secluded valleys." He noted that already the clan chieftains were charging rent from their tenants, and ridding themselves of the "surplus mouths" not needed to graze sheep. "The country affords no means of living without a possession of land, and how is that to be procured" by those dispossessed from that very land to make way for sheep? As a result of his observations, Selkirk concluded that emigration was "an unavoidable result of the general state of the country...."

In 1803, on the desirability of emigration, he cited a letter from a settler in Canada who exhorted his countrymen "to throw off the yoke of bondage and the shackles of slavery, and to quit the land of Egypt and come to this land of Canaan," adding, "How can I say otherwise when I never knew what actual freedom or the spirit of equality was till I came to Canada? We have wholesome laws and impartial judges; we have the blessings of the gospel, and peace in the midst of plenty. Here are no landlord, no factor, no threatening for your rents at Martinmas." (in *Third Report*, Appendix T, li)

Margaret Laurence, author: It was in the old days, a long time ago, after the clans was broken and scattered at the battle on the moors, and the dead men thrown into the long graves there, and no heather ever grew on those places, never again, for it was dark places they had become and places of mourning. Then in those days, a darkness fell over all the lands and the crofts of Sutherland. The Bitch-Duchess was living there then ... and her tacksmen [a leaseholder or tenant in the Highlands who sublets] rode through the countryside, setting fire to the crofts and turning out the people from their homes which they had lived in since the beginning of all time. And it was old men and old women with thin shanks and men in their prime and women with the child inside them and a great scattering of small children, like, and all of them was driven away from the lands of their fathers and onto the wild rocks of the shore.... *All the lands of Sutherland will be raising the sheep*, says the she-devil, *for they'll pay better than folk*. (Laurence, *Diviners*, 40)

Patrick Sellar, an Edinburgh lawyer: Lord and Lady Stafford [previously, Countess of Sutherland] were pleased humanely to order a new arrangement of this country: that the interior should be possessed by cheviot shepherds and the people brought down to the coast and placed there in lotts [or crofts] under the size of three arable acres, sufficient for the maintenance of an industrious family, but pinched enough to cause them to turn their attention to the fishing. I presume to say that the proprietors humanely ordered this arrangement, because it surely was a most benevolent action to put those barbarous hordes into a position where they could better associate together, apply to industry, educate their children and advance in civilisation. (in Hunter, *Last of the Free*, 258)

MK: Historically, emigration from Scotland to North America, as from most of Europe, was "aspirational," in the sense that individual families made the decision to emigrate to better their circumstances. But in the case of the Highland crofters in the early nineteenth century, an entire population en masse was compelled by the threat of utter destitution to leave their homeland, first by their eviction from the glens, then by the collapse of the kelp industry in which some families, driven to the seashores, had scooped and scraped a meagre living, and finally felled by a potato famine mid-century.

David Craig, author: I have interviewed direct descendents of people evicted from Strathnaver (in 1814 and 1819), who survived by licking oatmeal dust from the floor after their dwellings had been nailed up; from Strathfleet a few years earlier, where houses were torched by estate heavies while the men were away at the French wars; and from Kildonan, where people drove their sheep for miles to a temporary place only to have them savaged by dogs. By all means let us remember the majority of emigrants who made it through to a decent life in America and Australia – as long as we also remember the thousands rough-housed out of their homes (looms burned, fires dowsed with the day's milk), or the one in six who died of typhus, smallpox and cholera on the emigrant ships. (Craig, "Letter," unpaginated)

George Bryce: The Earl of Selkirk has been charged by those who knew little of him with being a man of feudal instincts. His temper was the exact opposite of this. When he saw his Scottish fellow-countrymen being driven out of the their homes in Sutherlandshire, and sent elsewhere to give way for sheep farmers, and forest runs, and deer stalking, it touched his heart, and his three Emigration Movements to the Red River, the last culminating in the Kildonian Colonists, showed not only what title and means could do, but showed a kindly and compassionate heart beating under the starry badge of Earldom. (Bryce, *Romantic Settlement*, 35)

MK: In 1807, Lord Selkirk married Jean Wedderbrun-Coville, member of a distinguished bourgeois family in Scotland. His new brothers-in-law also happened to be major stockholders in the HBC, and soon Selkirk joined them in buying stock of his own. Alexander Mackenzie of the NWC had the same idea for himself and his associates – to buy a controlling interest in the HBC – but by Spring 1810 Mackenzie had acquired a mere £800 worth of stock compared to the £12,000 acquired by Selkirk and his relatives, and the NWC was out of the game. Selkirk was now ready to make a proposal to the Governor and Committee of the HBC: that, in exchange for a grant of land within the territories owned by the HBC in the Canadian interior, he would build a settlement on the Red River at The Forks with the Assiniboine. It was in the Company's own interests to enable such a colony to be established, as the Committee itself explained later to the colonial Minister in these terms:

"The servants of the Hudson's Bay Company, employed in the fur-trade, have hitherto been fed with provisions exported from England. Of late years this expense has been so enormous, that it became desirable to try the practicability of raising provisions within the territory itself.... It did not appear that agriculture would be carried on with sufficient care and attention by servants in the immediate employ of the company; but by establishing independent settlers, and giving them freehold tenures of land, the company expected that they would obtain a certain supply of provisions at a moderate price. The company also entertained expectations of considerable eventual benefit from the improvement of their landed property by means of agricultural settlements.... With these views, the company were induced in the year 1811 to dispose of a large tract of lands to the Earl of Selkirk in whose hands they trusted the experiment would be prosecuted with due attention, as the grant was made subject to adequate conditions of settlement." (in A.E. Brown)

Grant of Assiniboia to Lord Selkirk, By the Hudson's Bay Company, June 12, 1811: This Indenture ... Between the Governor and Company of Adventurers of England trading into Hudson Bay of the one part and The Right Honorable Thomas Earl of Selkirk of the other part.... Now therefore this Indenture witnesseth that in pursuance of such Agreement and in consideration of the sum of ten shillings of lawful money of Great Britain to the said Governor and Company well and truly paid by the said Earl of Selkirk at or before the execution of these presents.... The said Governor and Company have given granted aliened enfeoffed[2] and confirmed And by these presents Do give grant alien enfeoff and confirm unto the said Earl of Selkirk his Heirs and Assigns All that Tract of Land and Territory being within and formerly part of aforesaid Lands and Territories of the said Governor and Company bounded by an imaginary line running as follows.... (in C. Martin, *Selkirk*, 201)...extending from 52° 30 north latitude (passing through Lake Winnipeg) on the north, to the height of land on the south, between the northern watershed and that of the Missouri, the Mississippi, and Lake Superior; and stretching from Lake Winnipeg and the Winnipeg River system (from its source near the Lake Superior watershed) on the east, almost to the source of the Assiniboine on the west. (C. Martin, *Selkirk*, 34)

MK: Some 116,000 square miles of territory (300,000 sq km, or 74 million acres) centering on the Red River Valley were conveyed to Lord Selkirk. Five times bigger than Scotland itself, and for the princely sum of $2.50, the grant of land extended from Lake Winnipeg down into present-day Minnesota and North Dakota. The colonists were not to trade in furs, they were to develop farms.

W.L. Morton: ... the colony would furnish provisions for the posts and boat brigades. It would supply country-bred men for the service and offer a sanctuary to retired servants and their dependents, relieving the posts of the cost of supporting them; finally, it would confirm the Company's title to the soil, flouted by the Montreal traders, through actual occupation. (Morton, *Manitoba*, 44–5)

2 1. (Law) To give a feud, or right in land, to; to invest with a fief or fee; to invest (any one) with a freehold estate by the process of feoffment.

George Bryce: **Sir Alexander [Mackenzie] ... was the guardian of the rights
of the North-West Company and manfully he stood for them....
To the fur trader or rancher, the incoming of the farmer is ever
obnoxious. The beaver and the mink desert the streams whenever
the plowshare disturbs the soil. The deer flee to their coverts, the
wolf and the fox are exterminated, and even the muskrat has a
troubled existence when the dog and the cat, the domestic animals, make their appearance. The proposed settlement is to be
opposed, and Lord Selkirk's plans thwarted at any cost.**

**The Nor'-Westers are frantic. The duel had begun! Who
will win? Cunning and misrepresentation are to be employed to
check the success of the Colony and also local opposition on the
other side of the Atlantic, should the scheme ever come to anything. At present their hope is that it may fall to pieces of its own
weight.** (Bryce, *Romantic Settlement*, 41–43)

John Strachan, Rector of York, Upper Canada, to his Lordship, 1811: **Your
projected settlement on Red River ... appears to me ... one
of the most gross impositions that ever was attempted on the
British public. [It] must be attended with the most baneful consequences to all those unfortunate men who, deluded by false
promises, shall leave their homes for such a dreary wilderness.**
(in Kelsey, 75)

R.G. MacBeth: **The [North West] Company regarded colonization as a distinct
enemy to their trading business, and as the organization that had
first pushed its way into the prairie country, they professed right
of occupation by precedence. They conveniently overlooked the
somewhat important fact that in point of law they were intrud-
ing on the territory which the Hudson's Bay Company held by**

royal charter; and these North-Westers wrought skilfully upon the credulity of the plainsmen by telling them that colonization would drive away the buffalo and destroy all their old methods of living. Hence the old Roman cry as to Carthage was revived under the modern form, "The Colony must be destroyed." (R.G. MacBeth, 39)

MK: In 1809, the NWC built Fort Gibraltar at The Forks of the Red and Assiniboine rivers near the location on the Assiniboine of Pierre La Vérendrye's Fort Rouge built some sixty years earlier. The Hudson's Bay Company had built a stores depot on the east side of the Red River. With the arrival of the first colonists and the building of Fort Douglas right under the nose of Fort Gibraltar in 1813, the looming confrontation of the two companies with the settlers caught between them could not have been more graphic.

Howard Angus Kennedy, newspaperman, author: The two companies were practically at war. In a 'civilized' land, with the law wide awake, unscrupulous competitors have to be satisfied with slower methods of ruining each other. In the wild west of our fathers' time the voice of civilization was feeble, and law was laughed at. The passion of gain was free to indulge its natural tendency to crime. Parties of rival traders, meeting in solitudes where no witnesses were to be feared, fought out their differences with gun and hatchet.... Many deeds of violence remained hidden in the breasts of the perpetrators. Of those that came to light, the most notorious was the 'Battle of Seven Oaks,' or 'Red River Massacre,' in 1816.... It was the foundation of the first white settlement in the West that led to that shocking event. (Kennedy, *The Book of the West*, 52, 53)

"Colonists on the Red River in North America."
Painted by Peter Rindisbacher.
(Library and Archives Canada, MIKAN no: 2835808)

TWO: COLONY 1811-12

Selkirk's Plans Go Ahead

Lord Selkirk, *The Collected Writings*: **Suffice it to say, that, from the first moment when the Hudson's Bay Company made a grant of land for the purpose of forming an agricultural settlement upon an extended scale within their territories, the North-West Company avowed the most determined hostility to the undertaking. The settlement in question having been formed in a district, which had been exhausted of valuable furs by the extirpation of the beaver, and the settlers, by the very tenure of their lands, being also debarred from interfering with the Fur Trade, it may appear extraordinary that any set of traders should have entertained such a determined animosity against its establishment. Nothing surely can be imagined more harmless in itself than the occupation of a farmer. (in Bumsted, *Collected Writings of Lord Selkirk*, 95)**

Jack Bumsted, interview: **In 1805, Selkirk wrote a book, *Observations on the Present State of the Highlands of Scotland*, which argued essentially** that Highlanders were being displaced by agricultural modernization, there was no place in Scotland for them to go, they were being shifted into fishing villages along the sea coast and being put into factories in Glasgow and Lanark. Selkirk insisted that these people had the right to continue with their agricultural way of life, their agricultural culture, and that they could do it best by moving from Scotland and Britain to North America where they could continue their agricultural ways.

And his book was exceptionally favourably received at the time. The Enlightenment social scientists of the day liked Selkirk's' argument and the various journals in London and Edinburgh were all sympathetic and very hard on the landlords, in a sense unnecessarily because, as I've argued in several places, in this early period the clearances were actually done by the people themselves, not by the landlords. This is to say that the Scots were actually emigrating to North America as a reaction to the modernization they were experiencing, not because the landlords were trying to get rid of them.

MK: Nineteenth-century historian of the Selkirk Colony, George Bryce, tells us that "Lord Selkirk, whose estates were in the south of Scotland, and who had no special connection with the Celts, nevertheless took pity on the helpless Highland exiles." (1909, 55) In fact, he had recruited among hard-up Irishmen as well, ostensibly eager to emigrate, and to prepare the settlement for the arrival of real farmer-settlers the following year.

Jack Bumsted, interview: Selkirk had discovered in research he had done in Scotland in the earlier years of the century, that the Red River Valley was rich agricultural land. But I don't think anyone in

Scotland quite understood how *cold* it was going to get in the wintertime but at the same time they knew it was rich dirt. And the people that Selkirk spoke to told him that it was going to grow good stuff, good foodstuff. So, why not? Good agricultural land because it's rich humus-filled soil. You just look at it — even today you look at it and you can see how *black* it is.

MK: Meantime, there was already a flourishing settlement on the Red and Assiniboia.

R.D. Garneau, historian: Many historians totally ignore the existence of the Metis Red River Settlement that is decades old. It is noteworthy that, prior to the European invasion of Red River, there were thousands of Metis settlers in the region called Red River. The Red River des Metis Settlement dates to about 1775 or earlier. It is noteworthy that there are over 180 Metis births at Red River Settlement. This is amazing considering most families travel on the two annual bison (buffalo) hunts as well as on freighting, trapping or trading activities. It is also not uncommon for one family in the Metis Settlements to care for 15 young children while the parents are away. (Garneau)

Edgar Stanford Russenholt, author: In 1811, it is past mid-April when the ice breaks up on the Assiniboine River and the Red. At "the Forks," where the two streams merge, ice piles up in booming commotion; grinding giant blocks to slush, until the backed-up flood sweeps all ahead on its muddy torrent.... June is the month when the Nor'West Company canoe brigades bring their harvest of furs from the remote interior, to Fort William [on Lake Superior]; and return with the year's supplies.... There are 20 or 30 Nor'West employees at Fort Gibraltar [on the Assiniboine]; and, probably, 150 free-men, with native wives and children numbering, perhaps 600. Indians – resident Saulteaux; and returning Cree and Assiniboines – may total 1000. Fort Gibraltar, for a few days, is a hilariously busy centre. (Russenholt, *The Heart of the Continent*, 23–4)

MK: Fort Gibraltar, complete with palisades five and a half metres high and a wooden watchtower dominating the surrounding countryside, encircled two houses that accommodated forty servants; stables, carpenter, and blacksmith shops; a meat-house, kitchen, and store; ice house; and the spacious quarters of the *bourgeois* [wintering partner] at the centre. (In Macleod, 10) But in the summer of 1811 in this "hilariously busy centre," the alarming news from Montreal has reached them – that the rival HBC is making plans to bring to the Forks – unbelievably – *settlers*.

Samuel Hull Wilcocke, Montreal pamphleteer: Lord Selkirk proceeded in the prosecution of his plans.... Agents were employed [in Scotland and Ireland] to circulate Advertisements, holding out the most fallacious prospects to Settlers in his intended Colony. The climate and soil were represented as superior to any in British North America, the culture of hemp and wool, held out as an inducement to the agriculturalist, when his Lordship must have known, it was impossible to transport the former to the sea, and that the plains, where the flocks were to be maintained, are principally characterized by the immense troops of wolves which infest them. (Wilcocke, *A Narrative*, 15–16)

George Bryce: To the philanthropist or the benevolent sympathizer like Lord Selkirk, who aims at benefiting suffering humanity, it is not the trouble, the self-sacrifice, or the spending of money in relief that is the worry, but it is the bitterness, the suspicion, the unworkableness, and the selfishness of the poverty-stricken themselves that disturbs and distresses the benefactor's heart.... Poverty in its worst form is a gaunt and ravenous beast.... So Lord Selkirk found it, when he undertook to help the poverty-stricken Celts of the Scottish Highlands and of the West of Ireland.... But the poor are timid, and they love even their straw-thatched cottages, and it needs active and decided men to press upon them the advantages which are offered them. The Emigration Agent is a necessity. (Bryce, *Romantic Settlement*, 45–6)

Margaret Laurence: But the people were afraid, see? They did not dare. Better to die on the known rocks in the land of their ancestors, so some said. Others said the lands across the seas were bad lands, filled with terrors and the demons and the beasts of the forest and those being the beasts which would devour a man as soon as look at him. *Well*, says Piper Gunn, *God rot your flabby souls then, for my woman and I will go and rear our daughters and sons in the far land and make it ours.* (Laurence, 41)

Preparations to Leave Scotland

MK: Undeterred, and requiring recruits, Selkirk engaged an agent, Miles Macdonell, to get them. Years earlier, he had made the acquaintance of this United Empire Loyalist and army officer in the Canadian militia who was a member of a well-known Catholic family of Highlanders. According to George Bryce, writing in 1909, Macdonell was a "man of standing and of executive ability" who had a brother, John, in the North-West Fur Company, who had kept a journal. In it he had written, and his brother surely read, that "From the Forks of the Assiniboine and Red Rivers the plains are quite near the banks, and so extensive that a man may travel to the Rocky Mountains without passing a wood, a mile long. The soil on the Red River and the Assiniboine is generally a good soil, susceptible of culture, and capable of bearing rich crops." Buffalo are plentiful as are the fish in the rivers, "plenty of sturgeon, catfish, goldeyes, pike and whitefish – the latter so common that men have been seen to catch thirty or forty apiece while they smoked their pipes." He might have mentioned that The Forks is embedded in 6000 years of history, back to camps of Aboriginal bison hunters. (Bryce, *Romantic Settlement*, 48)

George Bryce: To reach this land of plenty, which his brother knew so well, Miles Macdonell became the leader of Lord Selkirk's Colonists. He arrived in Great Britain in the year for starting of the Colony [1811] and immediately, as being a Roman Catholic in religion, went to the West of Ireland to recommend the Emigration scheme, obtain subscriptions of stock, and to engage workmen as colonists. Glasgow was then, as now, the centre of Scottish industry, and it is to Glasgow that the penniless Highlanders flock in large numbers for work and residence. Here was a suitable field for the Emigration Agent. (Bryce, *Romantic Settlement*, 48)

William Auld, HBC chief factor, Fort Churchill: If Lord Selkirk had advertized for a fool of the first magnitude he never could have better succeeded than he has done with the present man. (in Bumsted, *A Life*, 231)

George Bryce: And now as the time draws nigh for gathering together at a common port, the Stromness (Orkney), the Glasgow, the Sligo and the Lewis contingents to face the stormy sea and seek a new untried home, a fierce storm breaks out upon the land. Evidence accumulates that the heat and opposition of the "Nor '-West" partners ... were to break out in numberless hidden and irritating efforts to stop and perhaps render impossible the whole Colonizing project.... So the aid of the press was used to throw doubt upon the enterprise. Inverness is the Capital of the Highlanders, and so the "Inverness Journal," containing an effusion signed by "Highlander," [in fact Simon McGillivray, a partner in London of the company McTavish, Fraser and Company, marketing N WC furs and purchasing trade goods] was spread broadcast through the Highlands, the Islands, and the Orkneys, picturing the dangers of their journey, the hardships of the country, the deceitfulness of the agents, and the mercenary aims of the noble promoter. (Bryce, *Romantic Settlement*, 49-50)

MK: McGillivray went so far as to publish a letter in the *Inverness Journal* warning the hapless recruits to Selkirk's scheme that what lay ahead of them were "2000 miles of Inland Navigation — stemming strong currents and dangerous rapids & carrying boats and cargoes over numerous portages." That much was fair enough. But warlike "natives" would greet them on arrival and they would find themselves surrounded so that "Even if [they] escape the scalping knife, they will be subject to constant alarm and terror. Their habitations, their Crops, their Cattle will be destroyed and they will find it impossible to exist in the Country." (in Payne, *The Fur Trade in Canada*, 58)

Unsurprisingly, Macdonell was unable to recruit nearly as many men as the enterprise required. Some of those who did show up at Stornoway in May 1811 and waited around for the much-delayed HBC ships that would take them to Hudson Bay were full of doubts and soon deserted while others threatened to do so unless their wages were increased.

Donald Gunn, historian: [They] had time for reflection; unfavorable reports of the country to which they were to be transported were circulated; it was known then in the Highlands and North of Scotland by the significant and appropriate name of "The land of the cold," the abode of perpetual winter. They became terrified at the thought of being doomed to suffer the intense severity of the artic [sic] winter of Hudson's Bay and the extraordinary labor and drudgery to which they would be subjected in the Hon. Company's service. The effect of these fears soon became manifest ... [S]ome of those who had embarked refused to go further, threatened the captain's life, and at the same time declared that if they would not order them to be conveyed to the shore that they would seize the boats and go to the land. A few, in the height of their fury, sprang over-board, swam unmolested to the shore, and fled to the hills, and were never taken. (Gunn, A History of Manitoba, 69)

MK: Customs officials held up the ships' departure on "technical grounds," a naval press gang threatened the loiterers, and the livestock selected for the colony's establishment could not be taken aboard after all, because the decrepit hulk of a ship could not carry enough water for the crossing. But finally, on July 26, 1811, dangerously late in the Atlantic sailing season, the Edward and Ann shove off from Stornoway, its passengers, thirty-six workmen and Miles Macdonell, the newly appointed Governor of Selkirk's land grant, already at the end of their tether.

Vera Kelsey, author: Two dreary months later the *Edward and Ann* dropped anchor in Hudson Bay. The Selkirkers' eagerness to feel firm ground beneath their feet chilled at the sight of the barren shore, studded with rocks and blighted vegetation. And chilled again when the ungainly, lead-roofed buildings of York Factory proved hardly less cold than the reception tendered them by William Auld, overseas governor of the Company, and other officials. These officials were antagonistic on sight to Macdonell's energetic confidence in his own ability to overcome all obstacles. ... A really capable, conscientious man, Captain Macdonell did surmount both winter and obstacles. In spite of a riot among his cold, homesick flock that resulted in two being jailed for shipment to London. Of an armed insurrection, slyly abetted by York Factory, that lost nine more to Company employ. Of an epidemic of scurvy that took the life of one. (Kelsey, *Red River Runs North*, 76-77)

Winter on The Bay 1811–1812

Anne Matheson Henderson, historian: It was September 24th when they landed at York Factory on the Bay; they would never manage the inland trip to the Forks before freeze-up. They would have to winter over at the Factory. Unhappy as he was with their arrival, nevertheless Governor Auld, who would eventually join the North-west Company, chose a campsite for the party twenty-three miles up the Nelson River, and there in huts built Canadian style under the direction of Miles Macdonell, the winter was spent in hunting and fishing and when supplies were available in building York boats for their inland trip. Many of the men were troublemakers, quarrelsome and quite unsuitable for the work they were called on to do. (Henderson)

MK: The picture is a sorry one: shut out from York Factory, poorly-clad workmen awkwardly hacked away with axes at tree logs to fashion their winter quarters and heat them, while the Bay men watched and sneered; men subsisted on a monotonous diet, vulnerable to scurvy; the various groups – Irish, Orcadian, Glaswegian – frequently beat each other up. "Good souls they may have been in the eyes of God," writes J.G. MacGregor, but "they were a sorry selection. And so they proved during the long, cold, hungry winter." Meanwhile, Miles Macdonell, who could neither control them nor count on the co-operation of the fur traders in disciplining them, "wrung his hands." (MacGregor, 183)

E.S. Russenholt: [Meanwhile seven] hundred miles southward, at "the Forks," the inhabitants who know the country and its climate, likewise prepare for the winter. Hunters return from the fall buffalo hunt, their creaking carts loaded with meat and robes. They trade some to the fur-men. The remainder will provide plenty for their families, all winter. Some of the Indian hunters set up their teepees near the Fort; others go to Netley Creek, to harvest their bits of corn. The hybrid families re-occupy the cabins they left in June. The free-men take their families back to their log-homes, scattered along the Assiniboine and the Red; and harvest whatever potatoes and grain are in their little fields. The fur-men at Fort

Gibraltar pile up cordwood, buy provisions and moccasins; and wait for winter. At many forts there are crops to harvest; and grain to thresh. Fur-men hate, despise and fear farming; but at fur forts from Assiniboia to Edmonton and Athabasca, fields are tilled. (Russenholt, 25–6)

MK: Although Miles Macdonell remained high in Lord Selkirk's estimation, Selkirk's biographer, Jack Bumsted, judges him a bit of a prig (he disapproved of the "sleeping and living arrangements" of HBC employees with Aboriginal women) and a man stiff to the point of inflexibility who preferred to discipline men rather than seek their co-operation: "men who had not expected to be governed by martial law needed to be inspirationally led, not heavily disciplined." (Bumsted, *Selkirk: A Life*, 210)

By the beginning of July 1812, preparing to leave the Bay for the Forks, with only twenty-one workmen left, sickness and desertion having taken the other fifteen, the remainder still disputatious, Macdonell wrote to Selkirk: "a man of one nation is prejudiced against going with one of another . . . I shall go on with any number — take possession of the tract & hoist the Standard." (Bumsted, 217)

They Walk to The Forks July 1812

MK: Finally, on July 6, 1812, Macdonell set out with the men remaining to him to make the trek 1126 km south to the Forks of the Red and the Assiniboia where they would have only a few weeks to prepare the site for the arrival of Selkirk's settlers, the Highland farmers.

Vera Kelsey: When the ice left the rivers in mid-June, he and his twenty-two remaining colonists had built four crude copies of the York boat used by Bay brigades throughout the interior. Early on the morning of July 6, a bull, cow, and wheat seed were stowed aboard, though, strangely, for an agricultural colony at the junction of two fish-filled rivers, not an item of either farming or fishing equipment was included.... Sheepishly, under the mocking eyes of Company personnel and ex-Selkirkers, eleven Scots and eight Irish climbed into the boats. Escorted by experienced Bay traders returning to their posts, the little flotilla set sail. (Kelsey, 77)

Macdonell to Selkirk: At Oxford House [an inland post] I engaged 3 experienced men at advanced wages for one year with these & Tipotem a young Indian who volunteered to come with me from the Nelson, my number is augmented to 23 effective men as per enclosed Return. With this weak force I could not man all the small craft necessary for transporting the stores, & therefore procured two large boats that carry each the cargoes of 3 of the common size. One is a good new boat got from Mr Sinclair Chief of West Winipie the other is old & was condemned but by frequent repairs on every carrying place will I hope serve to bring us up.

    * * * * We have now got past all the bad navigation have a prospect of getting soon to the Land of Promise this navigation is not near so bad as was reported, & is very capable of improvement, but is yet entirely in the state of nature ... as if none but Indians had passed before us the Carrying Places are in a most wretched state. (*Selkirk papers*, vol. 2, pp. 443-449. Canadian Archives, M. 734.)

Donald Gunn: For miles, in the lower rivers, the boats had to be towed by men against a swift current, besides many discharges or landing places where part of the cargo had to be carried; and in other places the entire cargo had to be carried over on men's backs, the boats taken out of the water and launched over dry land. Besides lesser bodies of water they had to pass over Lake Winnipeg, a distance of three hundred miles. (Gunn, 105)

MK: The route they travelled between the Bay and the Forks was an old fur trader route that traversed eleven waterways and required thirty-four portages before they even got to Norway House on Lake Winnipeg, itself 480 km across. At the bottom of the lake they moved into the mouth of the Red River and onto the Forks.

They Reach The Forks

Vera Kelsey: Fifty-five days crawled away before Red River Valley's first European settlers — footsore, weather-beaten, mosquito and black-fly bitten — arrived at the forks of the Red and Assiniboine.... A group of Company traders camped there greeted them but did not welcome them. And the captain's cousin, Alexander Macdonell, as chief trader at Fort Gibraltar, made plain his loyalty to North West Company by sending mounted Métis, hideously painted as savages, to strike them cold with fear. (Kelsey, 77)

James J. Hargrave, HBC trader, author, and journalist: [At the Forks] they found themselves — metaphorically speaking — at home. They were in the centre of the American continent, 1500 or 1600 miles in direct distance from the nearest city residence of civilized man in America, and separated from the country whence they came by an impassable barrier. (Hargrave, *Red River*, 73)

MK: They had left the Bay July 6th and reached the Forks on August 30th, 1812. Here they found the Company stores depot on the east side of the Red River (not far from where St. Boniface Hospital now stands) and made camp there, directly across the river from the North West Company's Fort Gibraltar. Little, however, had been made ready for their arrival, in spite of Macdonell's instructions and expectations. Feeding these first colonists was an immediate concern and Macdonell was forced to buy supplies from the nearest trading post, which happened to be the NWC's Fort Gibraltar.

Macdonell to Selkirk: Not withstand all the orders, there was not one bag of Pemican or any other article of provision reserved for us. Cattle were now at a great distance & nothing was to be procured from the natives who never lay up any stock, & have only from hand to mouth. The river was therefore the main resource of us all, which, from our being very scarce of hooks, afforded but a scanty supply of fish for so many people. (*Selkirk papers*, vol. 2, pp. 443-449. Canadian Archives, M. 734.)

Vera Kelsey: Nevertheless, on September 4, 1812, flags flew at the junction of the Red and Assiniboine. Alexander Macdonell and his Nor'West traders, armed Hudson's Bay traders, colonists, Métis, and Indians stood more or less at attention. And Captain Miles Macdonell, as governor of Assiniboia, in the name of Lord Selkirk, took formal possession of Red River Valley. (Kelsey, 77)

Accordingly, Macdonell chose as the site of Red River Valley's first white settlement, a triangle on the west bank of Red River, just three-quarters of a mile north of the junction. Bounded on two sides by the thickly wooded River, on the third by golden prairies, it was a really pleasing location. To honour Lord Selkirk, he named it Point Douglas. (Kelsey, 81)

MK: Today, in La Vérendrye Park, in Saint-Boniface, the Franco-Manitoban city ward of Winnipeg, stands a bronze plaque recalling that, near this site — directly facing the forks of the Red and Assiniboia rivers — on September 4, 1812, the Red River settlement was formally proclaimed, with a guard of honour under arms. The plaque continues: "Macdonell, the first governor, was attended by officers and servants of the North West Company from Fort Gibraltar which lay across the Red River. The Patent and Macdonell's commission were read in French and English."

E.S. Russenholt: Thus, 2 or 3 dozen fur-men and settlers announce (to themselves) that Assiniboia has new owners. Few of the Canadian free-men, Saulteaux, Cree, Assiniboine or those of mixed parentage among the "populace" who drink the keg of rum, know or care about the proceedings. No one tells them that this, their homeland, is being handed over, by a few recent invaders, to owners who have arrived even more recently. "The populace" whose lives centre at "the Forks" number, perhaps, 2000 souls. They are multi-lingual. Only a minor fraction of them speak English or French; still fewer understand the legal verbiage. In fact, only "several Canadians and Indians" witness Macdonell's assertion of title. Most of "the populace" are a month away on the plains, exercising real ownership of the land by harvesting its wealth in the fall buffalo Hunt. (Russenholt, 28)

MK: Contrary to the assertions of Samuel Hull Wilcocke in his hostile *A Narrative*, that, at the "farcical ceremonies," the "Indians, attracted by the ceremony, were no sooner informed of its intent, than they expressed themselves hostile to the Establishment, as had been foreseen and foretold when it was projected," the situation was more nuanced. (*A Narrative*, 19) The "Indians" were likely the Saulteaux of Netley Creek, about fifty kilometres north of the Forks, and they welcomed the arrival of settlers. According to writer Maggie Siggins in *Marie-Anne: The Extraordinary Story of Louis Riel's Grandmother*, a settlement would provide the Saulteaux alternative customers to the Nor'Westers, "loathed" as bullies and cheats. When settlers finally arrived, the Saulteaux would provide them with much-needed food the first couple of seasons: wild rice, maple syrup, Indian corn, and of course meat. (Siggins, 210)

Anne M. Henderson: As soon as the formalities were over the Governor set about preparing for the coming of the Settlers. The land chosen was on the west side of the Red River north of the point of land that we know today as Point Douglas. This land was comparatively clear of timber, a bad fire having burned over it some years earlier, and this would, of course, enable the Settlers to get their land broken and crops in with a minimum of labor. The farms were 100 acres, facing on the river, running back two miles with another two miles as a "hay privilege," and directly across the river each Settler was granted a wood lot, where timber could be cut for his own use. Timber was cut for homes and farm buildings as well as for the Colony Fort, which was located at the base of the Point, south of the Settlement.

MK: It would have been an auspicious beginning but for the fact that, having arrived too late in the season for winter sowing of wheat or
raising potatoes, the colony would be dogged by the problem of
food supplies. They built a storehouse and hacked away at the
prairie sod — there was no blacksmith, thus no plough — turning it over for what they believed, optimistically, would be the
seedbed of their first crop of winter wheat. Miles Macdonell,
in his first trip to Red River in 1812, had carried a bushel and a
half of seed wheat and planted it dutifully. (The Selkirk Wheat
Monument in Winnipeg's Joe Zuken Park commemorates the
deed.) "Unfortunately," writes Grant MacEwan, "it was winter
wheat that could not survive the Manitoba brand of winter, and
the precious seed was wasted." (*Grant MacEwan's West*, 38)

Macdonell to Selkirk cont'd: **Next day 9 Septr I set off on horseback for**
Pembina [winter buffalo hunting grounds] with an escort of three
men, reached there the 12th a day after my people. The following day after reconnoitring on horse-back for two or three hours
the ground round about, made choice of the point south side
the Pembina at its junction with the Red R. to build on [the
future site of Fort Daer in present-day North Dakota]. That same
evening my men encamped on it, & next day began to work. A
Canadian free man [employee of the NWC remaining in the country after being discharged from his engagement] was engaged to
fish for us; he made his hooks out of nails & was tolerably successful. A great quantity of meat began to come in from free
Canadians & natives, which enabled me to send a Supply to the
party at the Forks. After building a Store House; sketching out
some other buildings and seeing the work fairly agoing, I went
off in a boat 1st Octr for the Forks took along two horses & a

Harrow we did not stop night or day, yet with Contrary winds & a weak crew, it took us three days to get down.

My people had not wrought well a quantity of Hay was made but they had not sufficient ground cleared for the winter wheat so that it was 7th Octr before it could be sown, & then put under with the hoe; there being no Blacksmitii to make teeth for the harrow * * * *

I hired a Canadian who had a general acquaintance with the Indians, to trade meat from them & also Skins when they should offer them. This man was also to fish & assist in putting up some buildings I projected. An Indian was engaged to hunt for the support of the party, & I left a quantity of pemican for the people expected up, with orders for them to proceed immediately to Pembina. (*Selkirk papers*, vol. 2, pp. 443-449. Canadian Archives, M. 734.)

MK: The people "expected up" were the settler-farmers who had sailed on June 24 1812 aboard the *Robert Taylor* from Sligo, Ireland, all from the west of Ireland and the Hebrides — some seventy of them including women and young children, as well as sheep.

Wintering Over 1812-1813

George Bryce: One morning nearly forty years ago, the writer wandered eastward toward the Red River, from Main Street, down what is now called Lombard Street. Here not far from the bank of the Red River stood a wooden house, then of the better class but now left far behind by the brick and stone and steel structures of modern Winnipeg.

The house still stands a stained and battered memorial of a past generation. On this October morning, of an Indian summer day ... was to be seen sitting on his verandah, the patriarch of the village, who was as well the genius of the place....

The writer was then quite a young man fresh from College, and with a simple introduction, after the easy manner of Western Canada, proceeded to hear the story of old Andrew McDermott, the patriarch of Winnipeg.

"Yes," said Mr. McDermott, "I was among those of the first year of Lord Selkirk's immigrants.... Thus the story-telling began.... (Bryce, *Romantic Settlement*, 10–11)

MK: Their voyage to Hudson Bay was no smoother than the one endured a year earlier by the working party on the *Edward and Ann*, when Miles Macdonell was leader of that expedition. The expedition leader on this sailing was an Irishman, Owen Keveny, judged a tyrant by his crew who almost rose in mutiny. (Keveny was eventually murdered by two employees of the nwc in September 1816.)

Samuel H. Wilcocke: While Mr Macdonell was thus employed at the Red River, Lord Selkirk was not less active in obtaining fresh recruits of Settlers.... Mutiny amongst the Emigrants was the first consequence of their cramped and uncomfortable state; the gaol-fever next broke out amongst them, which, it is understood, carried off a considerable number, either on board or soon after they were landed at Churchill or York Forts, in the Bay. (Wilcocke, *A Narrative*, 22)

MK: Keveny's party arrived safely at York Factory in early September, 1812. Rather than have them winter over on the Bay — a decidedly uncomfortable experience for families – Keveny decided they would all continue south to Point Douglas and Governor Macdonell, (who had only just arrived in Red River himself). Ever pessimistic, Samuel Wilcocke would write: "The cumulation of delays and instances of unforeseen circumstances outh to have signalled the lack of viability of the Red River project, at least as presently conceived." (A Narrative, 218)

On reaching the Forks in mid-October, the new emigrants discovered only five men at Point Douglas, Macdonell having escorted the rest of the colonists south, to winter over in Pembina, where they would be close to the buffalo herds, the Métis buffalo hunters, and food. They trudged on, south along the Red River to its junction with the Pembina River, guided by a band of Indians, to Macdonell and the others at the camp, a HBC post directly across the Pembina River from the NWC's Fort Pembina. They arrived October 27, 1812, and pitched in with the others to prepare their winter camp.

Macdonell to Lord Selkirk: Having but five old hands engaged below who were tolerably expert at the Axe three of whom only arrived with Mr Keveney, it was the 21st Novr [1812] before all the families & men got housed. The quarters for myself & officers were only habitable 27th Dec r some of the gentlemen remained some time afterwards in tents from choice to brave the winter. As soon as the place took some form & a decent Flag Staff was erected in it, it was called Fort Daer. (Selkirk papers, vol. 2, pp. 443–449. Canadian Archives, M. 734.)

Samuel H. Wilcocke: Settlers had to prepare for the ensuing winter, which already approached, and although the climate was less rigorous than that of York Fort, still, unprovided as they were with houses, clothing, or food, they could not but look forward to their situation with dismay. It was impossible to maintain them in a body, nor could the most active of the men procure subsistence by travelling over the immense lakes of snow in the plains, for want of deer-skin and snowshoes, like persons who had been accustomed to the Fur Trade of the country. The families were accordingly distributed, as there was a chance of escaping famine, some in the Forts of the Hudson's Bay Company, others in the huts of Freemen, and in the families of friendly Indians. (Wilcocke, A Narrative, 19)

Alexander Macdonell, fur trader and a partner of the NWC, cousin and brother-in-law of Miles MacDonell: [When herds were spotted, the freemen rushed to kill as many as they could, leaving the colonists to haul the meat back to camp, a job that sometimes took three days.] They were obliged to perform this duty destitute of all necessities, such as snow-shoes, caps, mittens, leather or blanket coats, socks, kettles, fire-steel or flint, and it is a fact that cannot be denied, that some of these wretches, for want of the means of making a fire, have buried themselves in banks of snow to prevent their being frozen to death, and have often been forced to eat the raw meat off their sledges." (in Wilcocke, A Narrative, 4)

MK: At the beginning of May 1813 they would return to Red River and do their best to build homes and plant crops.

Jack Bumsted, interview: There's no problem in understanding multiple miseries. For one thing, the first settlers who would have arrived here had no land cleared and they didn't have ploughs. They were doing it all with hoes and pointy sticks. And they were importing seed that was not necessarily properly acclimated to the growing conditions. The net result was that getting early crops was a pretty chancy business. It was hard to clear enough land with hand implements to really plant extensively.

Alexander Ross: [The colonists] sustained themselves in a wretched manner by means of hunting and fishing among the savages of the country, and often in their wanderings they endured every species of privation which misfortune could inflict or patience endure.... Every man, woman, and child now toiled from morning till night, to get a little seed in the ground; though, as events proved, they were only sowing for the fowls of the air to reap. (Ross, *The Red River Settlement*, 34)

Samuel H. Wilcocke: The following extract of a letter written from the spot, may convey some faint idea of their sufferings: "Take a view of the state of one family, and it will shew you what the sufferings are of these people: an old Highlander, his wife, and five children, the youngest eight or nine years of age, poor, and consequently badly provided with clothing to encounter the rigours of the climate, where the hottest summer never thaws the ground to any considerable depth – see this family, sitting on the damp ground, freezing for want of sufficient covering, pinched and famishing for want of food; and the poor woman had to take the well-worn rug from her own miserable pallet, to sell for a little oat-meal to give her dying children, and in vain, for two of them did not survive this scene of misery." (*A Narrative*, 17-18)

MK: The settlement would justify all the sacrifices of the colonists when, once established as agriculturally productive, it supplied the HBC with cheap food. But it had a secondary purpose, to have "feet on the ground" and secure the Bay's claim on the territory in the face of the NWC's defiance. But these two aims were in conflict with each other from the beginning: the presence of successful farmers was intolerable to a commercial trader. Even worse, to the NWC trader, Selkirk's settlers were an *instrument* of the Hudson's Bay Company's competition with the NWC for control of the interior fur trade.

Lord Selkirk to William Hillier 1812: Give them (the Nor'Westers) warning that the land belongs to the Hudson's Bay Company; and that they must remove from it.... They must not cut any timber, either for building or for fuel. What they have cut should be openly and forcibly seized; and their buildings destroyed. They should be warned that they are not to fish in our waters; and if they put down nets, seize them as you would in England those of a poacher! (in Russenholt, 27)

Auguste-Henri de Trémaudan, historian: Cultivation of the soil and animal husbandry were activities that did not agree well with the commerce in fur. The "Bourgeois" of the trade saw in these occupations of the new arrivals a serious threat to their interests, inasmuch as they had been led here by a man the Nor'Westers considered to be if not an enemy at least a troubling and dangerous adversary. By the same token, they viewed unfavourably the fact that the Métis who, up to this point and by force of circumstance had been very loyal to them [the NWC], were now gradually to change their practice as trappers, hunters and voyageurs and to begin to acquire the sedentary habits of one who plants crops and raises animals, occupations which "Messieurs" the Bourgeois affected to despise. (Trémaudan, *Histoire de la nation métisse*, 85 mk trans.)

Douglas Hill, author: The story of the first colonists in the west would be a nearly unbelievable account of hardships, dangers, misfortunes and mismanagement, even without the Northwesters' harassment. In many ways it is a heartbreaking story — mostly in terms of the colonists, torn out of their homeland, nervously going to a savage country where all their worst nightmares were to come true within months of their arrival, but also in terms of Selkirk, who had to watch his shining dreams of settlement grow tarnished and cracked, no matter how hard he worked or what compromises he made. Eventually his struggles and disappointments were to be the death of him. By then the process would have killed a number of settlers as well. (Hill, *The Opening of the Canadian West*, 26)

"Old Fort Douglas, circa 1815."
Painted by Ernest J. Hutchins.
(Library and Archives Canada, MIKAN no: 2837713)

THREE: THE COLONY IN CRISIS 1813–1815

Third Sailing

John Pritchard, trader of Red River, to Lord Selkirk: **But the real value of the country is the fertility of its soil, and the facility that nature offers to the industrious of obtaining the reward of his labour....** **In truth, I know of no country that offers so many advantages: an exceeding wholesome climate, a fertile soil, fish, flesh and fowls in abundance; and sugar and salt for the trouble of making them. In fact, all the necessaries and all the luxuries that are useful to mankind, are to be found there. Society only is wanting. (in Bumsted, *Collected Writings*, 22)**

MK: **The society Selkirk sought out further for his scheme was in the Highlands of Scotland, up the Strath, or broad mountain valley, of Kildonan Sutherlandshire, in the parish of Kildonan to be precise, described in the *Ordnance Gazetteer of Scotland* as consisting of "several small haughs [low-lying meadows] ... which yield good crops of oats and turnips. The soil on the higher banks along this strath consists of reddish gritty sand and peat-earth,** in which are embedded numerous detached pieces of granite or pudding-stone. The bulk of the agricultural population had been displaced by the introduction of sheep-farming between 1811 and 1831." (Groome) As unpromising as the soil must have been for the crofters, it represented nevertheless their livelihood and their explusion from their plots presaged their ruin.

Donald MacLeod, stone-mason and pamphleteer: The people meantime, dismayed and spirit-broken at the array of power brought against them, and seeing nothing but enemies on every side, even in those from whom they should have had comfort and succour, quietly submitted to their fate. The clergy, too, were continually preaching submission declaring these proceedings were foreordained of God, and denouncing the vengeance of Heaven and eternal damnation on those who should presume to make the least resistance. No wonder the poor Highlanders quailed under such influences; and the result was, that large districts of the parishes before mentioned were dispossessed at the May term, 1812.

The Earl of Selkirk hearing of these proceedings, came personally into Sutherlandshire, and by fair promises of encouragement, and other allurements, induced a number of the distressed outcast to enter into an arrangement with him, to emigrate to his estates on the Red River, North America. (MacLeod)

MK: June 28, 1813, Lord Selkirk himself was at Stromness to hail the group of colonists sailing aboard the *Prince of Wales* for Hudson Bay. Although he had received more than seven hundred applications for this sailing, in the end only one hundred could be accommodated: the North West Company had inconveniently leased all available ships precisely with the hope of thwarting the emigration to Red River. These settlers – who willingly paid Selkirk for their passage, 100 acres of land and a year's free provisions – came from the Highlands parishes, a few from the Islands, and others who were Company men from the Orkneys and Ireland, and they were sorely tried from the first day under sail: reportedly the captain was a bully, the officers lackadaisical, the steerage uncomfortably crowded, and the passengers tossed port to starboard in the foul weather – which contributed to an outbreak of fever claiming the life of the colonists' only trained doctor while still on board. Even after setting down at Churchill, the dying continued.

Hugh MacLennan, author: They were a race of hunters, shepherds and warriors who had discovered too late that their own courage and pride had led them to catastrophe, since it had enabled them to resist the Saxon civilization so long they had come to the end of the eighteenth century knowing nothing of the foreman, the boss, the politician, the policeman, the merchant or the buyer-and-seller of other men's work. When the English set out to destroy the clans of Scotland, the most independent of the Highlanders left their home with the pipes playing laments on the decks of their ships. They crossed the ocean and the pipes played again when they waded ashore. (MacLennan, *Each Man's Son*, vii)

Vera Kelsey: These were the Sutherlanders, nearly one hundred strong. By far the best settlers yet sent to Red River, they were the only ones to come joyfully. Of all the ruthless evictions of more than 450,000 tenants from Highland estates, those practised by Lady Sutherland were the most shameless. And of all the 15,000 people she dispossessed, those in the parish of Kildonan suffered most.

Memory of their homes a reeking mass of smoke and ashes, of the match applied while the sick and aged were in their beds, moved 700 of them to apply in one body to join Lord Selkirk's colony. . . . Hardly had the Sutherlanders sailed than typhus swept their ship. When it entered Hudson Bay, seven were dead, thirty dangerously ill. The captain, an obstinate man at any time, now in abject terror of the disease, anchored off a barren spot two hundred miles from York Factory, drove his passengers ashore. (Kelsey, 82)

MK: They had paid for passage to York Factory, which was prepared to provide accommodations and supplies. But they were abandoned, with only part of their luggage, at Fort Churchill on the Churchill River. Donald MacLeod painted a vivid picture: "on their arrival, after a tedious and disastrous passage, they found themselves deceived and deserted by his lordship, and left to their fate in an inclement wilderness, without protection against the savages, who plundered them on their arrival, and, finally massacred them all, with the exception of a few who escaped with their lives, and travelled across trackless wilds till they at last arrived in Canada."

In reality, the group, already weakened by fever, poorly dressed, and bereft of medical aid, managed to establish camp at a fresh water creek and called it Colony Creek in a fit of optimism about their prospects. But first they had to spend the winter.

Donald Gunn: Logs had to serve for chairs; the mud flooring had to supply the want of beds, sofas, tables, etc. We can easily fancy that these habitations were of the most simple construction, and very ill-adapted to defend the inmates from winter frosts, so often accompanied by heavy gales of wind, while Fahrenheit's thermometer ranged for months from 35 degrees to 50 degrees below zero, and many times in the course of the winter fell as low as 55 degrees or even to sixty degrees. To the above we may add, that they had to drag on flat sleds the scanty rations dealt out to them from the company stores, and in order to receive the same and return with it to their families they had every week to perform a journey of thirty miles on snow-shoes. (Gunn, 100)

Rev. John Strachan: On this route the rivers and lakes begin to break up in the latter end of May; but they are not sufficiently clear of ice to admit of a safe navigation till the middle of June; nor can a boat or canoe leave York Factory for the Red River later than the 6th of September. The settler can, therefore, depend only upon eighty-three days in the year for transacting the commercial business of the colony by Hudson's Bay.... During winter, when travelling on the ice and snow, things are still worse. Through all the distance, the country is extremely forbidding, being little more than one vast range of rocks, swamps, and morasses. Should any misfortune happen to the boat or canoe, the crew must inevitably perish. (Strachan, A Letter, 35)

Anne M. Henderson: After a cold, dreary winter [1813/14] on short rations and in cramped quarters, twenty-one men and twenty women, with guides and hunters, left Churchill for York Factory 5 April. They travelled in single file on snowshoes, drew their supplies on rough sleds, camped at nightfall, moved on at daybreak, a gunshot rousing them at 3:00 a.m. to have breakfast and hit the trail. Halfway down the line of march was the piper, and other stalwarts bringing up the rear gathered in the stragglers and helped the weary to keep up. In the same order as they left Colony Creek, we are told, they arrived at York Factory, having met with no serious mishap enroute. Archibald McDonald, who was in charge of the party, when reporting to Lord Selkirk tells of the progress made by the young women on snowshoes: "I must do them justice in the great reformation they made in science before they came to their journey's end." After a few days spent at York Factory in resting and preparing for their inland trip they left on 23 May and arrived at The Forks on 21 June, 1814 extremely good time for the trip. The balance of the party reached The Forks in August.

R.D. Garneau: The Metis, with much civility, placed themselves at the service of the poor Scottish party. [Charles?] Peltier showed them to land already cleared and ready for cultivation. He had provided horses and carts to assist in building Fort Daer. He also agreed to lend his cart and canoe for the summer to a family. Baptiste Roy received and took care of their seed grain. Francois Delorme and his Metis son supervised the building of their first dwelling. ... Fifteen Metis headed by Jean Baptiste Lagimodiere, alias Lagemodiere, Lagimodiere, and Lajimodiere (1778–1855), a French freeman, and included Bostonnias Pangman, b-1778, a Metis, conducted a hunting party to help feed and establish the Scots. The Metis Isham, likely the son of James Isham (a bigamist with a wife in Britain and Canada), supervised the preliminary work of breaking the soil and soon became their interpreter, while his son became a hunter for the Scots.

At this time there was no conflict between the English and French settlers. The Metis, however, were a bit apprehensive about what the real intentions of the H.B.C. were toward the Red River community. (Garneau)

THE SEVEN OAKS READER *Myrna Kostash*

At the Settlement

MK: Meanwhile, at HBC's Brandon House, Peter Fidler, who had furnished the settlement with pemmican and buffalo robes, with the return of Governor Miles Macdonell to Point Douglas at the beginning of May 1813, was employed to survey seven settlers' lots, each with ten-chain [201 metres] frontage north along the west bank of Red River. As it happened, this pattern of laying out lots in long and narrow strips along river frontage – as practised in Quebec – easily lent itself, according to Manitoba historian W.L. Morton, to the reproduction in the New World of the ancient Celtic infield and outfield system of Scotland. Now the spring sowing and land clearing could begin in earnest, in advance of the arrival of the Kildonan settlers. A sizeable building, 17 metres by 6.5 metres, that would become Fort Douglas, was under construction facing upriver and towards the NWC's Fort Gibraltar.

Grant MacEwan, Lieutenant Governor of Alberta, agriculturalist, and historian:
"Wha's a farm wi'out coos?" early settlers of Scottish origin were known to ask. There were children of seven and eight years of age in the pioneer farming community at Red River who had never tasted cow's milk, but it was almost impossible to obtain breeding stock. [In 1813 a bull, a cow, and a calf had been purchased by Peter Fidler for £100 and taken to the settlement at Red River.] But cattle raising is never without reverses. The bull bought from the North West Company turned ugly, and because they already had one bull, he was slaughtered for beef. Then Adam, exercising a bull's prerogative to explore, strayed away and became lost. The settlers hunted but did not see Adam again until the next spring, when his dead body was seen floating down the river on a slab

of ice. It left the settlement with three cows but no bull, a most unsatisfactory situation. (*Grant MacEwan's West*, 39–40)

MK: And, for all its fertility, the land was far from abundant.

Miles Macdonell to Lord Selkirk: 17th Julv. 1813. MY LORD Our crops from bad culture & the seed being old, do not promise great returns, the winter wheat being late sown has totally failed; as also the summer wheat, Pease and English Barley; of all these there must be fresh seed sent us. The appearance of the Potatoes promises good returns. The Indian Corn has almost totally failed; from a great drowth after planting grubs, &c. The sowing was chiefly done with the hoe, as well as the planting, only one imperfect plough was got agoing late in the season, there being no man here capable of making a good one. I feel the want of handy work-men in everything I attempt, A wheel-wright and a constructor of windmills would be great acquisitions to us. (Public Archives, Vol.2, 460–476.)

Rev. A.C. Garrioch: In the summer of 1813 the colonists suffered greatly for lack of food, and had to help eke out an existence by eating ber-ries and roots. Of the latter, the wild turnip (*cree*, miskoostusimin) received particular attention. Of this root it may be said, that being of a dry and fibrous nature, with no marked flavour of its own, it is more susceptible to flavouring than the potato, of which it may be remembered Sir Walter Raleigh wrote when introduc-ing this celebrated tuber to the British public: "To give them the greater relish in eating, they should be boiled with the juice of prunes." Probably, however, the poor·ex-crofter hadn't the juice of a thing in which to boil his miskoostusimin. (Garrioch, 26)

Margaret Laurence: Och aye, it was hard. It was so hard you could barely feature it. Locusts. Hailstorms. Floods. Blizzards. Indians. Half-breeds. Hot as the pit of hell in the summer, and the mosquitoes as big as sparrows. Winters so cold it would freeze the breath in your throat and turn your blood to red ice. Weather for giants, in them days. (Laurence, 69)

MK: In that same letter to Selkirk written in the summer of 1813, Macdonell had written also to alert him to a situation that, under his management, was destined to blow up into a genuine political and economic crisis at the Forks — in the judgement of Selkirk's biographer, Jack Bumsted, a "potentially fatal decision." (*Selkirk: A Life*, 231) The fact was that, for all their industriousness, the colonists, and the further party that would arrive that Fall, were a burden on the limited food supplies of the settlement. The NWC's John Pritchard, perhaps deliberately to starve the colonists out of the district, was ordered to buy as much Red River pemmican as possible. Pritchard succeeded in buying a third more than usual.

Miles Macdonell to Selkirk July 1813: In consideration of the number of people for whom I have to provide subsistence, I shall be fully justified in laying an Embargo on all provisions within our territory except what may be necessary to bring out the parties. (Public Archives)

MK: That the Kildonan arrivals of June 1814 were in good physical shape and spirits despite their arduous journey — plunging "lustily into the work of making their new homes habitable," in the words of historian Douglas Hill — cheered up those settlers from earlier arrivals: perhaps their colony had a fighting chance to flourish, after all. But, for all their high spirits, the colonists were not seasoned farmers, sowing too late in the season or helpless against drought and pestilence. As Reginald Buller reminds us, "these settlers had been fishermen in Scotland, not grain farmers. They did not have a single plough or harrow among them. They worked the soil with hoes. Although their grain crops had failed, they had a good harvest of potatoes and turnips in 1813 and 1814." (Buller, 1-12)

Vera Kelsey: Watching his charges grow thinner daily on the meager diet he could provide, Captain Macdonell grew bitter, too. For he was watching Indians and half-breeds stream into Fort Gibraltar with Red River pemmican, venison, bear meat, fish, waterfowl, cereals, fruits, even maple sugar and salt. North West's distribution depot needed every mouthful of food it could lay its hands on. Almost immediately after the United States declared war against Great Britain in June, 1812, American troops en route to attack Montreal had cut Nor'West's supply line. On Fort Gibraltar and Pembina, therefore, rested full responsibility for maintaining every North West post west of Lake Superior.

To Captain Macdonell, however, these Canadian trespassers on Lord Selkirk's private property were stealing foods that rightly belonged to the colonists. Now with the Sutherlanders added to his charges, he was forced to winter once more at Fort Daer. (Kelsey, 83)

Miles Macdonell, *Journal*, n.d.: The North West Company supply their own distant posts with provisions procured in this district, while we, to whom the soil belongs, are obliged to go to the expense of importing from Britain part of the subsistence of our people. (in Hamilton, *In the Beginning*, 285)

Vera Kelsey: There [Ft Daer] the weather was mild, food abundant. French
Canadians and Métis brought fiddles and drums to entertain the
settlers. Sutherlanders enthusiastically adopted the fast-paced
Red River Jig, made community festivals of the two marriages
and four births among the Selkirkers, assumed ways and buck-
skins of the country. Little by little, following their lead, all
the Scots and Irish began to put down roots in Red River soil.
Heartened by all this, the captain took the drastic step he had
long been considering. On January 8, 1814, as governor of Assiniboia, he posted a Proclamation. (Kelsey, 83)

Proclamation

MK: On January 8, 1814, in his capacity as governor of Assiniboia, Macdonell
issued a proclamation, known as the Pemmican Proclamation,
prohibiting the export of provisions of any nature from the
Territory of Assiniboia for a period of one year. It should be
remembered that this affected only provisions gathered within
the boundaries of Lord Selkirk's Grant, and that the provisions
were to be purchased, not confiscated without compensation.
Nevertheless, it did represent a provocative intervention into the
struggle for the control of (pemmican) food supplies at The Forks.

Proclamation, January 8, 1814: Wherefore it is hereby ordered, that no person trading in Furs or Provisions within the territory for the
Honourable Hudson's Bay Company, [for] the North-West
Company, or an Individual, or unconnected Traders or persons
whatever, shall take out any provisions, either of flesh, dried
meat, grain, or vegetables, procured or raised within the said

territory, by water or land-carriage, for one twelvemonth from the date hereof, save and except what may be judged necessary for the trading parties at this present within the territory, to carry them to their respective destinations, and who may, on due application to me, obtain a license for the same. The provisions procured and raised as above, shall be taken for the use of the colony; and that no losses may accrue to the parties concerned, they will be paid for by British bills at the customary rates. And be it hereby further made known that, whosoever shall be detected in attempting to convey out, or attempting to carry out, any provisions as prohibited above, either by land and water, shall be taken in custody and prosecuted as the laws in such cases direct. (in Bryce & Bell, *A Thousand Miles of Prairie*, 69)

Miles Macdonell, *Journal*, January 8, 1814: A Proclamation which had been some time in contemplation I had put up today on the South gate which was just hung (this prohibits all export of provisions of whatever nature so ever for one year from this date and also advertises the name and limits of the Territory of Assiniboia)... Gave a dance this evening to the people; the gentlemen, men and women enjoyed themselves and encroached on the Sabbath. (in A.S. Morton, *A History of the Canadian West*, 560)

R.D. Garneau: The major trading centers which are dominated by the Metis, Coureurs des bois and voyager settlers at this time are: Detroit, Mackinac, Chicago, Sault Ste Marie, Milwaukie, Green Bay, Prairie Du Chien, St Paul (called Iminijaska meaning White Rock), St Louis, LaPointe, Red River and many more lesser locations. The American British wars had driven many of the Metis into the west.... The Hudson Bay Company never had any rights to the Red River or the Saskatchewan Rivers. Selkirk was the first to suggest this preposterous idea of exclusive rights to these territories. . . .

The solution [to settlers' hunger] by Selkirk and the Hudson Bay Company is the Pemmican Proclamation stealing all food supplies in the area, including the North West Company supplies of pemmican and forbidding any to be shipped out. This was in effect a proclamation of War and led to the killings at Seven Oaks. It was fairly obvious that Selkirk was mentally unstable. (Garneau)

A.S. Morton, historian: Much can ... be said in favour of the embargo as a measure to protect the coming settlers – nothing can disguise the un-wisdom of precipitating at this early stage a struggle with the North West Company – especially as it gave the Northwesters, who were ready to take any means whatever to undermine the colony, excellent material for propaganda against the Hudson's Bay Company and Lord Selkirk. They denied that the territory involved was included in the Charter; they questioned the legality of the grant to Lord Selkirk, and insisted that the colony, and in particular the embargo, was a villainous device to destroy their trade in the interests of the English Company by destroying their system of transportation. Thus they made the issue the survival of the North West Company's business. As this was of the utmost importance to the colonies on the St. Lawrence, all Canada got behind the Company in its campaign against the colony. (W.L. Morton, 561)

MK: Whatever its effects and outcome, the first cause of the Pemmican Proclamation and the Pemmican War that followed from it was the critical shortage of food with which to provision the settlers. On their own, they did not have the money to buy supplies of pemmican from the Métis hunters to carry them over the winter, and, without horses, they could not follow a hunt themselves. They could only watch in amazement at the quantities of meat and pemmican the Métis hunters, employed by the NWC, took away from their hunts, in a good year some thirty tons, to provision the brigades servicing the NWC posts further west. Unsurprisingly, the direct threat of an embargo on the trade in pemmican not only infuriated the Métis in defense of their own economic interests and those of their employers, the NWC, but also put the two trading companies, the NWC and the HBC, on a collision course in defense of their ultimate objective, control of the lucrative fur trade in the north-west. As W.L. Morton argues, with the Pemmican Proclamation, the NWC had its long-standing suspicion confirmed that Selkirk's colony at the Forks was a tactical "front" for the HBC's strategy to disable the NWC's supply routes "for the purpose of crippling their trade." (Morton, *Manitoba: A History*, 51)

Donald Gunn: At this moment of imminent danger to their [NWC] concerns, a general system of aggression and violence against their property, and their servants, was begun by Mr. Macdonell under pretence that all the provisions collected in the country were required for the maintenance of the Colonists, who, at this time, be it observed, did not exceed twenty-five or thirty persons. [Historian] George Bryce reckoned at the end of 1814 the colony amounted to 180 or 200 persons. ("The Old Settlers") Parties of colony servants were sent to intercept convoys of traders on their way to their posts. Their boats and canoes navigating the river were fired at from

THE SEVEN OAKS READER *Myrna Kostash*

the Fort, and from batteries erected on the banks, brought to, and rigorously searched, and wherever provisions of any description could be found, they were plundered without hesitation. ...Great pains were taken to impress upon the minds of these servants and Indians that the ruin of the North-West Company was at hand, that it was equally dangerous and useless to resist such coercive measures as the Governor had it in his power to apply – to drive them entirely from the country. (Gunn, 108)

E.S. Russenholt: War between Nor'West and Hudson's Bay men – the inevitable outcome of unlimited competition for fur profits – engulfs the entire Nor'West.... Both Companies enlist more and more men – to fight each other.... Selkirk's Colony is ground like mincemeat between the two battling principals. Fur-men hate settlement! They believe (mistakenly) that farming must hurt their profits. Settlers, as people, do not enrage the fur-men; but, as farmers, they are to be eliminated! (Russenholt, 31)

Henry McKenzie "Mercator," merchant, politician: [Miles Macdonell dares] to prohibit in 1814 the sending of provisions out of the Red River, and then he seized upon those of the North West Company, by an armed force, thus commencing a system of pillage; and let it be observed that the provisions so taken were the produce of trade with independent natives, being the flesh of wild animals killed by them in hunting, and not a particle thereof acquired by the labor or time of a colonist. The Red River colony originated in avarice, has been prosecuted in deception and fraud, and must end in disgracing the character of a British nobleman [Lord Selkirk]. (in Ellice, *The Communications of Mercator*, 29)

George Bryce and Charles Bell, historian: Were the question asked, "Did the Governor act wisely?" subsequent events afford an answer in the negative.... The fact that the idea of law was yet new, that the feeling of the Nor'-Westers was hostile to a certain extent, and that they had the turbulent Bois-Brulés thoroughly under their control and ready to carry out any plans of attack, should have caused great caution on the part of the Governor, so newly created in his chair of authority. (Bryce & Bell, 70)

Margaret A. Macleod and W.L. Morton: The results of this act were two. One was to place the supply of pemmican for the North West Athabasca brigades at the discretion of the Governor of Assiniboia [Miles Macdonell], which to the Nor'Westers meant at the discretion of the HBC. The second was to assert the authority of the Governor of Assiniboia in an inescapable manner over the Red River country. That authority, in the eyes of Macdonell and his employer, Lord Selkirk, derived from the HBC charter of 1670. By that charter the officials of the Company were lords of the soil and rulers, under the British Crown, of all Red River.... This claim to jurisdiction and proprietorship the Nor'Westers flatly denied. (Macleod & Morton, *Grantown*, 20-21)

Jack Bumsted, interview: I think myself that the Pemmican Proclamation was absolutely necessary in January 1814. By January 1814, Miles had two lots of colonists at the Forks. He had just been to York Factory and received a letter from Lord Selkirk that a third lot, a larger lot, the so-called Kildonan settlers, was on its way in 1814. He still was not able to feed the entire complement with the agricultural activities they were able to engage in.

So he was short of food and I think it was perfectly under-
standable on his part that he would try to keep all the food that
he could in the colony. At the same time, it has to be said also that
Miles was feeling unnecessarily well off militarily in early 1814.
Which meant that he was prepared to rattle a few sabres and to
throw his weight around a bit. I think that even without that he
would have needed the Pemmican Proclamation but he certainly
made the Proclamation as unpleasant as he possibly could for the
NWC, which did not have the manpower in the region that he
had at that particular point.

And the Nor'westers said, "We don't think you can do this."
Although Miles thought privately to himself and might have said
to them, "Well, I can do anything that I can enforce at the point
of a gun." But that's the only kind of sovereignty you're going to
get out there, what you can get at the point of a gun.

Miles Macdonell to William Auld, trader, February 1814: I have sufficient force
to crush all the N Westers in this river should they be so hardy
as to resist openly authority. We are so well armed & I have a
parcel of fine active stout fellows that will execute any order they
receive. (in Bumsted, *Selkirk: A Life*, 236)

Jack Bumsted, interview: And we have to add also to this that in the winter of
1813/14 Miles still didn't have any handle on the mixed-bloods.
He doesn't understand what they are, who they are. And of
course who they are is largely the sons of liaisons between NWC
fur traders and Aboriginal women. And many of them are fairly
well-educated. Cuthbert Grant, for example, [NWC clerk at Fort
Esperance on the Qu'Appelle River] actually goes to Scotland.
He doesn't take a degree but he certainly has a formal education

and several of the others do as well. But you know, they're tough cookies, these guys.

Louis Aubrey Wood, historian: **Stormy days were coming.** Once Governor Macdonell had published his edict, he did not hesitate to enforce its terms. Information had been received at Colony Gardens that the Nor'westers had stored a quantity of provisions in their trading-post at the mouth of the Souris, a large southern tributary of the Assiniboine. It was clear that, in defiance of Macdonell's decree, they meant to send food supplies out of Assiniboia to support their trading-posts elsewhere. The fort at Souris was in close proximity to Brandon House on the Assiniboine, a post founded by the Hudson's Bay Company in 1794. Macdonell decided on strong action. His secretary, John Spencer, was ordered to go to the Souris in the capacity of a sheriff, accompanied by a strong guard and carrying a warrant in his pocket. When Spencer drew near the stockades of the Nor'westers' fort and found the gate closed against him, he commanded his men to batter it in with their hatchets. They obeyed with alacrity, and having filed inside the fort, took charge of the contents of the storehouse. Six hundred bags of pemmican were seized and carried to Brandon House. Already there was a state of war in Assiniboia.

The territory which comprised the colony was of great value economically to the North-West Company. The food supplies which supported its traders in the far interior were largely drawn from this area. In the eyes of the Nor'westers, Sheriff John Spencer had performed an act of pure brigandage at their Souris post. Still, they were in no hurry to execute a counter-move. In order to make no mistake they thought it best to restrain themselves until their partners should hold their summer meeting at Fort William on Lake Superior. (Wood)

Jack Bumsted: An exchange of seizures by the respective antagonists followed, the Nor'Westers complaining of the taking of two canoes at the foot of Lake Winnipeg, which should be released "unless you mean to declare war against us." Miles responded by freeing the crews of the canoes but keeping their arms, adding "you cannot suppose yourselves possessed of any civil or military authority here." (Bumsted, *Selkirk: A Life*, 244)

Douglas Hill: If it had been obeyed, the embargo would have ruined the Northwesters' organization; but of course Macdonell could not enforce the order, and they went right on moving pemmican out. Similarly, the fiery métis' blood was up and they ran the buffalo more often than they needed.... Macdonell, who had appointed one John Spencer as colony sheriff, then began the first manoeuvres of the Pemmican War. They were mild, almost funny for a while. (Hill, 35–6)

MK: Hill goes on to describe the almost farcical scenes of Spencer rushing about the colony looking for hidden caches of pemmican in canoe and riverbank, always running behind the Nor'westers who have the jump on him. Finally, he raids a NWC fort and impounds a big supply. In retaliation, the NWC captures a HBC man and sends him to Montreal to be tried for larceny. Eventually some of the pemmican is given back and the man freed. Macdonell sets up guns overlooking the Red River and captures canoes full of Norwesters.

On June 18, 1814, a truce of sorts was negotiated between the warring parties. The NWC sent John Mcdonald to meet with

Miles Macdonell: the Governor's river blockades and seizures of supplies, intended to secure the availability of food for the colony, were now threatening the starvation of the NWC. It was agreed that Macdonell could keep two hundred bags of the pemmican he had confiscated and the the Nor'Westers would continue to supply the colony with pemmican over the winter.

John Morgan Gray, biographer: Miles Macdonell was the same kind of man as those he faced – of similar background and temperament, stiffened by the same pride. Though trained at a less hard school, he was not soft, and for the moment he had more at stake. But his chief assets were intangible: the authority of his office as governor, the weight of the Hudson's Bay charter, and the backing of the Earl of Selkirk. The Nor'Westers might challenge and rail against them all, but they would not flout them as casually as they would the claims of a rival trader. Through several days of parleying, peace trembled in a balance that a loss of temper might at any moment upset.... Both parties had in a measure saved face while avoiding what must have been a bloody struggle. On June 28, 1814, John McDonald of Garth, the reckless old warrior who had turned peace-maker, signed first for the North West Company.... The ninety-pound bags of pemmican were hefted down the bank below Fort Douglas to the waiting canoes and the brigades swept out of the river heading for Fort William. As the voyageurs broke into song they did not look or sound like an expiring party. Miles Macdonell was left to contemplate his measure of victory, and to recognize the magnitude of failure ... to have had the pemmican and given it up seemed to these simple people [the colonists] the height of folly. (Gray, *Lord Selkirk of Red River*, 96–7)

Pemmican War

MK: But the War was on. Sheriff Spencer was "arrested" and shipped to Fort William. Métis went on hunting. Each side captured men from the other side, tit for tat, and then let them go. Moreover, Macdonell was not done with his proclamations. On July 14, 1814, he announced a prohibition on the running of buffalo with horses near the settlement, for the very good reason, in his view, that hunters on horseback drove the bison herds far out of the reach of the colonists, who, lacking horses, stalked the herd. But this angered the Métis — an insult added to the injury of the Pemmican Proclamation — for whom the running of the bison with horses was a tradition on the plains long before the HBC arrived. Their resentment was stoked by Nor'Westers Duncan Cameron, bourgeois, and partner, Alex Macdonell, of the Red River department, who pointed out to the hunters that their claim to the territory, through their mothers, gave them rights that superseded whatever legal authority the HBC pretended to assert. "And so," writes Margaret A. Macleod, "the alliance between the Nor'Westers and the *bois-brûlés* against Selkirk's colony began." (Macleod & Morton, *Grantown*, 23)

Jack Bumsted, interview: And Miles doesn't understand in 1814 that the Métis are a potential military force for the NWC. And that's really the key, I think. Up to this point he's been pushing these guys around, telling them they should stop hunting the buffalo on horseback, they should quit causing trouble. He doesn't appreciate the fact that they are a powerful fighting force in a countryside in which fighters are numbered in the dozens, not in the hundreds or thousands. These guys are all armed, they're all good hunters, they are all reasonably good shots. They're tough guys.

George Woodcock, author: To gain the support of the Métis, the Nor'Westers proceeded to cultivate, and in fact were the first to voice, the idea of a Métis nation with aboriginal rights to the land and special interests as hunters, at variance with the claims of the HBC colony. In doing so they were exploiting ill-defined sentiments of Métis identity and giving them shape and direction. Alexander Greenfield Macdonell and Cameron looked among their mixed-blood clerks for the leaders they could use to channel the energy and provoke the anger of the Métis on behalf of the NWC. (Woodcock, "Grant")

MK: The Nor'westers had the complete sympathy and understanding of Chief Grandes Oreilles of the Saulteaux who addressed the partners and servants at The Forks on June 19, 1814.

Grandes Oreilles, Saulteaux chief, holding a string of wampum: Traders, my Children, when I first heard of the troubles you were in at this place, my heart became sorry, and the tears ran down my cheeks.... I find that you as well as the Indians are surrounded with difficulties and dangers. We are placed as if all were encircled within the ring of beads which I hold in my hands. We have the Sioux to oppose from above, and now it appears that we have to contend with Landworkers from below. What are these Landworkers? What brought them here? Who gave them our lands? And how do they dare to prevent our Traders from purchasing whatever we have to give them, upon our own lands? But it would appear that these Strangers, these

makers of gardens, look upon themselves as the real possessors
of these lands, and presuming on this extraordinary right, would
wish to prevent you from returning here, by depriving you of
your stock of provisions traded on this River, in hopes thereby
to drive you from the country, and make slaves of the Indians
when deprived of their Friends and Protectors. (in Wilcocke,
A Narrative, 35)

The Memorial of Thomas Earl of Selkirk: **The partners of the North West
Company at their annual meeting in the year 1814 determined
to adopt more effectual measures for destroying the settlement, before it should be too late to make the attempt. For this
purpose they sent instructions to collect from various quarters a set of men whom they judged fit instruments for acts
of violence, viz: the sons of their Canadian, and other servants by Indian women, a great number of whom are reared
about their trading posts. . . . It was then for the first time that
they were taught to consider themselves a separate tribe of
men, and distinguished by a separate name, with the view
of ascribing their violences to the native Indians. These half-
breeds (or Bois Brulés as they were now to be called) have been
described as a Nation of independent Indians: but they are in
fact with very few exceptions in the regular employment and
pay of the North West Company, mostly as canoemen, some
as interpreters and guides, and a few of better education as
clerks. The latter are the progeny of partners of the Company,
at whose expense most of them have been brought up, and
through whose influence they may look to be themselves partners. These are the chiefs of this "New Nation." (in Bumsted,
Collected Writings, 113-14)**

MK: Such a one was the young Cuthbert Grant, clerk with the North West Company. Born 1793 in what is now Saskatchewan, he was the son of Nor'Wester Cuthbert Grant Sr. and a mixed-blood woman of Fort Tremblante on the Saskatchewan River. Brought to Montreal by his guardian, he was educated there and baptized in the Scots Presbyterian Church. His father died when he was six but provided for the boy's education. Under the guardianship of William McGillivray himself [head of the NWC], Grant was sent away, possibly to Scotland, for his education. In May 1812, he was back in Canada and was waiting in Montreal to embark by canoe for the Red River country. A young gentleman, and fluently bilingual, he had been accepted as an administrative officer in the running of the North West Company's posts. His first duties were clerking as an apprentice at the Qu'Appelle post, his father's old district.

Alfred Silver: He was dressed in the best that the tailors of Edinburgh and Montreal could make.... Against the perils of a spring night he'd added a sand-colored coachman's coat with double-caped shoulders. His head was bare, allowing the breeze coming off the river to ruffle his hair.... The eyes had a definite almond slant to them that had never come out of the British Isles. They were large and dark, the irises as black as the pupils, giving the disturbing impression that they would remain opaque and unreadable no matter how direct and level their gaze. (Silver, 13)

MK: Silver imagines Grant's view of the mixed-bloods he was to live and work among, their great variety, "dressed in everything from loincloths to corduroy trousers, from bead-worked black velvet waistcoats and embroidered antelope skin jackets to ermine-tail-tasseled hunting shirts and rawhide headbands."

Alfred Silver: Some had black hair, some red hair or blond, others chestnut; skin shades varied from yellow gold all the way to mahogany.... But it seemed there were two elements common to all of them. The first was that not one of them could be identified as a member of any previously defined race, not Gallic or Indian or Scots or English. The second was that there was a freedom, in their movements and expressions and laughter, that would have singled them out as aliens in any society that had fear or history to live up to. (Silver, 111)

Ron Bourgeault, interview: Métis emerged from the fur trade not simply as the result of intermarriage but of positioning children as adults into certain economic positions in the fur trade. (Métis emerged almost simultaneously in the HBC and NWC in the late 1700s.) The children born within these family formations, when they reached working age, were channelled into specific wage labour positions in the HBC together with the continued recruitment of labour from Scotland.

There were two class positions created, and there was a glass ceiling. Métis recruited as wage labour were paid the same wages as a Scottish labourer. They were not operating at lesser wage rates, as much as I can determine. Some of the male children born of the HBC officer class – the administrators at the fur trade posts – were sent to Scotland, for example, for education. They came back into HBC territory and they assumed junior positions in the HBC as post clerks. The "glass ceiling" prevented this middle class from rising into the ranks of the officer class.

They [the NWC] too had their administrative officers running their posts and had labourers underneath. You have the emergence of what became the French-speaking Métis as labourers in the NWC, and eventually buffalo hunters.

In the HBC the exploitation was of Indians as fur producers, including mixed-blood Indians born of intermarriage and not allowed to form around the fur trade posts or not allowed to gain access to higher positions such as wage labour and administrative positions in the HBC. *They* were the ones that produced the wealth, all the rest lived off it.

MK: By the autumn of 1814, Cuthbert Grant was one of four men — three of them of Scottish origin on their fathers' side — appointed at Fort Gibraltar by NWC factor Duncan Cameron as "captains of the Métis."

Duncan Cameron, NWC partner, to Cuthbert Grant, Esq., Lieutenant Grant:
I hear good word of your recruitment work along the Qu'Appelle. I think I do not exaggerate my own campaign here to say that by the spring the jardinières [gardeners] will need but a small push to see them all pack off for good. And I know just the lads to do it. Tell your jeunes gens [elsewhere, Young Fellows] that as soldiers of the New Nation they can expect to be fed and uniformed here at Red River, along with other presents. His Honourable Governorship and that ilk will turn tail soon enough when they see you and Seraphim et al in front of your cavalry. All their fine plans of harnessing your ponies to their ploughs and stealing your homes from under you and making you their servants. (in Silver, 268)

Skirmishes

MK: In July 1814, at the NWC's annual general meeting at Fort William on the northwestern shores of Lake Superior, when the wintering partners rendezvoused with the Montreal agents in annual council, the partners determined on a course of action to rid themselves of the farmers at Red River. Officially, they agreed to issue arrest warrants for Sheriff John Spencer and Governor Miles Macdonell and to induce the colonists to quit the settlement for a more advantageous situation in Upper Canada. Unofficially, it seems, they planned actual attacks on the colony. For, with their houses, garden plots, and crops, the colonists were beginning to establish a permanent foothold on the land, or so it was feared.

Louis Aubrey Wood: The grizzled partners, as they rubbed elbows in secret conclave, decided that something must be done to crush this troublesome settlement. Whether or not they formed any definite plan cannot be ascertained. It is scarcely believable that at this meeting was plotted the opposition to Lord Selkirk's enterprise which was to begin with deceit and perfidy and to culminate in bloodshed. Among the Nor'westers were men of great worth and integrity. There were, however, others in their ranks who proved base and irresponsible. During this conference at Fort William a bitter animosity was expressed against Lord Selkirk and the company which had endorsed his colonizing project. It was the Nor'westers' misfortune and fault that some of their number were prepared to vent this outspoken enmity in deeds of criminal violence. (Wood)

Heather Devine, historian: The assembled partners excoriated their colleagues in the Red River department who had surrendered pemmican to Miles Macdonell. The truce negotiated by John Macdonald of Garth was criticized by his associates and they angrily refused to recognize the agreement. The humiliated winterers returned to Red River with the understanding that they were to destroy the colony. (Devine, "Ambition Versus Loyalty," 261)

John Pritchard, colonist: The intention of the North-west Company was to seduce and inveigle away as many colonists and settlers at Red River as they could induce to join them; and after they should thus have diminished their means of defence, to raise the Indians of Lac Rouge, Fond du Lac, and other places, to attack and destroy the settlement; and that it was also their intention to bring the governor, Miles Macdonell, down to Montreal as a prisoner, by way of degrading the authority under which the colony was established in the eyes of the natives of that country. (in Bryce & Bell; in Blanchard, 71)

Herbert Mays, historian: Throughout June and July 1814 Macdonell was exhausted and depressed. The pemmican war, Selkirk's criticism of his conduct of the colony's affairs, particularly its accounts, and the lack of support he had had from the HBC men, especially William Auld, superintendent of the Northern Department, all played on his mind. On 14 July he wrote to Selkirk asking that "your Lordship be not prevented by any delicacy to send a suitable person to take my place, as I find myself unequal to the task of reconciling so many different interests." (Mays)

Heather Devine: In August of 1814 Duncan Cameron and Alexander Greenfield Macdonell appeared in military dress in Red River, announc-
ing to all that Cameron, and not Miles, was the "Chief of this
Country." A few weeks later Miles Macdonell suffered a nervous
breakdown at York Factory, an event that marked the beginning
of his descent into the mental illness which was to plague him
the rest of this life. (Devine, "Ambition Versus Loyalty," 261)

MK: As Devine notes in her study of Miles Macdonell, "Ambition Versus
Loyalty," for all his fractious relations with the NWC, he was
inextricably connected through an extensive web of kin-based
relations with various North West Company servants and partners in the Red River Department who "provided horses and
provisions at his request." Miles's brother John Macdonell, a
retired NWC wintering partner, had previously been in charge of
the Upper Red River Department. Duncan Cameron, was another
Macdonell relative, as was Alexander Greenfield Macdonell,
Miles's brother-in-law and second cousin, in command of Fort
Gibraltar. (Devine, "Ambition Versus Loyalty," 260)

George Bryce: The whole body of the traders were incensed against Lord
Selkirk, for had not one of the chief Nor '-Wester partners written two years before from London saying, "Lord Selkirk must be
driven to abandon his project, for his success would strike at the
very existence of our trade." The two men chosen at the gathering in Grand Portage were well fitted for their work. Most forward was Alexander Macdonell. (Bryce, *Romantic Settlement*, 97)

Alexander Macdonell to William McGillivray, head of NWC: You see myself and
our mutual friend Mr. Cameron so far on our way to commence

open hostilities against the enemy in Red River. Much is expected from us. One thing certain is that we will do our best to defend what we consider our rights in the interior. Something serious will *undoubtedly* take place — nothing but the complete downfall of the Colony will satisfy some, by fair or foul means — a most desirable object if it can be accomplished — so here is at them with all my heart and energy. (in Swainson, *Historical Essays*, 11)

George Bryce: **But the master-mind was his companion Duncan Cameron who, as a leader, stands out in the conflicts of the times as a determined man, of great executive ability, but of fierce and over-bearing disposition. The Nor'-Westers, having planned bloodshed, all agreed that Duncan Cameron was well chosen. He had been a leading explorer and trader in the Lake Superior district and knew the fur traders' route as few others did. His well-nigh thirty years of service made him a man of outstanding influence in the Company. Moreover, he could be bland and jovial. He had the Celtic adroitness.** (Bryce, *Romantic Settlement*, 98)

Louis Aubrey Wood: **Both these men, Duncan Cameron and Alexander Macdonell, had a wide experience of the prairie country. Of the pair, Cameron was unquestionably the more resourceful. In view of the fact that later in life he became a trusted representative of the county of Glengarry in the legislature of Upper Canada, there has been a tendency to gloss over some of his misdemeanors when he was still a trader in furs. But he was a sinister character. His principal aim, on going to the Red River, was to pay lavish court to the settlers in order to deceive them. He was a born actor, and could assume at will the gravest or the gayest of demeanors or any disposition he chose to put on. Alexander Macdonell, the** other emissary of the Nor'westers, was of an inferior type. He was crafty enough never to burn his own fingers. Macdonell had some influence over the Indians of the Qu'Appelle district and of the more distant west. His immediate proposal was to attract a band of redskins to the neighborhood of Colony Gardens with the avowed intention of creating a panic among the settlers. (Wood)

George Bryce: [Duncan Cameron] was a clever, diplomatic, and rather unscrupulous instrument of his company, and coming to command Fort Gibraltar, cultivated the colonists, spoke Gaelic to and entertained them with much hospitality, and ended by inducing about one hundred and fifty of the two hundred of them to desert Red River and go with him to Upper Canada. (Bryce, *John Black: The Apostle of Red River*, 56)

Louis Aubrey Wood: Towards the end of August the twain arrived at Fort Gibraltar, where they parted company. Alexander Macdonell proceeded to his winter quarters at Fort Qu'Appelle, on the river of the same name which empties into the upper Assiniboine. Duncan Cameron made his appearance with considerable pomp and circumstance at Fort Gibraltar.... Cameron decked himself in a crimson uniform. He had a sword by his side and the outward bearing of a gallant officer. Lest there should be any want of belief on the part of the colonists, he caused his credentials to be tacked up on the gateway of Fort Gibraltar. There, in legible scrawl, was an order appointing him as Captain [Commanding Officer, Red River Indian Territory] and Alexander Macdonell as lieutenant in the Voyageur Corps. The sight of a soldier sent a thrill through the breasts of the Highlanders and the fight-loving Irish. (Wood)

Alexander Ross: The partisans of the North-West Company used every art to involve the colonists in ruin, by fomenting dissension amongst them, and terrifying them with stories of Indian cruelty. Having thus heightened the terrors of their forlorn condition, it was easy to deceive them under the mask of friendship, and lure them away from the settlement, with the prospect of bettering their condition. For this purpose, they availed themselves of the most extraordinary means, even to the use of the Gaelic language; collecting men from all quarters, and conveying them to the Red River Colony, with the sole object of winning their confidence of the settlers, by the sound of their native tongue. This national charm the Highlanders could not withstand. All else they might have resisted: the influence of the Gaelic alone conquered them! (Ross, 33)

Louis Aubrey Wood: Some of the colonists were invited to [Cameron's] table. These he treated with studied kindness, and he furnished them with such an abundance of good food that they felt disgust for the scant and humble fare allowed them at the settlement. At the same time Cameron began to make bold insinuations in his conversation. He had, he said, heard news from the interior that a body of Indians would raid them in the spring. He harped upon the deplorable state in which the settlers were living; out of fellow-feeling for them, he said, he would gladly act as their deliverer. Why did they not throw themselves upon the mercies of the North-West Company? In their unhappy condition, abandoned, as he hinted, by Lord Selkirk to their own resources, there was but one thing for them to do. They must leave the Red River far behind, and he would guarantee that the Nor'westers would assist them. (Wood)

Letter to Cameron from a settler: Honoured Sir, I understand that your honour has proposed to relieve a poore distressed people By taking them to Montreal next spring. I hoap that you will count myself and family in the number, as I assure you that it is well known that I was still against the taking of the pimiken. (in Gray, 103)

Rev. A.C. Garrioch: [The colonists] had come out contrary to the wishes and advice of the North-West Company it is true, but considering their helpless plight in the old land, which so far was little changed in the new, one would think there might have been chivalry enough in the leaders of the North-West Company to at least have left them in peace, if they could not rise to the level of giving them a welcome and treating them with kindness. They did nothing of the kind, but continued their policy of obstruction, and in their treatment of the stranger showed an unmanly spirit. (Garrioch, 26)

William Wallace's Affidavit: William Wallace [colony labourer], late of Scotland, now at Montreal, deposeth and saith, That ... the Servants and Settlers of the Hudson's Bay Company were encouraged, and received succours and help from the servants of the North-West Company; and that the first winter they were there, this Deponent thinks they might have starved, if the servants of the North-West Company had not supplied them with provisions; that the North-West Company always continued to be friendly to Miles McDonell's people or settlers. (in Wilcocke, A Narrative, 33)

MK: As W.L. Morton relates in his classic Manitoba: A History, in Spring 1814 barley, oats, Indian corn, buckwheat — and this time spring not winter wheat — were all sown, as well as the usual complement of hundreds of kegs of potatoes. "The golden summer of 1814 rounded to its close," Morton writes, "and scythe and sickles swept through the abundant harvest." (W.L. Morton, 50) Abundant, perhaps, but still only yielding seed grain (for the 1815 sowing) and the indestructible potato. September 23: Peter Fidler writes that the settlers harvested their Indian corn, but that most is lost as "the horses and cows had broke the fences and ate the crop." (in Garneau)

In spite of his exhaustion and depression, Miles Macdonell nevertheless returned to the colony and Fort Douglas once more as its governor on October 20, 1814. It is historian Jack Bumsted's judgement that, although Macdonell was in command of his senses again, he continued to "behave strangely" (Bumsted, *A Life*, 250) over the next several months, preferred his own company, and, unlike the hospitable scene over at Fort Gibraltar, never invited a Métis man or woman into his quarters. He learned that Duncan Cameron, on taking up his own post at Fort Gibraltar, had repudiated the June compromise that had put a temporary halt to the so-called Pemmican Wars: he forbade the free traders to supply the colony with any meat. The next day, Macdonell ordered the Nor'Westers to quit Fort Gibraltar within six months. Then he organized a small militia armed with muskets from among the settlers and appointed himself commander.

Miles Macdonell Proclamation: *District of Ossiniboia. To Mr. Duncan Cameron, acting for the North-West Company at the Forks of the Red River.* Take Notice, that by the authority and on behalf of *your Landlord,* the Right Honourable Thomas Earl of Selkirk, I do hereby warn you, and all your Associates of the North-West Company, to quit the post and premises you now occupy at the Forks of the Red River,

within six calendar months from the date hereof. (Signed) Miles
Macdonell, this twenty-first day of October, 1814. (in Wilcocke,
A Narrative, 34)

Donald Gunn: Similar notices to quit the Hudson's Bay Company and Lord
Selkirk's territory were published throughout the country, one
of which we shall insert as it is well calculated to give the reader
some idea of the moving spirit which was at work and throw-
ing everything into confusion throughout the land. *By order of*
William Hillier, Esquire, Justice of the Peace. If after this notice your
building is continued I shall be under the necessity of razing them to the
ground. (Signed) A. Kennedy (Gunn, 114)

R.D. Garneau: Miles also served notice to quit on the other Canadian North
West Company Forts, including the Canadians at River Winni-
peg, Turtle River, Brandon House, Carlton House, Fort Dauphin,
Portage des Prairies and River Qu Appelle. The Metis Nation
had an instinctive hostility towards Englishmen, Orkney men
and Scots of the British Hudson Bay Company (or the North
West Company for that matter). They formed the first Canadian
Mounted Cavalry Division of the Red River Metis Nation,
who watched, with increasing resentment, the actions of Miles
MacDonnell. (Garneau)

Marjorie W. Campbell: Though they had attempted to ignore the Proclamation, this latest attack could not be ignored. Not only was it
a threat to the life-line of the North West Company, but it
was also a challenge from which the Métis could not easily
be restrained. Overnight the men and women living in Red
River Valley divided into two camps. Bostonnais Pangman and

Cuthbert Grant, sons of North West Company partners and Indian mothers, undertook to organize their people's defense. Soon many of Selkirk's people joined with the Nor'Westers. (Campbell, 211)

Deposition of Robert Sutherland: Deponent frequently heard Cameron say, that he was a King's officer, and that Miles Macdonell, Esq. had no authority from the King, or no lawful authority. Deponent heard a letter read by George Campbell, one of the settlers, from Duncan Cameron, saying, that it was necessary for the settlers to take possession of the cannon of the colony, in order to prevent mischief. ... That deponent was present when the settlers, in pursuance of this advice, did seize upon and carry away the cannon; that as soon as they had possession of them, a shot was fired; which deponent believes to have been intended as a signal; and that, immediately after, the said Duncan Cameron came out of a wood, where he had been concealed, at a short distance, along with Cuthbert Grant and William Shaw, clerks in the service of the North-West Company, and a party of armed men, who conducted the guns to the fort, or trading post of the said Company, when each of the settlers present at the taking of the guns got a dram. (in Halkett, *Statement*, xi)

Marjorie W. Campbell: A majority of the original labourers, by now completely disgruntled with the whole immigration project, sought employment with the Canadians as soon as their time with Selkirk was up. One small party of colonists, already friendly with the Nor'Westers, hauled a couple of Miles' cannon from Fort Douglas to Fort Gibraltar. By spring [1815] Duncan Cameron was ready. (Campbell, 211-12)

"Buffalo Hunting in the Summer, ca. 1822."
Painted by Peter Rindisbacher.
(Library and Archives Canada, MIKAN no: 2835795)

FOUR: FIRST DESTRUCTION OF THE COLONY

François-René Chateaubriand, London September 1822: **Only the great war of American Independence is famous. We forget that blood also** flowed on account of the minor interest of a handful of merchants. The Hudson's Bay Company sold, in 1811, to Lord Selkirk, land along the Red River; it was settled in 1812. The North-West or Canada Company took umbrage at this. The two companies, allied to different Indian tribes and supported by the Boisbrûlés, came to blows. This domestic conflict, horrid in its details, took place amongst the frozen wildernesses of Hudson Bay. Lord Selkirk's colony was destroyed in June 1815, exactly at the time of the Battle of Waterloo. In these two theatres of warfare, so different in their brilliance and obscurity, the woes of the human species were the same. (*Mémoires d'Outre-tombe* Book VII)

The Campaign Intensifies

MK: As we have seen, Duncan Cameron's "preparations" for his campaign to expel settlers from the Forks included various inducements to win their confidence and alienate them from any confidence in Lord Selkirk's plans for the colony. Their "sad condition" was exacerbated by the annual threat of hunger each winter.

Donald Gunn: During the winter and spring [1814/15] the settlers had often to apply to the North-West people for the means of saving their families from starvation. Mr. Cameron commiserated his unfortunate countrymen and did all in his power to relieve their wants, and we may believe that he and those of the settlers who were capable of reflecting would have talked over the present sad condition and of the dark prospect before them, and it might have been on one of those occasions the idea of leaving Red River, if possible, for Canada originated. (Gunn, 116)

Louis Aubrey Wood: As a result of Cameron's intrigues, signs of wavering allegiance were soon in evidence.... As many colonists as desired it, said Cameron, would be transported by the Nor'westers free of charge to Montreal or other parts of Canada. A year's provisions would be supplied to them, and each colonist would be granted two hundred acres of fertile land. Tempting bribes of money were offered some of them as a bait. An influential Highlander, Alexander M'Lean, was promised two hundred pounds from Cameron's own pocket, on condition that he would take his family away. Several letters which were penned by the sham officer during the winter of 1815 can still be read. "I am glad," he wrote to a couple of settlers in February, "that the eyes of some of you are getting open at last ... and that you now see your past follies in obeying the unlawful orders of a plunderer, and I may say, of a highway robber, for what took place here last spring can be called nothing else but manifest robbery." (Wood)

Marjorie W. Campbell: Numbers who had survived the horrors of a winter at Hudson Bay, the laborious trip inland and the hardships of the settlement coupled with the criminal ineptness of Selkirk's agent, longed to leave the Red River forever and as soon as possible. Cameron's offer, on behalf of the North West Company, to transport all who wished to leave for Canada in the company's canoes came as a blessed salvation. (Campbell, 212)

MK: In February 1815, the Métis (or the "Indians" of some menacing reports) set up camp on Frog Plain (la Grenouillière) north of the settlement, whose empty space opened out along the Red River above its confluence with the Assiniboine. They could be heard entertaining themselves with war songs, shooting their rifles and racing their horses around the camp. The NWC counted on their support in the campaign of harassment of the colony, through the Métis' sheer loyalty to the Company or through commitments even as free traders to re-enter Company service when bidden or through mutual commercial links as hunters and traders. What historian W.L. Morton calls their "esprit de corps" had been forged in the discipline of the buffalo hunt and they felt no kinship with "les anglais" of the HBC.

Margaret A. Macleod and W.L. Morton: [Cuthbert] Grant remained at Fort Gibraltar during these spring months, rallying the Métis with the aid of the three other half-breed clerks who, like himself, were sons of North West bourgeois — William Fraser, Angus Shaw, and Nicholas Montour. They drove home to the minds of their wild Young Fellows the idea that Cameron and [Alexander Greenfield] Macdonell had begun to circulate the autumn before. The Métis were, they assured them, lords of the soil and a new nation not bound by the pretended laws of Miles Macdonell and his colony, whose claim to the land and to the power to make laws was a violation of their rights in the soil and of their liberty as a free people. (Macleod & Morton, 27)

MK: Miles Macdonell took measures of his own, arming some men at Fort Douglas. The two sides took turns arresting, discharging, and re-arresting each other's personnel. Margaret Macleod and W.L. Morton write that "both Cameron and Macdonell paraded their men on the plain between the establishments in threatening demonstration of their military might." (Macleod & Morton, 26) The settlers took note.

Rev. A.C. Garrioch: Then although they had not pledged their word to fight in furtherance of Lord Selkirk's schemes, each man acted as if pledged to his God and himself to fight unto the death, especially in defence of the women and children. So when the time came, they stood up like true men and fought; they fought coolly and bravely as Highlanders have always done, and taught their foes what other foes before and since have learned — that "Britishers fight best with their backs against the wall." (Garrioch, 29)

J.G. MacGregor: Then about the middle of May Peter Fidler came from Brandon House to play his part in the excitement.... On May 19 he reported that five of the colony's horses were found dead and filled with arrows, while the Northwesters pretended that the Indians had killed them. On May 22 [his] journal reported that Elizabeth MacKay, the charming half-breed daughter of John MacKay, a long time Hudson's Bay factor and a friend of Fidler's, had run away from Point Douglas to share her lot with Cuthbert Grant. A few days later, the Northwesters tore down the fence at Fort Douglas and began taking pot shots at the building. (MacGregor, 196–7)

MK: Throughout April and May, 1815, the threat to the colony's security intensified. Their horses were shot at by arrows, their cows rustled or killed, their garden fences torn out and the cultivated plots torn up by the hooves of the Métis' horses, which had been let loose. Even some of the settlers' cottages were vandalized. (in Giraud, *The Métis in the Canadian West*, 433)

Louis Aubrey Wood: Meanwhile Cameron's colleague, Alexander Macdonell, was not succeeding in his efforts to incite the Indians about Fort Qu'Appelle against the colony. He found that the Indians did not lust for the blood of the settlers; and when he appeared at Fort Gibraltar, in May, he had with him only a handful of Plain Crees. These redskins lingered about the fort for a time, being well supplied with liquor to make them pot-valiant. During their stay a number of horses belonging to the settlers were wounded by arrows, but it is doubtful if the perpetrators of these outrages were Indians. The chief of the Crees finally visited Governor Miles Macdonell, and convinced him that his warriors intended the colonists no ill. Before the Indians departed they sent to Colony Gardens a pipe of peace, the red man's token of friendship. (Wood)

Deposition of Robert Sutherland arrived Red River June 1814: That the deponent never observed any appearance of hostility among the Indians, whom they, the settlers, saw during the summer, nor entertained any apprehension of danger, till they, the settlers, heard from the servants of the North-West Company, that Duncan Cameron, master of this trading post of the said Company, told deponent and his wife that the Indians would come in the spring, and murder all the settlers. (in Halkett, "Appendix," x)

Colony Under Attack

Duncan Cameron to Métis and freemen, June 1815: The purpose of our sending for you at this time is that you should engage with us [in] destroying or dispersing the colonists on the river for which you shall be supplied with all the necessaries for your equipment, such as horses, arms, ammunition and clothing. If they should disregard this warning, you are then to destroy and exterminate them by every means in your power, and you shall be rewarded with all the plunder and property which you may find in the Colony belonging to it.... If the colonists are allowed to increase, the consequence will be that they will make you slaves, put hoes and spades in your hands and oblige you to till the ground for them. (in MacEwan, *Cornerstone Colony*, 101)

John Halkett, brother-in-law to Lord Selkirk: On the morning of Sunday, the 11th of June (a day in which it might have been hoped some little rest from their troubles would have been allowed the harassed settlers) a number of loaded muskets, together with ammunition, were delivered out of the stores of the North-West Company to their clerks, servants and followers, for the purpose of an immediate attack upon the colony. Seraphim Lamar (the Voyageur Ensign), Cuthbert Grant, William Shaw, and Peter Pangman Bostonois, formed, as usual, part of this banditti. They marched from the North-West Company's post, and stationed themselves in a small wood adjoining the governor's house, which was the principal building in the settlement. They began their operations by firing a shot at Mr White, the surgeon, who was walking near the house, but it fortunately missed him. Another shot was at the same time fired at Mr Bourke, the store-keeper, and the ball passed close to him. A general firing then commenced from the wood, which was returned by those in the house, four of whom were wounded, and one of whom (Mr Warren) died of his wounds.

After the North-West Company's party had kept up their fire for a considerable time, they returned with Cameron, who, shortly after they had left the Forks, had followed them armed, and who, on their return, congratulated them, with much satisfaction, upon the result of their exploit, and on their personal safety — a circumstance not very surprising, considering that, during the attack, they were concealed in a wood, not one of them being visible to those upon whom they were firing.

After this cowardly and unprovoked attack, it would have been absurd in the remaining officers and settlers of the colony to have supposed they would be permitted to remain in security. (Halkett, 25–26)

Donald Gunn: Fortunately, for the cause of truth, in this case we have other information than that of the interested partisans of either Company. We have the evidence of living and reliable witnesses who were present when the above occurrences took place; who all agree in stating that the French half-breeds, under Cuthbert Grant, took possession of a grove of trees near the colony Fort, where the Governor resided. Being under the shelter of the bushes, they opened fire on the Fort, and most likely, as related above, the Fort men manned their bastions, of which there were four, one on each angle. These bastions were armed with small pieces and blunderbusses, which were always kept loaded, ready for any emergency. As Mr Warren was in the act of firing one of them the piece unfortunately burst, slightly wounding two or three of the men who were in the bastion, but dealing a mortal blow to poor Mr Warren, who died from its effects as he was on his way from Red River to Norway House. (Gunn, 118)

MK: Having made good their firing upon Fort Douglas, representatives of the NWC next demanded the surrender of Governor Macdonell. Judging this the better part of valour for the sake of the colonists, Macdonell surrendered, was placed under arrest and taken to Montreal to stand trial for alleged crimes committed against the North West Company in the Northwest. (His case was never tried.)

Rev. A.C. Garrioch: With Miles Macdonell out of the way, Duncan Cameron appeared in his true colours. Before he had sometimes come out in a scarlet uniform or some other showy costume – sometimes in kilts – a treat no doubt to them or the mosquitoes. Now he wore proper clothes and talked business. The offer with which he had tempted them [the colonists] during winter, and which two-thirds of them had accepted was as follows: Payment of wages that might be due either by Lord Selkirk or the Hudson's Bay Company, and assistance to obtain land. Duncan Cameron lived up to his promises, and the one hundred and thirty-four Colonists who had accepted his offer had to live up to theirs. Under his leadership they embarked June, 1815, and journeying via Lake Superior and Georgian Bay, arrived at Holland Landing in September. There they obtained land in the vicinity of New Market [in today's south-central Ontario] and many of their descendants are to be found there still. By this exodus of Colonists the number remaining on the banks of the Red River was reduced to forty; and the pick of souls they must have been, to thus place honour before every other consideration and to further brave the terrors of Nor'-Wester enmity. (Garrioch, 28)

MK: Two days after Macdonell's arrest, a jubilant Duncan Cameron, together with four mixed-bloods calling themselves "the North West free half-breeds," informed the remaining settlers, who had supposed they would be left in peace on their farms, that it was they, the half-breeds, who owned the land at Red River and that the settlers and the Hudson's Bay Company itself had two days to leave the settlement. To emphasize their seriousness, they put remaining houses to the torch.

William McGillivray June 24 1815: I am an utter stranger to any instigations or any determinations of the Indian nations to make any attack on the settlement in question; but I will not take it on me to say that serious quarrels may not happen between the settlers and the natives whose hunting ground they have taken possession of. (in Gray, 113)

J.G. MacGregor: Once more the perfidy of the Northwesters became obvious. They had promised to spare the settlement, but had made no promise that bound Cuthbert Grant's Métis — a body which by rumour, innuendo and active support they had built up into the North West Company's most potent weapon against the colony. A word from the Northwesters would have restrained the Métis, but that word they cunningly refused to give. In fact, their purpose was not to give it. Now, the Northwesters were in a position to stand by and see the Métis destroy the remnants of the colony, while at the same time they could say that they could not control them, and later, if and when a day of reckoning came, they could throw the blame on Cuthbert Grant and his Métis and appear at any trial with lily-white hands. (MacGregor, 198)

Alfred Silver: "...I am not leaving." [Cuthbert Grant] yanked the reins hard and looked back over his shoulder. "Not what?"

"Not leaving."

He turned the horse around to face [Kate Sutherland]...and when he spoke, his voice had altered to that of a stone statue magicked to life. "I had not taken you for a fool, Mrs. Sutherland,"

"Some have, Mister Grant, but either way I am not leaving."

"Your colony is falling to pieces around you."

"What the others choose to do is their business. I did not run five thousand miles from the Countess of Sutherland to be chased out by the North West Fur Trading Company."

"Do not make the mistake of thinking of this situation as merely a war between two trading houses ... consider this: The oldest and deepest dream of the human race is to someday return to Eden having eaten of the Tree of Knowledge. That is about to happen here. The New Nation can take possession of their mothers' Eden while still retaining their fathers' knowledge"...

"But surely a few tiny farms in this whole vast wilderness will make no difference to —"

"...The New Nation is not fighting for a few acres of riverbank or for a higher profit margin, it is fighting for its life." (Silver, 282–3)

Rev. A.C. Garrioch: The Bois Brules were mounted and armed with muskets, and outnumbered the Colonists and Hudson's Bay party two to one.... At one time it looked as though they were going to be overwhelmed, and then it was that [settler John] McLeod with the resourcefulness of the true general bethought him of a rusty old cannon that was laid away in the fort, and it was requisitioned now notwithstanding the popular opinion, that when discharged it would be a great menace to the safety of the man behind the gun as to those at whom it might be aimed. However, realizing that their desperate situation called for a desperate remedy, the gun was hastily hauled out, and a lot of cart chains were converted into chain-shot, and the ancient piece of ordnance was loaded to full capacity and pointed in the direction of the enemy, who with their savage Indian war-whoop, and an occasional spurt forward, appeared to be waiting the psychological moment, when they were to pounce upon and capture their prey. Once more they were coming; once more the air is filled with their horrid yells, when suddenly, as if the earth had opened her mouth and vomited a thunder bolt, accompanied with a league of chain lightning, there came fiendishly screaming about their ears, the curtailed cart chains, and the leaves and branches behind which they had concealed themselves flew hither and thither. The rusty cannon had spoken, and horses and riders as if by mutual consent lost no time in looking for safer quarters; and an occasional reminder from the brave little cannon kept them there, until convinced of its powers of execution they finally abandoned the siege.

This gave the harassed Colonists a breathing spell, which they turned to good account, by preparing to abandon their homes. ... No sooner had they left the settlement than the Bois Brulés commenced to destroy their houses, and generally to pull to pieces what they had put together with so much thrift, courage and perseverance. (Garrioch, 29–30)

Miles Macdonell (1767/69–1828), Governor of Assiniboina (1815–1817), wrote:

Our surrender to the enemy has not saved the colony. Our people, servants and settlers have been driven off by the N.W.C., who set fire to the houses and burned the whole to the ground. Simon McGillivray, Metis d-1840, son of William McGillivray and Susan Indian, said, "I am happy to inform you that the colony has been knocked on the head by the N.W.C." The Metis had no serious objection with the Scottish and Irish settlers, only with the British war invasion tactics. (in Garneau)

Colony Destroyed

Cuthbert Grant, Bostonais Pangman, Wm. Shaw, Bonhomme Montour, the four chiefs of the Half-breeds, James Sutherland, James White, Red River Territory, Forks, Red River, 25 June 1815:

Articles of Agreement entered into between the Half-Breed Indians of the Indian Territory, on one part, and the Honorable Hudson's Bay Company on the other, viz:

1) All settlers to retire immediately from this river, and no appearance of a colony remain.

2) *Peace and amity to subsist between all parties, traders, Indians and freemen in future throughout these two rivers, and on no account is any person to be molested in his lawful pursuits.*

3) *The honourable Hudson's Bay Company will, as customary enter this river with, if they think proper, from three to four of their former trading boats and from four to five men per boat as usual.*

4) *Whatever former disturbance has taken place between both parties, that is to say, the Honorable Hudson's Bay Company and the Half-Breeds of the Indian Territory, to be totally forgot, and not to be recalled by either party.*

5) *Every person retiring peaceable from this river immediately, shall not be molested in their passage out.* (in Macleod & Morton, 29–30)

MK: A community of Cree, Assiniboine, and Anishinaabe people under the leadership of Chief Peguis had settled at Netley Creek, south of Lake Winnipeg. Peguis thus became witness to the unfolding series of events troubling the peoples at the Forks, settlers and traders alike. Because of his reputation for negotiating and peace-making, more than once he had been appealed to by the settlers for protection when they were harassed and threatened by members of the NWC. As recorded by land surveyor and translator, Peter Fidler, Peguis responded to the settlers' appeal for help on June 25, 1815, after the men of the NWC had burned their buildings and demanded they leave the territory.

Chief Peguis: What do these people mean by driving you from these lands? Had we no other support than what they give us we might freeze in our tents die of want and be at the mercy of our enemies.

Look round & you will see our young men defended from the Inclemency of the weather & tormented of the musquitoes by your means, and we have even a Pipe of Tobacco to smoak and a round of ammunition to support our families — nor have we forgotten how pitiful & poor we were before your arrival here. ... The people of the other house [the N W C] are always breaking my ears with complaints & telling stories about my lands, but these are not my Lands — they belong to our Great Father — for it is he only that gives us the means of existence, for what would become of us if he left us to ourselves. We should wither like the grass in the Plains, was the Sun to withdraw his animating beams.

The hearts of my young men are vexed & inclined to war; it is with difficulty we can restrain them. I hope to procure you Peace but if my lands must be reddened with your Blood, my Blood and that of my Children shall be mixed with yours & like a stone we will sink together. (in Sinclair et al., 13–14)

A.S. Morton: Finally the Indians, ever friendly, came to them to advise them to depart, and promised to escort them in safety to their craft. Boats, crowded with men and women and children to the number of about sixty, accompanied by their cattle, bore the fugitives through Lake Winnipeg to its north end, to a spot near the narrows opposite Mossy Point. Here an encampment was made and events awaited. John McLeod, trusted and respected by all, even the Indians and half-breeds, was left with two or three men to guard the crop. The half-breeds, under their leaders, servants of the North West Company, plundered the houses and burned them down. Not so the Indians. Peguis, their chief, wept over the ashes of the Governor's house. The settlement was at an end. (A.S. Morton, 571-2)

Louis Aubrey Wood: Alexander Macdonell and his Bois Brûlés were now free utterly to blot out Colony Gardens. They visited every part of the settlement and set fire to everything. Not a single house was left standing. Cabins, store-, houses, the colony's grinding mill — all were reduced to a mass of ruins. Cameron's duplicity had been crowned with success; Alexander Macdonell's armed marauders had finished the task; Lord Selkirk's colony of farmers-in-the-making was scattered far and wide. (Wood)

George Bryce and Charles Bell: Had they [the Nor'Westers] a grievance, the courts of England, where they had much influence, were open to them. But no! Indians and Bois-Brules must be stirred up, like the letting out of water, to end no one could tell where; and the words of Simon McGillivray, a Nor'Wester partner, in writing from London in 1812: "Lord Selkirk must be driven to abandon the project, for his success would strike at the very existence of our trade," are seen carried out into action. The smoking home-steads of 1815, and the mournful band of three-score persons taking the route down the Red River, across Lake Winnipeg, and seeking Hudson Bay, as if the broad continent had no room for ever so small a band of peaceful and industrious settlers, tell their own tale. (Bryce & Bell, 71)

Margaret A. Macleod and W.L. Morton: Then, as the boats dropped down from the Red, the colonists watched the smoke rolling up from the last of their cabins and the whooping *brûlés* racing their buffalo-runners through the plots of tender wheat and barley. The Nor'Westers, the *brûlés*, and Mr Cuthbert Grant — clerk, captain, and chief — had "cleared the two rivers" of colony and company. Thereafter, except for the establishment at Fort Gibraltar, the Nor'Westers and most of the Métis left The Forks. Grant returned with Bethsy [his wife] to his post on the Qu'Appelle. The site of the colony was deserted during mid-summer of 1815. Only John McLeod of the Hudson's Bay Company at Point Douglas saw that the Métis had not done their work of destruction well. The trampled wheat and barley shot up strongly in the Red River sun, and the potatoes made dark green patches on the prairie. (Macleod & Morton, 30)

MK: Blissfully unaware of the catastrophe, the good ship *Hadlow*, under the command of one Captain Davison, sailed from Cromarty, Scotland, to Hudson Bay in June 1815 with thirty-four colonists mainly from Kildonan — the last of the Selkirk Settlers — and arrived in York Factory on 26 August 1815.

Lose the Battle, Win the War

J.G. MacGregor: But the North West Company had not won. Neither its might nor its money could hold back the clock of destiny, and destiny decreed that the Canadian prairies should become populous and prosperous. This trampled grain, these burned buildings, were not the end; they were just a turning point. John McLeod, who fought off the Metis and preserved his blacksmith shop from the flames, remained. He and three or four others. To them the prairie land displayed her graces, and as they watched, the grain sprang anew under the mild rains, and the potato tops spread out, basking in the sun. (MacGregor, 210)

E.S. Russenholt: To the Selkirk Settlers, the destruction of their Colony on Red River is overwhelming disaster. Historically speaking, however, this tragedy does not loom so large in the sweep of Assiniboia's development. If, as is suggested, more than 2000 humans are "more or less permanently" settled around "the Forks" of Assiniboine and Red, and along the wooded banks of these Rivers and their tributaries, it is highly probable that many of Assiniboia's people are not even aware that one of the communities in the area has been cruelly obliterated.... Apparently, none of the "hundreds of free Canadians... with families by Indian wives"... go with the deserting Selkirk colonists to Canada.... Some of them may be hired by the battling fur companies; most of them, probably, remain "free men"; and pursue the even tenor of their lives: hunting, fishing, wandering in summer, back to their homes in winter. They love this land. They are settled here – permanently. (Russenholt, 35)

MK: As for those Red River colonists who had taken advantage of Duncan Cameron's generosity and had emigrated to Canada to resettle on farms, their hapless situation was given due exposure by Lord Selkirk's sworn foe, the Rev. Dr. John Strachan, teacher and preacher in York, Upper Canada, who was active in public affairs and a friend of directors of the North West Company. Strachan published a statement, drawn from the evidence of the emigrants themselves, "and the delusions practised upon them," writes Donald Gunn in summary, "in order to warn the poorer classes of his countrymen against becoming, like these unfortunate people, the dupes of land-jobbing speculators, a class of persons well known in America, and of whom Lord Selkirk, from the magnitude of his operations, may be styled the chief." (Gunn, 120)

Rev. Dr. John Strachan 5 October 1815: Of the Settlers who went to the Red River, many died at Churchill, in Hudson's Bay, from the severity of the climate and the quality of their food. Others seriously injured their health; and not one of those who have escaped, saw a joyful day, from the time they left Scotland till they began their journey to Canada. (Strachan, 1)

MK: From Lord Selkirk's point of view, however, his and the settlers' efforts of the last three years to establish the settlement were not to be wasted. The settlement was to be reorganized; and in this he was advised and urged by Colin Robertson, erstwhile Nor'Wester and now working for the HBC. Colin Robertson, fur trader, merchant, and politician, was born in Scotland but sometime before the end of 1803 had entered the service of the NWC in Montreal. Perhaps chaffing at the slow pace of his promotion up the ranks, and because of a quarrel with one of its directors, he left the NWC in 1809. It is said that his favourite maxim was "When you are among wolves, howl!"

Chester Martin: Robertson despite the "natural impetuosity of his mind" ... knew the Northwesters and North-West methods.... A quarrel had thrown him into the arms of the Hudson's Bay Company, and since 1813 he had been urging upon the directorate the necessity of fighting fire with fire.... One hundred Canadian traders and voyageurs were to carry the trade-war into the enemy's territory [Athabasca]. In the spring Colin Robertson, with an advance-guard of twenty men, left Montreal in express canoes. (C. Martin, 97)

MK: Posing as an agent of Selkirk selling land in the Red River colony, Robertson and his men were camped east of Rainy Lake (now straddling the border between the United States and Canada) when he learned that Selkirk's colony had been broken up and that the Governor, Miles Macdonell, was a prisoner of the NWC. En route further downstream, they met up with some of the dispossessed settlers on their way to the Great Lakes and Upper Canada. Robertson persuaded them to turn back with him, agreeing to help them re-establish the colony. (In August, he would send the rest of his expedition on their way to Athabasca country.) Ten days later Robertson and company were at The Forks, surveying the situation.

A.S Morton: When Robertson arrived at the Red River, the blacksmith's shop inhabited by McLeod was all that remained. There, records Robertson, "they (Métis) told me frankly that they had been paid by the North West Company to drive away the Colonists." (A.S. Morton, 572)

Colin Robertson, *Journal*, Friday, 14 July, Red River: Left our encampment at midnight and arrived here this morning. At the entrance of Red River I found a large band of Indians encamped. Peegues [Peguis] was their chief. He made me a long speech, principally relating to the late transactions at this place. He found much fault with the N.W.Co. and seemed anxious that I should attempt to re-establish the Colony. About 11 o'clock a.m. I arrived at Frog Plain where a number of Natives and freemen were encamped. I went on shore and walked up to the Fort over the ruins of several of the houses that had been burnt by the white savages. A Blacksmith's shop was all that remained of the Colony [and it] was occupied by Mr. McLeod of the H.B.Co. as a store, which was supposed to be a great favour conferred on the Company by our amiable opponents. (Robertson)

Louis Aubrey Wood: He had done all that Lord Selkirk had instructed him to do, and he now took further action on his own initiative. At his command the sun-tanned voyageurs descended to the river bank and launched their light canoes on the current. Down-stream and northward along Lake Winnipeg, the party travelled, until they reached the exiles' place of refuge on the Jack River [later named Norway House]. (Wood)

MK: On August 19, almost a month after setting out from Red River to make contact with the settlers who had fled to Jack River, Robertson returned to the site of the settlement with all thirty-five. "To their surprise," writes Chester Martin, "the plots of ground which they had sown along the banks had suffered less than they had expected" and they brought in fifteen hundred bushels of wheat, "the first 'bumper ' crop garnered within the borders of what are now the prairie provinces of Canada." Historian W.L. Morton records "four hundred bushels of wheat, two hundred of barley, and five hundred of oats." (52) They had finally produced a surplus.

George Bryce: The return of the settlers to their homes in 1815 had filled the minds of their enemies with rage. The contempt of the wild hunters of the plains for the peaceful tillers of the soil can hardly be conceived. They despised them for their manual labor; they named them, by way of reproach, "the workers in gardens;" and their term "pork-eaters," formerly applied to the voyageurs east of Fort William, was now used in derision to the Scotch settlers. During the whole winter the fiery cross of the Nor-Westers had been flying; and they looked forward to a grand gathering in the spring at "The Forks," to give a final blow to the infant colony. (in Blanchard, 72)

Overview 1815

R.D. Garneau: Some claim Selkirk established the first permanent settlement in the Northwest, totally ignoring the Metis Red River Settlement that was over 20 years old.... Peter Fidler's journal of 1814-15 called an account of Canadian Free Traders at Red River. It listed 42 families at the Forks at Pembina, 10 families at Swan River, 7 Families at Riviere La Appelle and 7 other families; totaling 64 families in the vicinity. This is interesting given that in 1805, Alexander Henry (1764-1814) and David Thompson (1770-1857) recorded 240 families in the Red River region. (Garneau)

Chester Martin: It is difficult to estimate the number of actual settlers at Red River at the close of this first period of its history. It is to be remembered that the numbers were changing almost continuously through fluctuations in "the service" between the [Hudson's Bay] Company and the Settlement.... The numbers taken to Upper Canada by the North West Company are given in the imperial Blue Book, Hudson's Bay 1819 as about 140. Those who were driven off to Jack River, according to the list to be found in the Selkirk Papers, numbered approximately about 45 souls. There is record, therefore, of about 185 from the actual lists of some 205 who are recorded to have come out as settlers or servants at Red River.... Further research at Hudson's Bay House may supply three or four names which are needed to complete the full list of those whose arrival at the "Land of Promise," as [Miles] Macdonell called it, will be celebrated in 1912. The brilliancy of that promise, only now about to be realized, will lend something of additional interest to the names of these pioneers of settlement in the Canadian West. (C. Martin, 3)

MK: It was long to be the contention of Lord Selkirk and the HBC that the "bois brûlés" responsible for the attacks on the settlement at Red River had been inflamed to their purpose by the partners of the NWC, who had aroused them with spurious arguments that they had inalienable land rights, and who urged them on in their defense. Granted, Governor Macdonell didn't "have a handle" on who these Mixed-bloods really were. But neither, argues, Jack Bumsted, did the NWC.

Jack Bumsted, interview: One of the problems of this entire episode is the fact that nobody understands that it is not Aboriginals who are causing any trouble; it is mixed-bloods who may or may not have aboriginal claims to the soil. It is not entirely clear whether *they* have the claims or whether the NWC develops the claims for them.

MK: "The evidence," Bumsted writes, "is simply not available to ascertain the extent to which those of mixed descent developed such demands and grievances on their own, but it is certain that these people had grievances against the settlement." They were aggrieved at Selkirk's lofty unconcern about their long-term presence on the land he claimed for the HBC and were especially aggrieved that his local agent, Miles Macdonell, whatever his reasons, had treated them so high-handedly, "as mere interlopers on the region." (Bumsted, *Selkirk: A Life* 268–9)

Alfred Silver: "Falcon said I don't have to be Cree no more. Is that true? I never was Cree, just my mother was, and it didn't feel right to pretend like I was Cree — but a man can't just be a tribe of his own. Not for long. Sooner or later a bunch of Cree or Assiniboine or Blackfoot are going to knock him on the head." ... Over the first half of the winter he [Grant] had grown accustomed to the fact that there were a great many young men like Jumps High. They could track a lizard through a dust storm, shoot the eyes out of a squirrel, or take on a grizzly bear with a hand axe, but inside them all was the same unease and yearning. (Silver, 267)

"Winter fishing on ice of Assynoibain & Red River, 1821."
Painted by Peter Rindisbacher.
(Library and Archives Canada, MIKAN no: 2835803)

FIVE: COLONY WINTER/SPRING 1815–16

Rev. Roderick George MacBeth: **Meanwhile, over in Scotland, Lord Selkirk,** whose courage was unbroken, and whose interest in the colony was unabated, was arranging in 1815 to send out from Kildonan the largest and ablest band of colonists he had yet gathered together; and in order to ensure some stable form of oversight in the Red River country, he had a new governor, a military man, Robert Semple, sent out to take charge. It was with this band that my father came out as a lad; but, young though he was, the scenes through which they passed on arrival at the Red River were never effaced from the tablets of his memory. These new settlers had expected to find their relatives and friends in free and happy homes in the colony on a new continent. With these friends they might well hope to find shelter, renewing old memories, until they too could have homes of their own in the free land of the West, but instead of all that they found only a few huts and tents amid the ashes of the homes that had been built, and without houses or food, and with very inadequate clothing, these people were facing the icy breath of an approaching winter in an environment to which they were wholly unaccustomed. (R.G. MacBeth, 40)

Elusive Peace

Louis Aubrey Wood: **The occupants of Fort Gibraltar viewed the replanting of the settlement with baleful resentment. Their ranks were augmented during the autumn by a wayfarer from the east who hung up his musket at the fort and assumed control. This was none other than Duncan Cameron, returned from Canada [and his rendezvous with the Montreal partners], with the plaudits of some of his fellow-partners still ringing in his ears. To Colin Robertson the presence of Cameron at Fort Gibraltar was not of happy augury for the settlers' welfare. (Wood)**

MK: **On October 13, Chief Peguis, together with a sizeable number of his people, arrived at the beleaguered settlement on a friendly visit, to judge from the gifts he sent ahead, wild rice, dried meat, and sturgeon, and the ceremonial formalities.**

Colin Robertson, Friday, 13 October, Fort Douglas: **Peegues arrived this morning with his Band consisting of 65 men. When they doubled Point Douglas and were in sight of the Fort they fired a volley which we returned by a three pounder. We then hoisted our flag. Peeguis immediately returned the compliment by mounting his Colours at the end of his canoe, and then the whole Squadron came in sight consisting of nearly 150 canoes, including those of the women and children. It had a wild but grand appearance — their bodies painted in various colours — their heads decorated, some with branches and others with feathers. Every time we fired the cannon the woods re-echoed with that wild whoop of joy, which they gave to denote the satisfaction they received. When they came in front of the fort the women and children paddled** past the men's canoes to a spot where I had fixed upon for their encampment, where they mounted their lodges. The men accompanied by their chief, as soon as the families had passed debarked under a volley from my men. They then entered the hall with three hearty cheers from our people. The room was rather small but they managed to seat themselves in tolerable good order. I then ordered the large Peace Callimate to be lighted and after taking two or three whiffs out of it, I presented it to Peeguis who after smoking about a minute passed it to the next in respectability to himself, and in this manner it went round the band. During this ceremony not a single word or even a whisper was heard.

MK: But peace on the Red River was elusive: a few days later Colin Robertson received word that Alexander Macdonell, partner of Cameron, who had also returned from Canada, had left Fort Gibraltar and attacked the HBC post at Qu'Appelle.

John Perry Pritchett, historian: [Macdonell] was greatly displeased at finding the Hudson's Bay traders building storehouses and putting up new stockades around their fort. At once he sent Alexander Fraser, a métis clerk, to John McKay, the officer in charge of the rival post [Qu'Appelle], with an order to leave the place in twenty-four hours, and if the order was not complied with he would "blow him and the Fort to hell." Fraser added, for himself, that as long as he had a heart in his body he would never allow a colony to be established in Red River. McKay's answer was to send an express to Robertson for advice or assistance. (Pritchett, 170)

MK: There are multiple accounts of Duncan Cameron's actions on October 15. In one, Duncan Cameron imprudently went out for a stroll on the prairie, and in another, he went "riding on the plains" (Wikipedia). In one source hostile to Selkirk, *A Narrative* by Samuel Wilcocke, "while passing quietly along a public road," (48) Robertson seized him, took him hostage, and in a show of strength in retaliation for the NWC's attack on Qu'Appelle, forced entry to Fort Gibraltar, a mere half-mile from the colony, where he regained possession of some of the weapons and field-pieces that had been taken or delivered from the colony in the spring. Point made, Robertson released Cameron the next day.

J.P. Pritchett: At first [Robertson] seems to have intended to send Cameron to England by way of York Factory; but upon the prisoner's "solemnly promising that he would write to his Colleague at River Qu'Appelle to cease further proceedings on the part of the N.W.Co," and pledging himself "in the most solemn manner that neither he nor any of his associates should in any manner debauch, seduce, or in any other manner disturb the peace & prosperity of the Colony," he released him after twenty-four hours' detention. Cameron gave little trouble for the rest of the winter. (Pritchett, 170-1)

MK: This was unconvincing, according to Louis Aubrey Wood, writing a century later, for Cameron was "a born actor and a smooth talker. In all seeming humility he now made specious promises of future good behavior, and was allowed to return to his fort."

Lord Selkirk's Defense

MK: Alarmed by reports of his colonists' difficulties, Lord Selkirk had set out for New York in September 1815, but it wasn't until he had arrived in North America, on November 15, that he received the news of the actual destruction of the colony, "through the machinations of Duncan Cameron and Alexander Macdonell," as Louis Aubrey Wood wrote. Selkirk had written in one of the last letters he posted before setting sail, that "it is necessary that I should obtain justice for those who have thrown themselves on my protection." (in Bumsted, *Fur Trade Wars*, 130) Selkirk had long suspected there had been collusion between the bourgeois of the NWC and the Bois Brûlés and now he was eager to prove it, especially from the testimony of those colonists who had accepted Duncan Cameron's offer of assistance in resettling in Upper Canada.

Louis Aubrey Wood: At once he hastened to Montreal, where he received from eye-witnesses a more detailed version of the occurrence. Many of the settlers brought to the east were indignant at the treatment they had received at the hands of the Nor'westers and were prepared to testify against them. In view of this, Lord Selkirk applied to magistrates at York (Toronto) and Montreal, desiring that affidavits should be taken from certain of the settlers with respect to their experiences on the Red River. In this way he hoped to accumulate a mass of evidence which should strengthen his plea for military assistance from the Canadian government. (Wood)

Lord Selkirk in a letter to the Lieutenant-Governor of Lower Canada, Sir Gordon Drummond, November 1815: It would surely be most disgraceful to the British government, if these lawless ruffians should be suffered to make open war upon their fellow subjects." The culprits were "Canadians, mixed with the bastard sons of others, who have thrown off the restraints of regular society, & cohabiting with Indian squaws have formed a combination of the vices of civilized & savage life." (in Bumsted, *Fur Trade Wars*, 130)

MK: Making reference to the charter granted him by the HBC, "We do give and grant unto the said governor and company free liberty and license in case they conceive it necessary to send either ships of war, men or ammunition unto any of their plantations, forts or places of trade aforesaid for the security and defence of the same," Selkirk raised a force consisting of 180 Hudson's Bay Company employees and around 150 soldiers recently discharged from the De Meuron and De Watteville regiments, Swiss veterans of the Napoleonic Wars. Selkirk provided them with muskets, bayonets, and cartridge pouches and paid them out of his own pocket. (Wikipedia, "Pemmican Wars") For his part, Robert Semple, the new Governor-in-Chief of Rupert's Land, writing September 1815 from York Factory to the Committee of the Hudson's Bay Company in London, also called for the intervention of the British government in this affair, warning that their failure to do so would result in violence.

Robert Semple: It would be useless in my opinion to enter into a war of Posts when a decisive and open attack has been made on a great point of the Company's Territories in open violation of all law.... Should our Government refuse to interfere the inevitable consequence will be that two great Trading Company's of the same nation will be reduced nearly to the state of Two Indian Tribes at war and scenes of bloodshed and Confusion will mark the whole of our tracks. (in Gray, 141)

MK: Along with the final party of Kildonan settlers, Robert Semple finally arrived at the Red River colony in November, 1815. They were to help in rebuilding the colony but by then Colin Robertson was in full control of the situation, and the two men were eventually at loggerheads. Opinions about the character of Semple, American by birth and well-travelled, a writer not inexperienced in business, and a retired British army captain, are wildly divergent. Margaret A. Macleod and W.L. Morton, for instance, have averred that, for all his capacities, "he was, however, somewhat impulsive, yet at the same time stiff and unimaginative." (Macleod & Morton, 33) Writing a history of Red River in 1871, James Hargrave admires Semple without reservation: "[Semple's] personal qualities are reported to have been such as to qualify him well for the task he had undertaken. He was a man with a high sense of honour, endowed with a character gentle, just and firm." (Hargrave, unpaginated Appendix)

The ever-loquacious Louis Aubrey Wood, judged him "a man of upright character and bull-dog courage, but he lacked the patience and diplomacy necessary for the problem with which he had to deal." But author Vera Kelsey cuts Semple no slack: "Had Lord Selkirk scoured the British Empire for the most unsuitable successor to Miles Madonell, he could not have made a better choice.... A pompous ass personally, he knew nothing of farming, military service, or government. He was not impressed by the buckskinned Nor-Westers at Fort Gibraltar. He understood at once that the destruction of Colony Gardens stemmed from Captain [Miles] Macdonell's 'grossest mismanagement.' To a man of action like Robertson, a man of words like Semple was a disaster." (Kelsey, 88)

Governor Robert Semple to Lord Selkirk, November 1815: "The Colours were hoisted, the guns were fired, at night we laughed, and drank and danced and now the serious Calculations of the Colony Commence." (in Siggins, 238)

A Troubled Spring

James J. Hargrave: The fact that the settlement had been entirely destroyed the previous year by the agents of the North West Company, who were confessedly much annoyed at the perseverance of the colonists in returning, after their expulsion, to the scene of their sufferings, and altogether opposed to Lord Selkirk's project of colonization, prepared the settlers and the agents of the Hudson's Bay Company to expect a determined attack in the spring, as the next probable step in the progress of what had been a long time an irregular series of skirmishes, in the course of which Forts and other property had been seized by way of reprisal for pervious acts of violence by either party with varying success. (Hargrave, unpaginated Appendix A)

John Pritchard, settler: In the course of the winter [1815-16] we were much alarmed by reports that the Half-breeds were assembling in all parts of the North for the purpose of driving us away, and that they were expected to arrive at the settlement early in the spring. The nearer the spring approached, the more prevalent these reports grew, and letters received from different posts confirmed the same.... Likewise a report was very current, that a party of Half-breeds, and Cree Indians, were expected to arrive from Fort des Prairies [Fort Edmonton], on the Saskatchewan River, as soon as the melting of the snow would admit of their traveling; and the language of every free Canadian we saw was: 'Mefiez vous bien pour l'amour de Dieu; mefiez vous bien.' ['Be on your guard, for the love of God. Be on your guard.'] (in Halkett, 74–5)

Cuthbert Grant to Seraphim Lamar at Fort Gibraltar, 2 December 1815: My dear sir,... speaking of this new Governor, he gives every indication that we shall really be forced to shut him up if we are to spoil his game.... Give my best wishes to all the Young Fellows of the *bois-brûlés* that you see and impress upon them that they keep up their courage and take good care what they do for come spring we shall see the *bois-brûlés* from Fort des Prairies and from all sides. (in Macleod & Morton, 34)

George Bryce: After New Year in 1816, Governor Semple returned from Fort Daer to the Forks and took counsel with Colin Robertson, who seems to have been the most sane of Lord Selkirk's colonial staff. Their conference led to the conclusion that the North-West Company plan was clearly so hostile that to capture Fort Gibraltar and thwart Duncan Cameron's schemes was the only satisfactory course. (Bryce, *The Life of Lord Selkirk*, 67)

Cuthbert Grant, 13 March 1816 to Cameron from Fort Qu'Appelle: My Dear Sir, I received your generous and kind letter last fall, by the last canoe.... I am yet safe and sound, thank God, for I believe it is more than Colin Robertson or any of his suit dare to offer the least insult to any of the Bois-Brules. He shall see that it is neither fifteen, thirty, nor fifty of his best horsemen, that can make the Bois-Brules bow to him. Our people of Fort des Prairies and English River are all to be here in the spring; it is hoped we shall come off with flying colours, and never to see any of them again in the colonizing way in Red River, in fact the Traders shall pack off with themselves also, for having disregarded our orders last spring; according to our arrangements, we are to remain at the Forks & pass the Summer, for fear they should play us the same trick as last Summer, of coming back; but they shall receive a warm reception [if they do]. (in Macleod & Morton, 36)

MK: In March, Duncan Cameron singled out Cuthbert Grant as "Captain-General of all the Half-Breeds."

Alfred Silver: There was the swearing-in to do and papers to be written up. Captain Cameron was all for rousting out one of the junior clerks, until Grant pointed out that that was, after all, what the company had educated him for. They found some ink and pens and paper in a drawer, and Grant took Duncan Cameron's dictation. Seraphim Lamarr said: "Who you figure we'll have to defend the country from?"

"It's more your country than anyone else's, so I suppose you'll have some say in that."

Alex Fraser said: "Do you really think we're going to be invaded?"

"Some would say you already have been." (Silver, 235)

Margaret A. Macleod and W.L. Morton: But the Nor-Westers were rejoicing, not making war, that day, and [James] Sutherland [chief factor, Ft Douglas], learned why from an inebriated Canadian who came over to his post:

The flag was flying in honour of Cuthbert Grant having been appointed Captain-General of all the Half-Breeds in the country, and likewise as a rejoicing for the news brought by Swan River MacDonald that the Half Breeds in Athabasca, English River, Saskatchewan and Swan River were collecting under their several chiefs and had sent information that they would all join Grant early in the spring to sweep Red River of all the English.

Sutherland did not take this drunken talk too serious, but later learned that it was indeed intended to renew the war against the colony in the spring [1816]. The crisis of the fur-trade war was near. (Macleod & Morton, 37)

MK: In March 1816, Governor Semple, touring the HBC posts in the district, left Colin Robertson in charge of the colony. Robertson was already aware from the Saulteaux and others that the partners of the NWC, who had met once again at Fort William, had plotted a second and definitive attack on the settlement. He decided on a pre-emptive strike of his own: hearing that a party of Métis, Indians, and NWC voyageurs was converging on Fort Gibraltar, Robertson with some twenty of his men marched on the fort on March 17 and seized it. This gave Fort Douglas a commanding control of the waterways at the Forks in the crucial season of the transport of pemmican from the NWC's posts.

Donald Gunn: Apparently Mr Robertson did not relish a life of peace and inglorious ease.... [On] the night of the 17ᵗʰ of March, 1816, between seven and eight o'clock, Mr Robertson, at the head of an armed party of Hudson's Bay Company's servants, attacked Fort Gibraltar. The assailants rushed, with drawn swords, into Mr Cameron's sitting room, where that gentleman, unsuspicious of danger, was passing the evening in conversation with his clerks. On entering the room Mr Robertson collared Mr Cameron.

Captain McLean, Mr Bourke and others seized his sword, pistols and other arms. The captured gentleman, as soon as he had recovered from his surprise, asked Mr Robertson what he meant by his unexpected visit and extraordinary conduct. He replied, "you will know that by and by." Cameron, his clerks and servants, were for several hours kept in confinement, with a guard of armed men placed over them. The behaviour of some of the Hudson's Bay clerks was rude in the lowest degree, threatening to blow out the brains of one of the North-West Company's clerks who was their disarmed prisoner. (Gunn, 138)

Marjorie W. Campbell: Robertson's real reason for the arrest soon became apparent; while his armed gang held the bourgeois, he not only read the letter Cameron had been writing — it was an appeal to James Grant at Fond du Lac [Lake Superior] for help against Selkirk's "machinations" — but went on to ransack the room for further letters. (Campbell, 214)

MK: Two days later, March 19, Robertson detained the eastbound NWC express with its cargo of letters and correspondence from posts upriver at Qu'Appelle, Swan River, and Fort des Prairies and among the papers read a note from Alexander Macdonell at Qu'Appelle to Duncan Cameron. "A storm is gathering to the Northward ready to burst on the heads of the rascals who deserve it; little do they know their situation; last year was but a joke. The new nation under their leaders are coming forward to clear their native soil of intruders and assassins." (in Garrioch, 33)

Manitoba-based historian, Chester Martin, went rummaging in the Selkirk Papers in the early 1900s:

Chester Martin: At Moose Lake the half-breeds were urged to "join in extirpating those Miscreants out of the Country." ... Alexander Macdonell [wrote], "You will see some sport in Red River before the month of June [1816] is over." "'It must end,' said Laughlin McLean, 'in some sickly work at the long run." ... As early as March, it has been noticed, Grant considered his men "all united and staunch." (C. Martin, 108-09)

Donald Gunn: After the Hudson's Bay Company's servants had taken possession of the place, they removed all the arms, public and private, likewise the trading goods, provisions of every kind, furs, books, and papers, to the Hudson's Bay Fort. In due time the furs were sent to York Factory. (Gunn, 139)

MK: As fur trade historian Jack Bumsted argues, this was not yet evidence that the Nor'Westers were inciting the "new nation" to violence. However, in another letter, Macdonell wrote that NWC clerk William Shaw "has actually taken every Halfbreed in the country to the Forks from Fort des Prairies, it is supposed they will when collected together form more than one hundred, God knows the result." (in Bumsted, *Fur Trade Wars*, 144) These revelations were followed by the capture on March 20 of the NWC post at Pembina [winter hunting grounds in the Dakotas].

Donald Gunn: The Canadian traders had but few persons to feed at this place and were enabled to lay up a great stock of provision procured by the chase, with large quantities of Indian corn and potatoes. Bostennois Pangman, a half-breed, was in charge of the place, and two clerks and six or seven tripmen [hired for temporary duty on a fur brigade] constituted all his available forces. On the night of the 20th of March, three days after Fort Gibraltar had been captured, Bostennois' house and all the little shanties in which his men lodged, were secretly surrounded and simultaneously assaulted.... [The spoils taken away] consisted of arms, ammunition, trading goods, four or five packs of furs, great quantities of dried buffalo meat, Indian corn and potatoes; everything, whether the produce of the chase or the fruit of the earth, was taken away by the victors. (Gunn, 140)

MK: The HBC "victors" also arrested the traders and sent them down in bond to Fort Douglas, where, Gunn continues, "they underwent a rigorous confinement for the space of a week or two, and were at last turned out of the Fort ... and, finally, like their fellows taken in Fort Gibraltar, had to seek for an asylum among their kind countrymen [Métis] who were passing the spring among the buffalo on the plains." (Gunn, 140)

At the end of March, Governor Semple returned from his tour of the territory and, having read Cameron's intercepted papers for himself, wrote him personally, threatening legal consequences to the NWC's campaign against the colony.

Robert Semple to Duncan Cameron, 31 March 1816: Sir: I regret that an indisposition subsequent to my arrival here has prevented my addressing you till now. I think it my duty to tell you as soon as possible the charges alleged against you and wh[ich] I assure you will demand yr. most serious consideration.

1st. You are accused of seducing His Majesty's subjects settled on Red River and the servants of the Earl of Selkirk to desert and defraud their masters and one to whom the former were largely indebted.

2nd. Of collecting, harbouring and encouraging Halfbreeds and vagabonds with the avowed purpose of destroying an Infant British Colony.

3rd. Through the means of these men thus collected, of firing upon, wounding and causing the death of His Majesty's subjects defending their property in their own houses.

4th. Through the means of these men headed by yr. clerks or the clerks of the N.W.Co., such as Cuthbert Grant, Charles Hesse, Bostonais Pangman, William Shaw and others of burning a fort, a mill, sundry houses, carts, ploughs and instruments of agriculture belonging to the said infant colony.

5th. Of wantonly destroying English cattle brought here at an immense expense and of carrying off horses, dogs, and other property of large amount. The horses were collected in your own fort and distributed by yourself and your partner Mr A. McDonnell, to those men who had most distinguished themselves in the above act of robbery and mischief.

6th. Of encouraging Indian tribes to make war upon British subjects attempting to colonize, representing to them according to their ideas that cattlemen would spoil their lands and make them miserable, and expressing your hope they would never allow it.

7th. Without unnecessarily multiplying charges it appears now by your own letters that you were making every preparation to renew the same atrocities this year, if possible on a more extensive scale, collecting the Halfbreeds from points still more distant than before and endeavouring to influence both their rage and avarice by every means in yr. power. You even breathe the pious wish that the Pilleurs [plunderers] may be excited against us here saying "they may make very good booty if they only go cunningly to work."

Such are the principal charges you will be called upon to answer. … The whole mass of intercepted pages now in my hands appears to disclose such wicked principles and transactions that I think it my duty to forward them to be laid before His Majesty's ministers by the director of the Honourable the H.B. Co., advising them of this my resolution and the motives wh. have determined me to it, a copy of wh. shall be handed you meantime. (in Oliver, *The Canadian North-West*, 23–4)

MK: Yet, for all his bluster, Semple appeared immune to fears of the impending danger, to be confronted by the settlers if not by himself. The settlers had returned from Pembina at the end of April, and Governor Semple lost no time in encouraging them to get to their spring work on their lots, providing them the seed to plant extensively. And here is where the "difference of opinion" between Robertson and Semple finally reached breaking point, and Robertson debated leaving the settlement if proper measures to protect the community of settlers were not undertaken at once.

Jack Bumsted, interview: And what was Colin Robertson unhappy with in Semple's policy? He was allowing people out in the fields to plant, where they were likely to run into mixed-bloods, and something nasty was going to occur. Robertson wanted the settlers kept within the fort and under control while the mixed-bloods were riding around out there. Semple had no military experience whatever that I can find – most of his experience seems to have been as a spy in Europe.

MK: Robertson's *Journal* records: "He (Semple) appears full of confidence – rather too much so … guided by the opinion of others." (in Russenholt, 38) Robertson persistently referred in his writings to Semple as Mr. Simple. (in Bumsted, *Fur Trade Wars*, 145) With his leader a prisoner of the HBC, his posts on the lower Red River plundered, and his enemy, Semple, secure in Fort Douglas, Alexander Macdonell had reason to be very concerned for the NWC's organization of business.

Alexander Macdonell: It was my duty therefore, to take whatever steps I lawfully could for the preservation of the property under my charge. I consequently, with as little delay as possible, stated briefly in a general letter to the Partners to the northward of Red River, the state of their affairs in that department; the necessity of sending forward with all possible expedition some of the most active men, Half-breeds and others, with a supply of arms and ammunition for the defence of the depot of provisions at Qu'Appelle, Robertson having captured the greater part of those stores in the lower posts. (in J. Martin, "150th Anniversary")

MK: In the month of April, the Métis, some by horseback and others by canoes, made their way in small groups toward Qu'Appelle, where they were concentrated under the command of Cuthbert Grant and Alexander Macdonell.

Deposition of Pierre-Chrysologue Pambrun, HBC post at Qu'Appelle, appearing before Lord Selkirk 16 August 1816: That when he arrived to take up his post at Qu'Appelle, he found that at the fort or trading post of the North-West Company, near the same place, were assembled a great number of the men, commonly called Brulés, Metifs or half-breeds, *viz.* the bastard sons of Indian concubines, kept by the partners or servants of the North-West Company; that these people had been collected from a great distance, some of them having come from Cumberland House, and others from the Upper Saskatchewan, or Fort de Prairies, that they uttered violent threats against the colonists on the Red River, in which the deponent understood them to be encouraged by Mr Alexander McDonell, then commanding for the North-West Company. (in Halkett, xxxii–xxxiii)

Marcel Giraud, historian: All of them, when they arrived, were imbued with hostile intentions toward the Red River settlers, and were resolved to sweep them from the territory they had usurped from the Métis nation. As buffalo hunters, most of them came armed with their muskets. The rest had provided themselves with pistols, daggers, bows, or swords. On the Qu'Appelle River, near the North West Company's post, a smith had set up a stall where he repaired their arms and forged lances on request. (Giraud, 452)

MK: Giraud goes on to describe how the "energies" of this "New Nation" of mixed-bloods on the plains were then rallied by a flag of their own, unfurled before them, a horizontal figure eight on a blue background, a "nationalist" insignia which nevertheless had been "devised" by the Nor'Westers. The implication is that Métis patriotism was a consciousness manipulated by the Company.

Ron Bourgeault, interview: Where and how *consciousness* arises, well, consciousness arises by virtue of their position between the overall Indian population and the European. The consciousness of being Métis is not the product of a primordial instinct that arises out of intermarriage. It's not biologically transmitted. It's the rise of consciousness within the political economy of the mercantile capitalist fur trade. The consciousness of being loyal to one mercantile fur trading company, for what they get out of it, and seeing themselves as indigenous.

Attacks and Counter-attacks

MK: In May, Cuthbert Grant and his Nor'Westers canoed down the Assiniboine, "more like a war party than a fur brigade." (Gray, 142) He and about seventy Métis were on their way to intercept a HBC transport of pemmican meant as provisions for the settlement. This would be no mean feat, as Fort Douglas, with its block houses and artillery commanded the river, so close to the river's edge that "even armed with musketry, no craft could pass in safety without the permission of those who occupied it." (Gunn, 141)

William B. Coltman's Report: On May 8, 1816, James Sutherland, P.C. Pambrun, and twenty-two men, in the service of the Hudson's Bay company, in charge of five boats, containing twenty-two packs of fur and about six hundred bags of pemmican, whilst embarrassed in the rapids of the river Qui Appelle, were attacked by a party of about forty-nine persons under the command of Cuthbert Grant, Thomas McKay, Roderick McKenzie, and Bostonais, clerks or interpreters, and Brisebois, a guide in the service of the North-West company. (in Barkwell, *The Battle of Seven Oaks*, 30)

Margaret A. Macleod and W. L. Morton: Grant left the ponies back in the trees and set his men in ambush along the willow-lined shore. As the boats came round one at a time, their crews were forced to put into shore by the *brulés'* levelled muskets and, unarmed, they marched into the willows. Sutherland and Pambrun with their whole party were taken neatly, boat-load by boat-load, by the politely smiling Grant. The smoothness of the operation was marred only by one boat grounding in the rapids. It was a coup of much distinction, simple and clever, which rejoiced the hearts of the *brulés*. (Macleod & Morton, 42)

Pierre-Chrysologue Pambrun: I was kept a prisoner for five days. Cuthbert Grant, Peter Pangman, and Thomas McKay were of the party who made me prisoner. I was taken back to River Qu'Appelle, to the Northwest Company's post. I was kept there for five days. Mr Alexander Macdonell was in command at this station, and I asked him why I had been made a prisoner, or by whose orders I had been arrested? He said it was by his own. There were about forty or fifty Bois-Brules at this fort. Cuthbert Grant frequently said they were going to destroy the settlement, and I was told Mr. Macdonell said the business of the year before was a trifle to what this should be. Cuthbert Grant frequently talked with Bois-Brules about going, and they sang war-songs as if they were going to battle. (in Bryce & Bell; in Blanchard, 74–5)

MK: As coordinator of history research at the Louis Riel Institute, Lawrence Barkwell has compiled fascinating biographical information about the men who rode with Grant. Not all were Métis: Francois Firmin Boucher was a French Canadian employed by the NWC as a clerk; Jean-Baptiste Desmarais was a voyageur, interpreter, and foreman who travelled with his Saulteaux wife, Josephte; Machicabou (Stepping Ahead or Starts to Stand) was a Chief long associated with the NWC and also described as a Midewewin Medicine man. But the main body of men in Grant's party were Métis, and a typical biography might be that of, say, Pierre Falcon, born at Elbow Fort in the Swan River valley to Jean-Baptiste, fur trader, and to a daughter of Pas au Traverse, a Cree Indian, who clerked with the NWC; or Baptiste Lafontaine, later a renowned buffalo hunter, born in the North West Territory to Jean Baptiste Lafontaine and a Sioux woman (unnamed); or the hunter André Trottier, son of André Trottier and Louise (Chippewa). (in Barkwell, *Battle*, 13ff)

Louis Aubrey Wood: After five days' imprisonment George Sutherland and the servants of the Hudson's Bay Company were released. This did not mean, however, any approach of peace. Pierre Pambrun was still held in custody. Before the close of May, [Alexander] Macdonell caused the furs and provisions which his men had purloined from Sutherland's party to be placed in boats, and he began to move down the Qu'Appelle, taking Pambrun with him. A band of Bois Brûlés on their horses kept pace with the boats. (Wood)

Alexander Macdonell: [On their way, Cuthbert Grant and Macdonell met a band of Saulteaux Indians and declared their intentions. Macdonell spoke through an interpreter, Joseph Primeau.] My Friends and Relations, I address you with Bashfulness for not having more Tobacco to present to you. It is the English people who are the cause of it. They have stopped the supplies that were coming for you. You know who I mean — those that make you believe they are cultivating the lands for the good of the Indians, but don't you believe them. They are spoiling the Lands that belong to you, and to your Relations, the Metifs (*sic*) only. They are driving away the Buffaloe, and will render the Indians poor and miserable, but the North West Company will drive them away, since the Indians do not choose to do it. If the Settlers resist, the ground shall be drenched with their blood. None shall be spared. We do not need the assistance of the Indians, but we shall be glad if some of the young men would join us. (in Pritchett, 174)

Pierre-Chrysologue Pambrun: The chief said he knew nothing about it, and should not go himself; if some of the young men went, it was nothing to him.... The next morning, the Indians went away. (in Bryce & Bell; in Blanchard, 75)

MK: For good measure, on June 1, 1816, en route for Red River, Cuthbert Grant and company captured Brandon House and its stores of pemmican. A showdown was inevitable. As Bruce Sealey and Antoine Lussier write in *The Métis: Canada's Forgotten People*, "[T]he Nor'Westers and the Metis had the pemmican and were determined to open the river, while the settlers under Semple were equally determined to keep the river blocked and to retain all the pemmican within the District of Assiniboia." (Sealey & Lussier, 41)

Peter Fidler: At ½ past noon about 48 Half Breeds, Canadians, Freemen & Indians came all riding on Horseback, with their flag flying blue about 4 feet square & a figure of 8 horizontally in the middle, one Beating an Indian Drum, and many of them singing Indian songs, they all rode directly to the usual crossing place over the river where they all stopped about two minutes, and instead of going down the Bank and riding across the River they all turned round and rode at full speed into our Yard — some of them tyed their Horses, others loose & fixed their flag at our Door.... Cuthbert Grant then came up to me in the Yard & demanded of me to deliver to him all the Keys of our Stores Warehouses & I of course would not deliver them up — they then rushed in the House and broke open the warehouse Door first, plundered the Warehouse of every article it contained, tore up part of the Cellar floor & cut out the Parchment windows ... they also plundered every person in the House of part of their private property

& took away every horse belonging to the Company & European Servants... all these men were armed with a Gunsack, a pike at the end of a pole, some bows & arrows swords.... Bostonais told that it was Mr. Robertson's fault they had plundered our House – for taking their Fort at the Forks. (in MacGregor, 213-4)

MK: From Brandon House, the expedition moved on to Portage la Prairie, where they were reinforced by small groups of Métis from outlying posts. Cuthbert Grant's party now numbered some sixty-two men, most of them sporting war paint, according to Peter Newman's lively account of events, and taking on the aspect of an army on the march (Newman, *Caesars of the Wilderness*, 229) "The Generalissimo," wrote J.P. Pritchett, "was now ready to move against Red River." (Pritchett, 173)

Showdown at Red River

MK: Finally ceding to Colin Robertson's urgent appeals that he act to protect the settlers and that Fort Gibraltar be razed so that he would have one less post to defend and could use the timbers to strengthen the walls of Fort Douglas, Semple decided to act.

Chester Martin: Fort Gibraltar was demolished, the stockades were drawn up to be taken in rafts down to Fort Douglas, and what remained was burned to the ground. The same day, June 11, "lord Chesterfield," as Robertson was popularly known among the Northwesters, left the settlement at open variance with Semple, the two men still disagreeing vehemently about the need, in Robertson's view, or not, in Semple's, of further protection of the settlers by sequestering them inside the fort. Robertson took his prisoner, Nor'wester Duncan Cameron, down the river towards York Factory. "I had no participation," Robertson afterwards wrote, "in suggesting or approving these incautious measures, which had a great tendency to produce the second destruction of the colony." (C. Martin, 108)

MK: It is said (in Wikipedia), of Robertson's and Cameron's departure, that instead of flying the HBC's Red Ensign behind his canoe, Robertson had rigged up an empty pemmican sack — as an insult to the HBC governor he now spurned or to the NWC whose *bourgeois* he had prisoner is unclear. As they drew away, Cameron had his last look of Fort Gibraltar. He would not be returning to the Red River. (Cameron was sent held at York Factory for a year and eventually moved overland to Montreal for trial.)

George Bryce: The Nor'-Westers House at Pembina near Fort Daer was dismantled in the same way, and its store of provisions taken by the colony. This policy, which Lord Selkirk would not have approved, had much of the spirit of the military martinet, and brought the heavy penalty of death upon Governor Semple himself. (Bryce, *Life of Lord Selkirk*, 68)

Marjorie W. Campbell: The sight of the great fort [Gibraltar] in flames was too much for the Métis; soon the fire which had been smouldering in every one of them also burst into flame. To each the destruction of the North West Company post was a warning of what might happen to his own small home. Or like a prairie fire news of the destruction of Fort Gibraltar raced from post to post, and from camp to camp wherever Métis and Indians gathered to

hunt buffalo. The ancient war spirit of their Indian mothers, augmented by many a strain of fighting French and Highland Scots
paternity, urged them to defend their very existence; and the
Nor'Westers were no longer in any mood to enforce restraint.
(Campbell, 215)

Louis Aubrey Wood: Then the combined force of half-breeds, French Canadians, and Indians, in round numbers amounting to one hundred and twenty men, advanced to Portage la Prairie. They
reached this point on or about June 16, and proceeded to make
it a stronghold. They arranged bales of pemmican to form a rude
fortification and planted two brass swivel-guns for defense. They
were preparing for war, for the Nor'westers had now resolved
finally to uproot Lord Selkirk's colony from the banks of the Red
River. (Wood)

Grant MacEwan: But while he was a hero to the Métis, Cuthbert Grant was
soon to be the most feared and hated man of the country to the
settlers, at least for a few years. In the course of time, with the
help of the Hudson's Bay Company, he won the respect of almost
everybody along the two rivers. But as of this moment, he was
entering the lives of the Red River residents like an evil monster.
(MacEwan, *Cornerstone Colony*, 104)

Robert Henry, Nor'Wester: I would not be surprised if some of us left our
bones there [at Red River]. If it comes to a Battle many lives must
be lost. . . . I am very much afraid it will be a serious business but
we must hope for the best. (in Pritchett, 173)

"The Fight at Seven Oaks, 1816."
Painted by Charles William Jefferys.
(Library and Archives Canada, MIKAN no: 2835226)

SIX: THE BATTLE OF SEVEN OAKS

Donald Gunn: But, alas! man's lot on earth is but a checkered scene at least; and as the serenest sky and brightest sunshine are often obscured by dark and threatening clouds, so was the sunshine of [the colonists'] anticipated happiness darkened; adverse clouds were swiftly gathering around their devoted heads, which speedily poured forth an irresistible tempest that desolated their habitations and drove them out homeless and helpless wanderers on the voyage of life. (Gunn, 145)

Métis on the Move

MK: It wasn't as though Governor Semple had not been warned. On June 17, two Métis men had approached Fort Douglas to let him know that a large and hostile expedition, camped at Portage la Prairie, would march on the colony in two days. Disbelieving, Semple nevertheless began a twenty-four-hour watch at the Fort, although, characteristically, he turned down an offer of help from Chief Peguis to protect the colony. On June 19 he received a second warning that the large force of Métis and Nor'westers would soon be on the move. (Cuthbert Grant's group included "four Saulteaux, two Cree, six Canadiens and fifty-two Half Breeds.") (Barkwell, *Battle*, 10)

Among partisans and historians of the event, there was never to be agreement on the motives of the Alexander Greenfield Macdonell and Cuthbert Grant parties in choosing the movements to and around Frog Plain those June days, the 17th to 19th: innocent or ill intent? They were always to argue that they moved to and around Frog Plain simply to ensure contact by land with the Nor'West canoe brigade arriving up river on the Red.

Donald Gunn: [Alexander Greenfield Macdonell] and his half-breeds made their appearance, about the middle of June, at Portage la Prairie, being desirous, as he professed, to prevent a contest between his men and those under Governor Semple's command. A brigade of canoes, from Fort William, was expected to arrive in Red River about the 20th of June. Mr. [Alexander Greenfield] McDonell knew that those in possession of Fort Douglas could blockade the river, at that point, and cut off all communication between the expected canoes and the North-West Company's servants encamped at Portage la Prairie. He knew that any attempt, made by his people, to pass up or down by water, would end in a collision of the rival parties and the probable discomfiture of the Canadian traders and the ruin of their interest in the Red River country. To avoid this dreaded result, the North-West Company's servants essayed to open the communication, by land, between the stations on the Assiniboine and Lake Winnipeg, to effect that object. (Gunn, 145)

George Bryce: In order to show their intentions at this point, it is necessary to say that the concerted plan of the Nor'-Westers was to send to meet this western rally organized by Alexander Macdonell, another party of Nor'-Westers coming from Fort William, under the command of a prominent Nor'-Wester officer, Alexander [actually Archibald] Norman MacLeod. The plan was that these should meet on the banks of the Red River, and then no doubt it was their intention to capture Fort Douglas as a reprisal for the pulling down of Fort Gibraltar by Governor Semple. (Bryce, *Life of Lord Selkirk*, 71)

Alexander Macdonell: [On June 18th ... Grant and about fifty men and boys ... were instructed that on] their arrival at Passage, a place on the Assiniboine River, nine or ten English miles above the settlement and garrisons at the forks of the Red River, they should land and unload the canoe, secrete it in the woods and put the pemmican into two carts sent for that purpose, with which they were directed to proceed in an orderly and peaceable manner, avoiding if possible, being discovered or seen by the Hudson's Bay people and settlers; to keep at as great a distance as possible from Forts Gibraltar and Douglas; to avoid the Settlement in like manner and upon no account to molest any of the settlers. (in Joseph Martin," 150th Anniversary")

Lawrence J. Barkwell: June 18 to 19: Cuthbert Grant's party was mounted and traveling east along the Assiniboine River, they had two carts and canoes with 15 bags (1.150 pounds) of pemmican. He brought the canoes ashore at Sturgeon Cree and they proceeded overland to Catfish Creek (now Omand's Creek) then headed north to Frog Plain. He reached Catfish Creek on the late afternoon of the nineteenth, a location three miles west of the forks. Because of the large swamp drained by the creek, Grant's horses were up to their bellies in water and had to travel further east than they had planned. They had to veer east to within one and a half miles of Fort Douglas. (Barkwell, *Battle*, 9)

George Bryce: The half-breeds were mounted on their prairie steeds and formed a company of sixty men under the command of Cuthbert Grant. Dressed in their blue capotes and encircled by red sashes the men of this irregular cavalry had an imposing effect, especially as they were provided with every variety of arms from muskets and pistols down to bows and arrows. They were all expert riders and would equal in their feats on horseback the fabled Centaurs. Down the Portage road which is a prolongation of [today's] great business street to Winnipeg running to the west, they came. On the 19th of June, 1816, they had arrived within four miles of the Colony headquarters — Fort Douglas. Here at Boggy Creek, called also Cat-Fish Creek, a Council of War was held. (Bryce, *Romantic Settlement*, 121)

MK: For his study, *The Red River Valley 1811–1849*, American historian John P. Pritchett compiled contemporary sources that included John Pritchard, Peter Fidler, John Bourke, and Michael Heden for an account of the battle.

J.P. Pritchett: At this time Governor Semple was fully aware of the hostile designs of the Metis, and his scouts kept him carefully informed of all their movements. He also knew from letters he had intercepted that a force was coming from Fort William to join the band from the west. Hence he was on the lookout for trouble, and apparently was determined to prevent, if possible, the junction of the two enemy bands. (Pritchett, 174–5)

Governor Semple Musters His Men

MK: But suddenly they were right there, in Semple's spy-glass. The evening of 19 June, a party of some fifty to seventy armed Métis and aboriginals on horseback had been spotted from the watch-house of Fort Douglas. "The half-breeds are coming, the half-breeds are coming!" Ostensibly, in their wide sweep across the plain, they were skirting the Fort and the settlement — but not wide enough. When they reached some settlers weeding potatoes in their fields beyond the Fort, they detained five of them, to prevent them from alerting the Fort. Back at the Fort, Semple immediately organized a small platoon of twenty-five volunteer settlers and Baymen to march out and confront the horsemen as to their intentions. But these latter had already reached Frog Plain/La Grenouillère (a kilometre north of Seven Oaks) and were unsaddling when the rumour reached them that Semple's men were preparing an attack.

Marjorie W. Campbell: Late on the day of June 19, 1816, Grant was within sight of the rubble of Fort Gibraltar. He might continue to follow the river bank, but in doing so would run the risk of fire from the cannon at Fort Douglas. Instead he led his men — some of them Indians in war paint — on a line across the prairie, avoiding the angle between the rivers to regain the Red River below Fort Douglas. As he headed his men toward a point known as Seven Oaks he saw a group of some thirty men emerge from the fort gate, headed by Robert Semple. Now on the alert, he watched their movements carefully. (Campbell, 216)

Deposition of John Bourke, storekeeper to the colony, 1816: On the nineteenth day of June last, about five o'clock in the afternoon ...

[t]he deponent, with others, went into the watchhouse for the purpose of viewing the said party of horsemen, with a spy-glass, and they then distinctly perceived that the said party consisted of sixty or seventy men on horse-back, all of them armed, and approaching the settlement in a hostile manner. The said governor having viewed the approach of these men, who appeared to direct their course towards the settlement below the fort, desired twenty men to follow him, for the purpose of ascertaining what was their object; and upwards of that number, among whom the deponent was, immediately collected and went with him out the fort. (in Halkett, xlix-xlx)

Vera Kelsey: In all his travels to foreign lands, Semple had found the Anglo-Saxon to be above challenge, the natives docile and obsequious. These barbarous Red River half-breeds wouldn't dare to defy a British governor and man of letters! Ordering every male Selkirker within earshot to follow, he rushed out. Twenty-six men, muskets in hand, obeyed. (Kelsey, 89)

James J. Hargrave: The party under Governor Semple were provided with guns, but they were in an unserviceable state, some being destitute of locks and all more or less useless. This fact was of course unknown to their opponents, who were apparently sincere in their belief that the Governor was prepared to offer serious resistance to them before the carnage commenced, after which their entire want of order and discipline rendered them incapable of reason or consideration. The infatuation which led the Governor's party to attempt by a vain exhibition of useless weapons, to intimidate nearly three times their number of men to whom the saddle and gun were instruments of their daily occupation, is almost incomprehensible. All the victims of the tragedy claim our commiseration, but most of all, I think, compassion is called forth by the untimely fate of that high minded gentleman who led the party, whose valuable life was doomed to so sudden, so revolting and so unprofitable an end. (Hargrave, 487)

Jack Bumsted, interview: I think Seven Oaks was basically an inadvertent disaster, that is to say, I think the Métis — or mixed-bloods, as I prefer to call them because there was no Métis yet; Métis is a term which is later developed — the mixed-bloods were obviously out to intimidate the settlers who were planting. They were planting around Seven Oaks. But I don't think, there is no evidence that I can see, that the mixed-bloods had a particular intention of having a military encounter. On the other hand, if they weren't looking for trouble, they could have gone wider around the farmers than they did. The fact that they went in so close to the farmers suggests intimidation, I think.

Rev. A.C. Garrioch: When the colonists met the French half-breeds at Seven Oaks there followed what some have called a fight, but which is as often and more correctly designated a massacre, and of which the account considered the most reliable is that of Mr John Pritchard, grandfather of Archbishop Matheson; and it must be admitted that his version of the affair bears the impress of candour, and shows a desire to tell the whole truth, for we are informed that one of the Half-breeds greeted him with the remark, "*Petit chien* (you little dog). What are you doing here?" This question in which Mr Pritchard is classed as a diminutive specimen of the canine race, is accounted for by the fact that though he was now a settler in the Red River he had been previous to his retirement, an officer in the service of the North-West Company. (Garrioch, 36)

Affadavit of John Pritchard: The governor said: "We must go out and meet those people; let twenty men follow me." We proceeded down the old road leading down the settlement. As we were going along we met many of the settlers running to the fort, crying, "The half-breeds! The half-breeds!" When we were advanced about three-quarters of a mile along the settlement we saw some people on horseback behind a point of woods. On our nearer approach the party seemed to be more numerous, on which the governor made a halt and sent for a field piece, which, delaying to arrive, he ordered us to advance. (in Bryce & Bell; in Blanchard, 78–9)

Alfred Silver: As the governor began to amble down the path again, Lieutenant Rogers gave the order for the escort to march on. Mister Macbeth [a settler] stood aside and shouted as they passed: "Keep your backs to the river! Form up with a broad front and, whatever else you do, do not let them outflank you!"

...As they marched on, John Pritchard loudly reassured everyone that there was nothing to fear, that one white man was worth five half-breeds in a fight, and the half-breeds knew it. Michael Heden, the colony blacksmith, said he hoped the half-breeds would be stupid enough to start something so he could teach them a lesson. The governor announced confidently that the day was yet to dawn when a disciplined body of white men couldn't face down a ragtag batch of savages. (Silver, 387–9)

John Pritchard: We had not proceeded far before the half-breeds, with their faces painted in the most hideous manner, and in the dresses of Indian warriors, came forward and surrounded us in the form of a half moon. (in Bryce & Bell; in Blanchard, 79)

The Battle of Seven Oaks

Peter C. Newman, author: The Métis halted in half-moon formation. Semple and his men advanced in single file. And then all grew quiet — a silence more intense than the absence of noise, with even the sweet sounds of nature temporarily stilled. A horse snorted. The Métis, reinforced by new arrivals at the edges of their formation, began to tighten their half-circle, pressing Sample's irregulars towards the river bank. Grant signalled one of his subalterns, a Métis named François Firmin Boucher, to order the governor and his men to lay down their arms or they would be shot. As Boucher urged his horse forward, Grant covered Semple with his gun. (Newman, 229-30)

Auguste-Henri de Trémaudan: And it is here, on the 19th of June 1816, that the incident known as Frog Plain or Seven Oaks intervenes. As with all dramatic incidents of this nature, and because of the bias existing on all sides, it would be unfair to lay responsibility on anyone in particular. Chance, especially, was the biggest culprit. (Trémaudan, 105 M K trans.)

Affadavit of John Pritchard: We then extended our line and moved more into the open plain, and as they advanced we retreated a few steps backward, and then saw a Canadian named Boucher ride up to us waving his hand and calling out, "what do you want?" The governor replied, "What do you want?" To which Boucher replied, "We want our fort." The governor said, "Go to your fort." They were by this time near each other, and consequently spoke too low for me to hear. (in Bryce & Bell; in Blanchard, 79)

Marjorie W. Campbell: "We want our fort," snapped Boucher. "Go to your fort, then!" retorted Semple, to which the *Canadien* answered angrily: "Why did you destroy our fort, you damned rascal?"

Probably stung out of his senses by the insult from one whom he considered his inferior, Robert Semple grabbed Boucher's gun. It was the opening act of battle. Even as Boucher slid from his horse to retrieve his gun, the Métis opened fire. (Campbell, 217)

Donald G. McLean: The Metis men, who seconds ago were astride their horses, were now concealed behind them. Volley after volley of gunfire came from Grant and his men. At the same time, some of the concealed Metis came in from behind the settlers, completely surrounding them. They were now doomed. Some, like John Maclean and an HBC official named Rogers, fixed bayonets and charged savagely at Grant. They were cut down by a sharp volley. A few men broke and ran. They were ridden down and speared. Governor Semple was dispatched with a shot in the chest. Most of the settlers were killed in the first few seconds of battle, falling where they stood, in a straight line across the trail. (McLean, 43)

Affidavit of John Pritchard: Captain Rogers, having fallen, rose up and came towards me, when, not seeing one of our party who was not either killed or disabled, I called out to him, "For God's sake give yourself up!" He ran towards the enemy for that purpose, myself following him. He raised up his hands and, in English and broken French, called for mercy. A half-breed (son of Col. William McKay) shot him through the head, and another cut open his belly with a knife with the most horrid imprecations. Fortunately for me, a Canadian (named Lavigne), joining his entreaties to mine, saved me (though with the greatest difficulty) from sharing the fate of my friend in that moment. (in Bryce & Bell; in Blanchard, 79)

Louis Aubrey Wood: The wounded governor lay stretched upon the ground. Supporting his head with his hand, he addressed Cuthbert Grant: "I am not mortally wounded," he said, "and if you could get me conveyed to the fort I think I should live." Grant promised to comply with the request. He left the governor in charge of one of his men and went away, but during his absence an Indian approached and shot Semple to death. (Wood)

William B. Coltman, merchant, justice of the peace: After the battle, Cuthbert Grant informed Pritchard that Governor Semple was wounded by a shot from himself, and that lying on the ground, his thigh bone being broken, he asked him if he was Mr. Grant, and being answered yes, he said, "I am not mortally wounded, and if you could get me conveyed to the fort, I think I should live." Grant promised to do so, and left him in the care of a Canadien, but that the governor was afterwards shot through the breast by an Indian. These particulars agree nearly with what Grant stated in his deposition and he further added, that the name of the Indian was Machicabaou, and that Machicabaou had told Grant that he had killed the Governor. Nolin, in his deposition states that he was told at the time that it was Deschamps, a Canadien who killed him; but this report probably arose from people having seen Deschamps plundering the Governor's body. (Coltman, *Papers Relating*, 186)

Nor'Wester Archibald McLeod: The Governor begged for his life after he was wounded severely, which the half breeds granted and one of them stood by to protect him, but an Indian whose child had died in the winter and to whom the governor told on the plenitude of his confidence that he lost his child for his attachment to the NWC, told the governor, "today you must follow my child as you boasted it was medicine killed him," so saying shot him. (in Siggins, 246)

Solicitor-general to Grand Jury at Assizes, York, Upper Canada 1818: On receiving his wound [Semple] called out to his people to do what they could for themselves, but they, perceiving him struggling in the agonies of death, almost immediately, whether from panic or from affectionate attachment to their governor and friend, you will judge, gathered round him, and made no resistance. Whilst they were thus situated, gathered round the dying man, a volley was poured in by which nearly the whole were killed. (in Wilcocke, *Report*, 63)

MK: Of those killed, only three were colonists, from one or another party of settlers to Red River: Reginald Green, Alexander MacLean of Kengharair, and Adam Sutherland. Others were HBC employees or labourers, such as Bryan Gilligan, Duncan MacNaughton, Henry Sinclair, or HBC officers, among them Captain John Rogers, Dr. James White, Lt. Einer Holte, as well as Governor Robert Semple himself. (Barkwell, *Battle* rev., 31ff)

Louis Aubrey Wood: Of the party which had left Fort Douglas with Governor Semple there were but six survivors. Michael Heden and Daniel M'Kay had run to the riverside during the melee. They succeeded in getting across in a canoe and arrived at Fort Douglas the same night. Michael Kilkenny and George Sutherland escaped by swimming the river. In addition to John Pritchard, another prisoner, Anthony Macdonell, had been spared. The total number of the dead was twenty-three. Among the slain were Rogers, the governor's secretary, Doctor Wilkinson, Alexander M'Lean, the most enterprising settler in the colony, and Surgeon James White. The colonists suffered severely in proportion to their number: they lost seven in all. The Nor'westers had one man killed and one wounded. This sanguinary encounter, which took place beside the highway leading along the Red River to Frog Plain, is known as the massacre of Seven Oaks. (Wood)

Jack Bumsted, interview: Now the *massacre* of course comes because Cuthbert Grant cannot control his mixed bloods. Semple surrenders to him and despite that surrender to Cuthbert Grant – Semple says, "I've been hit but I don't think I'm mortally wounded; I surrender" – nevertheless someone comes up to Semple and whacks him over the head. And he's dead. Most of the settlers are killed in the same vein. Lack of discipline. Anyway, it seems to me it's inadvertent and in a situation which is explosive, to say the least.

Joseph Tassé, historian: The smell of powder seemed to make the *Bois-brûlés* drunk with rage; thus Milord's men (as the voyageurs referred to Lord Selkirk) were utterly decimated. In less than fifteen minutes, more than twenty English bodies had tumbled onto the bloody plain. (Tassé, 342 mk trans.)

Bruce Sealey and Antoine Lussier: Experienced hunters and sharp-shooters, the Métis fired a volley of shots and then fell to the ground to reload. The naïve settlers cheered for they thought that their few aimless shots had killed all the Métis. The Métis reloaded their guns and charged the settlers. With the notable exception of two or three, the settlers turned in terror and tried to escape by running to the river and hiding along the bank. The Métis horsemen then charged and shot them with the ease of men accustomed to "running the buffalo." The battle lasted only fifteen minutes. (Sealey & Lussier, 41)

Lawrence J. Barkwell: Up until recent years, historical writings have focussed on the Selkirk Settlers who were killed (only three) whereas there is barely a mention of the seven Irish HBC labourers who were killed in the battle [among them James Bruin, Daniel Donovan, and James Gardiner, and three from the Orkneys and five from northern Scotland]. No one has commented previously on the relative youth of Cuthbert Grant (age 23) and his men: Francois Deschamps Jr. was 12 or 13 years-of-age; Joseph Letendre dit Batoche, the only Metis killed in the battle, was 16, and Baptiste Lafontaine was [16]. (Barkwell, *Battle*, 4)

Jack Bumsted, interview: Semple had decided in his infinite wisdom to raise an armed force and go out and confront the mixed bloods. Of course he went out with his force — less than thirty people but they had guns, which they didn't know how to use, against seventy armed buffalo hunters on horseback. Who knows who issued the first call to violence? Whether done by Semple, whether done by one of the mixed-bloods. But I think there was enough animosity and the situation was tense enough that you got what you got, which was, shooting starts and it doesn't stop until a number of settlers are dead. And it's the settlers dead rather than the mixed-bloods dead because the mixed-bloods are by far the better fighters on the day.

Ron Bourgeault, interview: The military prowess is important because they are already schooled in it as buffalo hunters, all the skills that came from firing from a horse and taking steady shot by putting their rifle on the back of a horse and shooting. And they use those skills against the HBC and early settlers who were not schooled in those skills. So it was a one-sided fight, those who were trained to do it and those who were not trained to do it.

Martin McLeod, traveler and diarist: The hunters are exceedingly expert, notwithstanding which many accidents occur. I have seen many of them with broken legs, broken arms and disabled hands. This latter accident frequently occurs from their manner of loading their guns. They never use wadding. The powder is carelessly thrown in more or less quantities the ball is then tumbled in upon it, and off goes the shot. This is done to save time, and it is almost incredible what a number of shots one person will discharge in riding the distance of 3 to 4 miles, the horse at the top of his speed.

Who Fired the First Shot?

Marjorie W. Campbell: Indeed, every man present at the little site marked by the seven oaks had his own version of what had happened. (Campbell, 217)

Voluntary Declaration of François Firmin Boucher, accused on oath of having, on the 19th of last June, killed at the colony of the Red River, twenty-one men, among whom was Governor Semple, says: That he did not kill any person whatever.... That as [he and his companions] proceeded towards Frog Plain, they observed a group of Hudson's Bay people — upon which a certain number of men in the service of the North-west Company, called Bois-Brules, joined the deponent and his companions. That these, thinking the Hudson's Bay people meant them harm, because they advanced with their muskets in their hands, the Bois-Brules wanted to fire on them; but the deponent opposed their doing so. That at last he advanced alone to the Hudson's Bay party to speak to them, and came so near Governor Semple, that the latter took hold of the butt end of the deponent's gun, and ordered his people to advance; that they, not obeying him, and the deponent saying that if they fired they were all dead men, Governor Semple said that they must not be afraid, that this was not the time for it, and they must fire. Immediately the deponent heard the reports of two muskets fired by the Hudson's Bay people. (in Bryce & Bell; in Blanchard, 81)

Deposition of Michael Heden, colony blacksmith: The said Boucher jumped from his horse, and a shot was instantly fired by one of the party of horsemen.... The said Boucher then ran to his party, and another shot was fired from the same quarter, by which Governor Semple was wounded. (in Halkett, lvi)

William B. Coltman: Not one [witness] except Haydon states the contrary, even on belief; and all others who have spoken on the question concur in stating that such was the general report [that the colonists fired first]; whilst the opposite statement of Haydon remains unsupported by a single evidence, either direct or indirect. Other collateral circumstances have also combined, with this weight of evidence, to convince me that the declaration made by him is, in this respect, unfounded. (in Barkwell, *Battle*, 7)

Alexander Ross: As might be expected, the advocates of either party in this catastrophe strenuously denied having fired the first shot, and perhaps it will ever remain in some minds a matter of uncertainty. In the country where the murder took place, there never has been a shadow of doubt, but rather a full and clear knowledge of the fact, that the North-West party did unquestionably fire the first shot, and almost all the shots that were fired. (Ross, 36–7)

A.S. Morton: The evidence rather shows that there was no firing on the Governor's side.... The settlers averred that the Governor cautioned them not to fire without his command — which was never given.... It is scarcely necessary to reconcile these conflicting testimonies. It is certain that Governor Semple had drifted into the struggle without the precaution of a plan of action. He fell the victim of his own unpreparedness — of his strange disregard of a simple principle that the best of all defences is a carefully devised attack. The half-breeds knew better and had no scruples. They attacked. (A.S. Morton, 577)

Meanwhile, Back at the Fort

Donald Gunn: Many of the colonists were in the Fort, either on business or for protection, before the Governor and his party left it. These, or at least some of them, made him an offer of their services, which he declined, as we have stated before. Others, alarmed by the constant report of discharged firearms, which took place in the afternoon, hastened to their "city of refuge," the Fort, so that before night came on most of the settlers were within its defences. However, their lodgings were not of the most desirable kind. Men, women and children had to crowd together in a house that was in course of erection; the walls had been logged but the seams were open and the apertures for the windows had neither parchment nor glass in them. The night passed quietly without any alarm, yet it was passed in the most agonizing terror. They had heard the sad tale of the savage butchery of Seven Oaks, and they did not know how soon a similar fate might be their own. (Gunn, 151)

Deposition of John Bourke: When the attack was made on Governor Semple, as above-mentioned, there was an encampment of Sautoux and Cree Indians opposite to Fort Douglas. These Indians took no part whatever in the hostility which had been evinced against the colony, nor in any of the atrocities which were perpetrated for its destruction. On the contrary, they lamented the fate of Governor Semple, and those murdered with him, hardly less than the colonists themselves, and were anxious to shew their good disposition towards the colony, by every act of kindness in their power. They assisted in bringing some of the dead bodies of those who had been murdered to Fort Douglas, and burying them. (in Halkett, lii)

Grant MacEwan: Surviving men were crazed by frustration; women and children could not curb their tears as the dead from the brief but conclusive battle were counted, and all responsible adults were obliged to consider their next move forthwith.... Almost a score of the cabin homes along the river were suddenly without husbands and fathers.

"Will Miles Macdonnell's Pemmican War never end?" some were asking in anguish. "Does it have to be a war of extermination?" (MacEwan, *Cornerstone Colony*, 101)

Deposition of John Bourke: The next day the said Cuthbert Grant and one Fraser, both of them clerks in the service of the North-West Company as aforesaid, with about sixteen or seventeen of their associates in the murders of the preceding day, came to Fort Douglas, and threatening everybody in the fort and settlement with immediate death, if their orders were not complied with, insisted on the immediate abandonment of the fort and of the settlement, and that property of every kind should be delivered up to them. (in Halkett, li)

Vera Kelsey: That evening Cuthbert Grant sent an ultimatum to the stricken Colony Gardens. If one gun was fired from Fort Douglas, every man, woman and child would be shot. But if all properties were surrendered peaceably, he would give them safe conduct. (Kelsey, 90)

Alexander Ross: The colonists who survived the massacre, were ordered once more to leave their homes without further warning or preparation, on pain of being hunted down and shot like wild beasts, if they should ever appear there again. It is doubtful, indeed, whether one innocent head would have been spared; and that any escaped was due to the generosity of Mr Grant, the chief of the hostile party, who rushed before his own people, and at the imminent peril of his life kept them at bay, and saved the remnant of the settlers from extirpation. (Ross, 36)

Rev. A.C. Garrioch: By the death of Governor Semple, Sheriff Alexander Macdonald became officer in command; and it required no arguments from him to convince his little mixed garrison of the seriousness of the situation, and to persuade them of the necessity of standing by one another as a solid unit.... Accordingly on the following day Mr Grant with his followers approached the fort, and was met by Mr Macdonald with a flag of truce.... After having completely crushed any opposition that it may have been in the power of the Colonists to offer, the Bois Brules showed sufficient love for them to allow them three days in which to pack up and be off; also all the boats they needed, and enough provisions to last them until they had gotten themselves far off.... More than that, a Nor'-Wester was placed in each of the boats as they floated down the river, and Mr Grant with a few men rode abreast as a precaution against an attack from some unforgiving Metis.... Once more they left the land of their adoption which had been so plentifully moistened with their tears and their blood, and they skirted the eastern shore of Lake Winnipeg till they reached that haven of refuge, Jack River. (Garrioch, 38–40)

Deposition of Pierre-Chrysologue Pambrun, HBC post at Qu'Appelle, appearing before Lord Selkirk 16 August 1816: That in the evening of the 20th of June, a messenger arrived [at Qu'Appelle where Pambrun had been held prisoner since May 12] from Cuthbert Grant, who reported that they had killed Governor Semple, with five of his officers and sixteen of his men, on which the said McDonell, and all the gentlemen with him ... shouted with joy. — That Alexander McDonell then went to announce the news to the rest of his people, crying out, "Sacré nom de Dieu! Bonnes nouvelles, vingt-deux Anglois de tués." [Good news — 22 Englishmen killed!] — That [Peter Pangman] Bostonais [NWC clerk and interpreter] then inquired whether any of the half-breeds had been killed, and on being told of one, he said the deceased was his cousin, and his death must be avenged, that the affair must not end there, that the settlers must all be killed, and not one allowed to leave the river, for as long as one of those dogs was alive they would be coming back. (in Halkett, xxxiv-xxxv)

Marjorie W. Campbell: The "battle" of Seven Oaks had temporarily relieved the Nor'Westers of any fear of "being imposed upon." Once more the unhappy remnants of the colony had taken off down the Red River, and [NWC Partner Archibald Norman] McLeod had already interviewed them on his way from Lake Winnipeg, commandeering such papers as he considered of value. No doubt to impress the Métis, who as much as the Indians loved a show of arms, he ordered a small salute to be fired. Then he formally took possession of Fort Douglas as at least partial recompense for Fort Gibraltar. His final official act was to call together the Métis whose action had defended their homes as well as the company's property, rewarding those whose deeds seemed most outstanding in the light of the circumstances. (Campbell, 218)

George Bryce: It was now about a week from the time of the massacre.... Human bodies [lay] scattered on the plain, and in most cases the flesh had been torn off to the bone, evidently by dogs and wolves. Far from discouraging the talkative half-breeds, whose blood was up with the sights of carnage, McLeod and his fellow-officers expressed their approbation of the deeds done, and the Bois-brulés became boisterous in detailing their victories.... The Bois-brulés bedecked their naked bodies with Indian trinkets and executed the dance of victory, as had done their savage ancestors. The effect of these dances is marvellous. By a contagious shout they excite each other. They reach a frenzy which communicates itself with hypnotic effect to the whole dancing circle. At times men tear their hair, cut their flesh or even mutilate their limbs for life. The "tom-tom," or Indian drum, adds to the power of monotonous rhythm and to the spirit of excitement and frenzy. (Bryce, *Romantic Settlement*, 137–8)

Vera Kelsey: At Colony Gardens the united North West forces plied the *Métis* with feasts and rewards for three days. Then leaving the half-breeds to raze the Settlement, they returned to Fort William to report this that time Selkirk's "Rascally Republic" had fallen forever. (Kelsey, 90)

Marjorie W. Campbell: Cameron arrived [at Fort William] with word of the swift tragic little battle of Seven Oaks. Word flashed through the entire depot. In French and English and native *patois* it echoed throughout camps of northmen and pork-eaters, the Indian tent villages along the shore and on every street within the stockade. Most fervently of all it was discussed again and again in the great hall where the bust of Simon McTavish was a reminder of how recent was the continent-wide trade achieved by their own effort and enterprise. The news that a hundred and thirty of Selkirk's colonists had accepted the Nor'Westers' offer of sanctuary in Canada and were already on their way east strengthened the feeling of satisfaction.... The Nor'Westers had suddenly won a reprieve. Semple's rash act relieved them of the probable necessity of taking the offensive against the colony thrust across their life-line by Selkirk and the Hudson's Bay Company. (Campbell, 224)

Deposition of John Bourke: [After the departure of the colonists] the deponent and his fellow-prisoners were placed by the said McLeod under the guard of these murderers, and even detained some days at the same place until the said McLeod went to Fort Douglas to make some arrangements and then returned.... He then took charge of the whole party and came with them to a trading post of the North-West Company called Fort William. The morning of their departure, the deponent was put in irons, and all his clothes were taken from him, together with his watch, and a pocket case of mathematical instruments; and in this situation he was placed on top of the baggage, in the canoe, without any attention being paid to his wound, and was conveyed to Fort William. After his arrival there, he was put in confinement in a place that had been used as a privy, into which light was not admitted, except through crevices between the logs, of which the building was constructed and in which an intolerable stench prevailed. In this place the deponent was confined twenty days. (in Halkett, liii-liv)

Marjorie W. Campbell: During the long summer days, moccasins and European leather boots trod deep paths in the grass and bracken along the portage trail. At night bourgeois and clerks danced in the great hall, singing tender Scottish ballads and naughty French songs to the sensuous slip-slap of moccasined feet and the haunting cadence of bagpipe and fiddle; now and again a Chippewa girl's throaty murmur blended with a man's exulting laughter in one of the cabins or from under the canoes beached along the riverside. Fort William had never seemed more secure. (Campbell, 225)

George Bryce: The departure of what was called the Grand Brigade [N WC brigade to Athabasca country] was signalized by an artillery salute from Fort Douglas, which resounded through the wretched ruins of the houses burnt the previous year, and over the fields deserted by the Colonists and left to the chattering blackbird and the howling wolf. (Bryce, *Romantic Settlement*, 139)

Fixing Blame

MK: Accusatory fingers have pointed in all directions, as to who and what was to blame for the melee at Seven Oaks/Frog Plain and its violent aftermath. Historians and writers, partisans of one fur trade company or the other, of the settlers or the Métis, come to mutually exclusive conclusions, or, rather, represent, each of them, a truth that contributes to a compendium of truths, some more reliable than others.

Samuel H. Wilcocke: Thus was this devoted Colony for the last time dispersed; ... As far as the Canadians were concerned, in having employed these people [Métis] solely for the transport of their provisions, and without the most distant apprehension of the fatal conflict which ensued, they [the NWC] were entirely blameless. (Wilcocke, *A Narrative*, 55)

Deposition of Pierre-Chrysologue Pambrun, militia officer and HBC fur trader:

> The deponent has reason to believe that all the partners [of the
> NWC] who are now at Fort William ... looked upon the crimes
> which had been committed in Red River by the half-breeds and
> others under the command of Alexander McDonell, as services
> done to the North-West Company, and have rewarded them
> accordingly. (in Halkett, xxxv)

Donald G. McLean: The nameless, faceless directors of the Hudson's Bay
Company had placed the Highland Scots and Irish labourers into
the mouth of a loaded gun; the Métis hunters, dupes of the North
West Company, joyfully pulled the trigger. (in Newman, 231-2)

Alexander Ross: We must in fairness remark that Governor Semple was ill
advised in going out with an armed party at all on this occasion, unless he had been able to command a sufficient force to
awe his opponents and protect the settlers. His better plan was
negotiation, or stratagem, and he should have gone out alone, or
at most taken one or two with him, unarmed. By a little flat-
tery, and good management, the half-breeds and Indians might
have been diverted from their mischievous projects, since they
are by no means unreasonable people when an appeal is made to
the better feelings of their nature. On the contrary, Mr Semple
and his party being all armed, must have suggested an idea of
their hostile intention, and was no doubt the leading cause of
the catastrophe that followed. (Ross, 40)

E.S. Russenholt: Of all the tragic mistakes which culminate in Seven Oaks,
perhaps the most tragic is the contempt in which the Governor and his "gentlemen" hold the free-men, Indian and hybrid

peoples of Assiniboia. Europeans have found arrogance and over-powering weapons against other "lesser breeds." Against buffalo-hunters, it back-fires! (Russenholt, 40)

Auguste-Henri de Trémaudan: In our view, this bloody brawl originated especially in the impudence of a man who, ignorant of the peculiarities of the country to which he had just arrived, without giving thought to the consequence of his actions, sinned by an excess of zeal.... Is it also not proved that the first shot fired came from the English side?... That the Métis — nothing more natural — defended themselves?... One cannot repeat too often that chance and circumstance, aided by the rashness of Semple and his men, were the principal cause of this regrettable episode in which — in conclusion — the Métis found themselves embroiled as individuals, not as a nation, as can clearly be seen from the fact that they were involved on both sides. (Trémaudan, 109, 111 mk trans.)

Samuel H. Wilcocke: That it was necessary to employ the Half-Breeds and Indians in defence of their property, the North West Company must lament; and they must long feel the consequences of having been obliged to resort to their assistance; but it is *positively denied* [ital in original] that there was the most remote intention on the part of Alexander Macdonell, or any Partner of the North-West Company, to place the lives or property of the Colonists at risk, in any attack or retaliation on the Settlement.... Mr. Pritchard, who certainly cannot be accused of any good will towards the North-West Company (as well as all the other witnesses) admits the facts of Mr Semple having marched out and pursued the Indians ... and although he does not admit the first firing to have taken place from Semple's party, he will not go the length of the other two witnesses, [settler John] Bourke and [blacksmith Michael] Heden, in positively affirming the contrary. The latter witness is an ignorant person, whose memory seems to have been refreshed by those who had a case to make out from it, and does not seem much relied upon. (Wilcocke, A Narrative, 138–9)

MK: On the other hand, it was the opinion of Alexander Ross writing in the 1850s that" the guilt of this bloodshed rests on the North-West party," and concludes with a macabre flourish that their guilt pursued them with "the violent or sudden death of no less than twenty-six out of the sixty-five who composed the party," to their graves. He includes the cases of François Deschamps, Jr., stabbed to death by his own comrade, his wife shot and his children burnt to death, all at the same time, near Fort Union, Missouri River. Coutonahais, who suddenly dropped dead while dancing with a party of his comrades at the Grand Forks, below Pembina. J. Baptiste Latour, who died a miserable death by infection. Duplicis, killed by a wooden fork running through his body while he was jumping from a hay stack at Carlton, on the North Saskatchewan River. Louison Vallé, put to death by a party of Sioux Indians in the Pembina plains, and in sight of his companions.

The Ballad of Pierre Falcon

MK: But the Battle of Seven Oaks was to have its very first historian, first and only Métis witness on record, and first point of view, in a man who had been there, Pierre Falcon. One of Cuthbert Grant's men, he had been escorting provisions on the way to Lake Winnipeg and seems to have arrived in the middle of the battle.

James J. Hargrave: I have been fortunate enough to secure from the lips of its author a metrical account of this battle, composed on horse-back while on his way home from the scene of its occurrence by Monsieur Pierre Falcon, who is now a petty magistrate in the colony, aged about 76 years. He neither reads nor writes. This composition was, however, like the Saxon Bards of Old England, caught up by friendly ears and conveyed from mouth to mouth till it might be heard throughout the country wherever the axe of the woodcutter fell or the paddle of the canoe kept time to the cadence adapted to its measure. In reading the poem it must be borne in mind that the author was a zealous member of the North West party, and that his prejudices have seriously inter-fered with the accuracy of his description of the battle, if indeed the skirmish ought to be so spoken of. It is, however, a genu-ine production of the country, and a curious relic of the times. (Hargrave, 75)

Margaret Laurence: Well, my old man, he told me about Rider Tonnerre, away back there, so long ago no one knows when.... He wasn't all Indian, though. He was Métis, only back there, then, our people called themselves *Bois-Brûlés*. Burnt wood. I dunno why. Maybe the fires they made to smoke the buffalo meat. Maybe their own skins, the way they looked.... Now, one time there was a bunch of Englishmen – goddamn *Anglais*, as they used to be called – and they came in to take away the Métis land and to stop the people from hunting buffalo. And these guys had a bunch of Arkanys with them.

(Arkanys?)

That is how my dad called the Scotchmen. Men from Orkney, I guess. So a bunch of the Métis, there, they said *Shit on this idea: they're not coming here to take over our land and stop us from hunting.* But they sat on their asses all the same and didn't move. So that Rider Tonnerre, he says *We're gonna hunt these Anglais and Arkanys like we hunt the buffalo, so c'mon there, boys.* It was some place around Red River, there, and they see all these Englishmen and their hired guns the Arkanys.

(Hired guns? I bet they weren't!)

Sure, they were. Anyway, it's just a story. So Rider Tonnerre and the others, they make an ambush, see, and the other guys fall for it and ride straight in. So Rider, he starts picking them off with this rifle, *La Petite,* and the other Métis do the same. The English and the Arkanys try to shoot back, but they're not doing so hot, and in the end every single one of them got killed. And one of Rider's men made up a song about it, only my old man, he don't remember it. But he said his father, Old Jules, used to sing it sometimes. (Laurence, 118)

Joseph Howard, author: **And there was an anthem, called "Falcon's Song," because it had been created by a man named Falcon. It was not a very good song: the images were crude and the sentiment not at all elevating; it was a hymn of hate and thus like some other national anthems. But it was unique in this: it was not written** down. Pierre Falcon himself could not write and his song was perhaps the only national hymn in history which was transmitted exclusively by singing it.... The song was born on June 19, 1816. On that day, too, the nation was born in the minds of the people, if not yet in political fact. (Howard, *Strange Empire*, 31-2)

MK: When Margaret A. Macleod compiled her *Songs of Old Manitoba*, she noted that "this [French] version was sung by his grandchildren as Falcon taught it to them, and taken down by Henry L. Caron, Winnipeg;" (Macleod, *Songs*, 6-7) while the translator, James Reaney, added that "in making this translation I have followed Ezra Pound's practice. Since there can be no translation so inaccurate as that which sticks closely and literally to the surface of a song, I have attempted to make only an English equivalent of Falcon's ballad and so translate the really important thing — its high spirits." (in Macleod, *Songs*, 9)

NWC clerk Pierre Falcon:

Would you like to hear me sing
Of a true and recent thing?
It was June nineteen, the band of Bois-Brûlés
Arrived that day,
Oh the brave warriors they!
We took three foreigners prisoners when
We came to the place called Frog, Frog Plain.
They were men who'd come from Orkney,
Who'd come, you see,
To rob our country.
Now we like honourable men did act,
Sent an ambassador — yes, in fact!
"Monsieur Governor! Would you like to stay?
A moment spare —
There's something we would like to say."
Governor, Governor, full of ire,
"Soldiers!" he cries, "Fire! Fire."
So they fire the first and their muskets roar!
They almost kill
Dead on the ground lots of grenadiers too.
Plenty of grenadiers, a whole slew.
We've almost stamped out his whole army
Of so many
Five or four left there be.
You should have seen those Englishmen —
Bois-Brûlés chasing them, chasing them.
We won this day.
Yes, she was written this song of praise —
Come sing the glory

Well we were just about to unhorse
When we heard two of us give, give voice.
Two of our men cried, "Hey! Look back! Look back!
The Anglo-Sack
Coming for to attack."
Right away smartly we veered about
Galloping at them with a shout!
You know we did trap them all, all those Grenadiers!
They could not move
Those horseless cavaliers.
Our ambassador!
Governor thought of himself a king.
He wished an iron rod to swing.
Like a lofty lord he tries to act.
Bad luck, old chap!
A bit too hard you whacked!
When we went galloping, galloping by
Governor thought that he would try
For to chase and frighten us Bois-Brûlés.
Catastrophe!
Dead on the ground he lay.
From bluff to bluff they stumbled that day
While the Bois-Brûlés
Shouted "Hurray!"
Tell, oh tell me who made up this song?
Why, it's our own poet, Pierre Falcon.
Yes, she was written this song of praise
For the victory
Of the Bois-Brûlés.

(in Macleod, *Songs*, 7–9)

Sketch of Cuthbert Grant.
(Archives of Manitoba, Kerr, John 5 N12762)

SEVEN: AFTERMATH

Lord Selkirk Strikes Back

Jack Bumsted: Then, in 1816, a morally outraged Lord Selkirk went on the
offensive. Within months, he completely altered the course of the
conflict.... The liberal lord, the high-minded philanthropist, met
the Nor'Westers on their own violent terms, without scruples,
which surprised them considerably. (Bumsted, *Fur Trade Wars*, 154)

MK: Selkirk had already set out from Montreal for his (only) visit to the Red
River colony when the news arrived on 20 June that it had been
destroyed once again; that Fort Douglas was now in the hands of
the NWC; and that some Baymen, including P.C. Pambrun, John
Pritchard, and John Bourke, were being held at the NWC's Fort
William on Lake Superior.

In July 1816, a flotilla of 130 canoemen as well as officers and
men of foreign regiments in British service, the De Meuron and
De Watteville, engaged by Selkirk, pushed on from Kingston to
York in Upper Canada and then northward to Lake Simcoe and
Georgian Bay.

Finally, mid-August, Selkirk and company arrived by canoe in the precincts of an undefended Fort William, on the northwest shore of Lake Superior, at the very starting point of the great canoe route to the western plains.

Alexander Begg, journalist and author: [Selkirk] at once arranged his men and artillery so as to command the approaches to Fort William, the cannon being loaded and pointed as if for a siege and bombardment of the place. On the following day, two men acting as constables entered the fort and arrested Mr William McGillivray who was in command, soon after which Lord Selkirk arrived and, placing the principal officer in confinement, took possession. The place was then searched, and all the furs, valued at $60,000 and other property seized, notwithstanding the formal protests of the Nor'-Westers against such proceedings. (Begg, *History*, 186)

MK: The retaliation by written protest began when William McGillivray and several others drew up a document against "the general terror, the uncertainty as to what were the Earl's designs, and the acts of violence" of their situation.

We the undersigned, Agents and Partners of the North-West Company, being this day, the thirteenth of August, 1816, in a body assembled at Fort William, in the district of Kaministiguia, do hereby formally protest against the violent proceedings done and committed upon our persons and property, at the above mentioned place in the afternoon of the above-mentioned day, by a troop to the number of between fifty and sixty disbanded and intoxicated soldiers, formerly belonging to the Regiment of De Meuron and at present in the service and pay of the Earl of Selkirk ... who forcibly entered the Fort Gate, spread out their troops in every direction having their bayonets fixed, and shouting a most horrid huzza! Which spread a general terror amongst the inhabitants of the Fort. (Signed) Wm McGillivray, Kenneth Mackenzie, John Macdonald, Simon Fraser, Allan Macdonell, John McLaughlin, Hugh McGillis, Daniel Mackenzie. (in Wilcocke, A Narrative, 72–3)

Jasper Vandersluys, a NWC clerk at Fort William: Captain D'Orsonnens, the leader of these disbanded, intoxicated, and almost uncontrolled soldiers, cried out *"aux armes, aux armes!"* and immediately the bugle was sounded, and an armed force of about sixty in number, with loaded muskets and fixed bayonets, rushed forcibly into the Fort, shouting, cursing and swearing, and threatening death and destruction to all persons and all property. The soldiery were strongly countenanced in this by their officers. (in Wilcocke, A Narrative, 71)

MK: As historian Jack Bumsted summarizes the scene, Selkirk "was prepared to operate on the fringes of a legality which the NWC never expected to confront. The NWC stood in awe of legal British authority." (Wars, 159) Partisans of the NWC, however, describe their reaction differently.

Marjorie W. Campbell: "What right have you to assume the powers of a governor of Canada?" McGillivray demanded of Selkirk. Without the courtesy of an explanation, Selkirk ordered his men to arrest [NWC partners] [Kenneth] McKenzie and Dr [John] McLoughlin as well as McGillivray. He refused to grant them bail, claiming that the charges against the three were too serious to allow bail. In view of Selkirk's military strength, McGillivray and his colleagues submitted with what dignity they could muster; McGillivray doubtless recalling bitterly his comment to [his uncle and scion of the NWC Simon] McTavish that there was dishonour in being fooled by this "piddling" lord. They were, they all realized, in the hands of a man at least temporarily deranged. (Campbell, 227)

Jasper Vandersluys: All this while the above-mentioned [NWC] Gentlemen did not offer the least resistance, but on the contrary, patiently submitted to the outrageous and lawless conduct of their assailants; and they were carried off to the Earl's Camp, guarded by an armed force. (in Wilcocke, A Narrative, 71)

Marjorie W. Campbell: Tonight all were prisoners in their own great stockade depot. A thousand miles from Montreal, there was no hope of adequate help arriving within a couple of months.... With an army across the river and under command of a dictator periodically bereft of his senses, only one course was open: to burn such of their records as they could before Selkirk confiscated them to whatever ends his warped mind might suggest.... Great batches of such papers as Selkirk might use to their disadvantage were piled on the fireplaces in the mess hall. Others were carried to the kitchen stoves by the armful. A few small arms were loaded and cached in the hayloft, a barrel of gunpowder carried out of the rear gate into the swamp, and hidden: under cover of darkness skilled voyageurs silently paddled a canoe-load of arms up the river, passing under the very shadow of Selkirk's camp. When morning came only the blackened ashes of paper on the hearths and in the kitchen stoves, and a patch of trampled grass in the swamp, indicated the precautions they had taken. (Campbell, 228-229)

MK: Selkirk then began an examination under oath of the arrested partners, who, unsurprisingly, denied any participation in the sequence of violent events at Red River. In their defense, they pleaded that, in any case, they had little influence over the decisions and behaviour of the wintering partners and servants of the NWC. Foreshadowing future historical debates, they said also that they objected to the word "massacre," preferring "battle" or "affair." (Bumsted, *Fur Trade Wars*, 160) On 17 August, they were all under guard in canoes dispatched to the governor-general of Upper Canada, Sir John Coape Sherbrooke, to whom Selkirk wrote that he was sending him "a Cargo of Criminals of a larger Calibre than usually came before the courts of York." He had ample evidence of "the most detestable system of villainy that was allowed to prevail in the British Dominions." (in Bumsted, *Fur Trade Wars*, 160)

Alexander Begg: It was next decided to take the North-West officers to Montreal for trial, and accordingly they were sent off in canoes under charge of a guard of Selkirk's men, the Hudson's Bay Company force in the meantime remaining in possession of the fort. The charge upon which Lord Selkirk arrested these officers was based on the plea that they in some way were connected with or instrumental in bringing about the outrages committed on the Earl's property in June, but this, it is apparent, was only a pretext to serve Lord Selkirk's purpose. (Begg, *History*, 186)

Rev. A.C. Garrioch: It speaks well for both sides, and shows the value of education and discipline, that though feeling ran very high, no blood was shed on this occasion, and that there was no recourse to brute force on either side, although Lord Selkirk acting in his magisterial capacity, arrested, tried, imprisoned and sent

east for trial, those whom he considered most guilty. Even the
De Meurons were kept within bounds; and the Nor'-Westers,
although they considered Lord Selkirk's actions quite unjusti-
fiable, had no recourse to physical force, although some of their
supporters afterwards made the claim that they had the advantage of numbers, and could have annihilated Lord Selkirk and
his whole party had they felt so disposed; and that they did not
defend themselves by force because they had made the resolve
that there was to be no more bloodshed, and therefore restrained
themselves, confining their resentment to protests either verbal
or written. (Garrioch, 43)

MK: In early September, 1816, Selkirk drafted another letter to Sir John in
which he described Red River country in a "state of rebellion,"
occupied by "Banditti who avow their determination to set the
laws of their Country at defiance," (in Bumstead, *Wars*, 163) and,
in view of what had happened to his colony, a destruction carried
out with impunity, made the case for a Commission to investigate who and what had been responsible. In October, W.B.
Coltman and John Fletcher were duly appointed as magistrates
in the Territory to lead such a commission.

Chester Martin: Selkirk received word of the appointment of the Commission
with unfeigned enthusiasm. "I am greatly rejoiced that it is determined upon." Though the sacrifice of the principles for which he
had been contending — "the lawful authority of the [H B] Company," the "unimpeachable validity of these rights of property"
— was not made without a reservation, there was to be "voluntary acquiescence" and therefore no "dereliction of their rights
of Jurisdiction." (C. Martin, 132)

MK: Then, 9 November 1816, a warrant for Selkirk's arrest (he was still at Fort William) was served for "forcible entry and detainer;" he gave the serving constable short shrift, expelled him from the Fort, and saw the De Meurons off for Red River, making their way on foot and snowshoe They were joined in late December by a small group of aboriginals who acted as scouts for the expedition as it made its way to the Forks which they reached 10 January 1817. They took (re)possession of Fort Douglas without a violent struggle with the n w c occupiers whose chief, Cuthbert Grant, took to heart the command of the Royal Proclamation – the soldiers brandished a copy of it – to "all persons in the Indian territories to desist from any hostile aggression."

Alexander Begg: This was accomplished in true military style by taking advantage of a dark and stormy night, when the de Meurons approaching the fort succeeded in scaling the walls before the garrison was even aware of their presence in the neighbourhood. Taken thus by surprise, the Nor'-Westers yielded without firing a shot, and Fort Douglas once more passed into the hands of the Hudson's Bay Company. (Begg, History, 187)

A War of Words

Mercator: The Red River colony, originated in avarice, has been prosecuted in deception and fraud, and must end in disgracing the character of a British nobleman. (in Ellice, The Communications of Mercator, 29)

MK: Meanwhile, the n w c's friends in the Lower and Upper Canadas defended the Nor'Westers vigorously, challenging the authority of the

Hudson's Bay Company Charter and impugning Lord Selkirk's character. In York, Archdeacon John Strachan, related by marriage to mercantile interests in Montreal, wrote privately in September 1816 that, concerning the grievances of Lord Selkirk of the HBC against the NWC during the course of the fur trade wars in Assiniboia, "there is a great feeling here as it appears to be a mercantile quarrel and people here have not sympathy with a Peer of Great Britain turning fur Merchant and applying the power which an ample Inheritance gives him in destroying a trade which has given bread to them for two centuries." (in Bumsted, *Selkirk: Life*, 318) In August 1816, a series of hostile letters began appearing in the *Montreal Herald* under the nom de plume, Mercator, in fact Henry McKenzie, a business agent in charge of public relations for the NWC.

Mercator: How superlatively sordid must be the avarice of that man, who could descend from the high rank of a Peer, to endeavour to take the bread out of the mouths of a thousand, who had no other dependence but their industry. And who could deliberately throw into this community to serve his private views, the firebrand of disunion, discord, and personal animosity, which may outlive his existence. (in Ellice, 49)

Lord Selkirk: After the experience they have had of impunity, for all their crimes, it is not wonderful that the North West Company should consider themselves altogether above the law; and when they foretell that violence and bloodshed will be the consequence of attempting to enforce legal warrants against them, the audacity they exhibit is no greater than might be expected after so much encouragement. All former experience shows that the North West

Company are never at a loss for a pretext, to justify or to excuse any crime which it is for their interest to perpetrate; and where they have resolved upon a course of criminal conduct, it is their policy to prepare the public, as early as possible for the misrepresentations by which it is to be cloaked. (Selkirk, *Memorial*, 195)

MK: John Halkett, Selkirk's brother-in-law, published anonymously *Statement Respecting The Earl of Selkirk's Settlement Upon the Red River*, opening his defense of Selkirk's actions in rebuttal to the on-going slanders and distortions of the record by partisans of the N WC, as he saw it.

John Halkett: The plans of colonization, promoted by the Earl of Selkirk in British North America, have, for some time past, given rise to much, and gross, misrepresentation. More than common pains have been taken, by his opponents, to mislead, and to prejudice, the public; but such attempts, when the opportunity for strict investigation arrives, can have no other effect than to recoil upon those whose studied object has been to calumniate an individual, and to conceal the truth. (Halkett, 1)

Jack Bumsted, interview: The *Narrative*, which was written by Samuel Hull Wilcocke, was designed as an answer to a work which had been brought out by one of Selkirk's relatives, John Halkett. And the Narrative was *intended* as an indictment of the H BC and of Selkirk, written by a hired pen who was hired to be as nasty as possible. The net result is that you shouldn't pay any attention to the *Narrative* as a work of history or of journalism. It's pure venom and intended in that context. He is merely answering another work which is deeply sympathetic to Selkirk because it's written by his brother-in-law; and he's being paid to be as evil and nasty as possible.

The Selkirk Colony Rebuilds, Again

MK: With Fort Douglas once more under HBC control, Selkirk prepared to leave Fort William in early May 1817 (it was promptly repossessed by William McGillivray and the Nor'Westers). By June 21, he and his party had arrived at the Forks. Macdonell had already arranged for the return of the colonists, who had fled north after the destruction of Colony Garden in June, 1816: "Some of the more venturesome settlers were so eager to try again in Red River that they returned over the ice of Lake Winnipeg to be in time for spring planting." (A.E. Brown)

Donald Gunn: The fame of the above exploit [the recapture of Fort Douglas] spread like wild fire over the country. A special messenger was dispatched to Jack River to bear the welcome tidings to the fugitives, inviting them to return, and setting before them the prospect of protection and security in future. To this invitation these distressed people gladly responded, and a few of the men set out at once for Red River, where they safely arrived before the breaking up of the ice. But, as usual, provisions were very scarce. Great privation and its consequent attendant, discontent, prevailed among the various classes who had to dwell on empty stores for their daily support. However, as the spring advanced the snows of winter disappeared, wild fowl became abundant in every marsh and pond, and soon after the ice on the river broke up and was carried off by the weight and force of the accumulated waters poured in it by its numerous tributaries from the east and from the west. The few settlers that were at the place commenced farming operations. The hoe was the only implement at their service, and with it each one applied himself heartily to the work and managed to sow a few gallons of wheat and barley, and planted a few pecks of potatoes each. (Gunn, 195–6)

Vera Kelsey: They had just returned and buried the bleached bones of the massacre's still exposed dead when Lord Selkirk arrived. What were his emotions as he beheld his colony a pinpoint of ruin in that vast green sea of prairie? When he met the gaze of his tragedy-worn people? The answer lies in the strenuous efforts to place Red River Settlement on a firmer footing. For this, too, an unexpected ally appeared. In Lord Selkirk, that astute Chippewa chief, Peguis, recognized the shaping hand of the future. Forthwith, he transformed his young hunters into a food battalion and in all things made himself provider and protector of the great white chief's people. (Kelsey, 98)

Chester Martin: Selkirk appeared for the first time in the role which may be taken to typify his plans of colonization. His activity and practical knowledge of agriculture upon his own estates in Kirkcudbrightshire.... Selkirk's generous and wise supervision at the Red River Settlement created an impression in less than four months that still survives in narrative and tradition.... [quoting Alexander Ross's *The Red River Settlement* published in 1856] "So correct and unerring was his judgement that nothing he planned at this early date could in after years be altered to advantage." ... There is a sense in which these obscure months must be considered the practical consummation of an active life. Seldom has immediate reward been so paltry, outlay so enormous, and ultimate vindication of practical foresight at once so tardy and so complete. (C. Martin, 132–3)

Donald Gunn: The colonists, as we have already stated, had hitherto met with nothing but a series of disappointments and unparalleled sufferings. Humanity and policy dictated to his Lordship not only the necessity but the wisdom of dealing liberally with them; and now the time had arrived when he had the opportunity of giving some proof of his appreciation of their endurance and perseverance; and for the accomplishment of that object he invited the colonists to meet him on a certain day in the centre of the incipient colony – which, in August, 1817, was the lot on which St John's Cathedral now stands. ... On this occasion he made them a present of two lots of land ten chains frontage each, and addressed them saying: "This lot on which we are met today shall be for your church and manse; the next lot on the south side of the creek shall be for your school and for a help to support your teacher, and in commemoration of your native parish it shall be called Kildonan." At this meeting an urgent application was made for the [Presbyterian] minister, and again solemnly promised by his Lordship. Yet thirty-four years had run their course before a Presbyterian Minister appeared in the colony.... Unfortunately for the settlers, their noble patron was too deeply involved in litigation in the Canadian Courts with the North-West Company to leave him any time to ... think of the protracted disappointments of his confiding and faithful settlers. (Gunn, 200–01)

R.D. Garneau: Thomas Douglas and the British issued land claims to Scottish squatters which were marked out in river front lots, three to ten chains in width, consistent with the French system of the past forty years in the region. The English would later challenge the Metis river lot system with no regard to the Scottish, French or British-Hudson Bay Company common law [precedent]. The English are notorious for changing the rules of the game, during play, to their advantage. (Garneau)

MK: Nevertheless, the layout of the original twenty-four river lots given to the settlers in 1817 became the foundation for the neighbourhood street alignments and urban grid that one sees over much of Winnipeg's North End; and the wagon trail on the west side of the Red River would become Main Street. (Goldsborough)

Rev. R.G. MacBeth: This visit of Lord Selkirk to the Red River in 1817 was, in many respects, the most outstanding event in the early history of the Selkirk Colony in the minds of the settlers themselves. In my boyhood days I often heard the old men, who had seen and conversed with the Earl, and had heard his addresses, talk the matter over and seek to impress upon us younger folk the greatness of their benefactor and friend. They spoke of his tall, slight, aristocratic figure, his gentleness of speech, his beauty of manner; of the way in which he expressed appreciation of their endurance, of the pains he took to assure them that they had a right to their Red River home, and that they would never again be disturbed in their possession of it. (R.G. MacBeth, 44-5)

MK: One means of securing an undisturbed possession of the land under their feet was to trade "one hundred Pounds of good and merchantable Tobacco" annually for the land. On July 18, 1817, Selkirk with five of the Saulteaux and Cree chiefs including Peguis signed the agreement.

Lord Selkirk, 20 July 1817: The bearer Peguis, one of the principal chiefs of the Chipeways or Saulteaux of Red River, has been a steady friend of the settlement ever since its first establishment, and has never deserted its cause in its greatest reverses. He has often exerted his influence to restore peace, and having rendered most essential services to the settlers in their distress, deserves to be treated with favour and distinction by the officers of the Company, and by all the friends of peace and good order. (in A.N. Thompson, 448)

Alexander Morris, treaty commissioner: The Indians then inhabiting the region were described as being of the Chippawa or Saulteaux and Killistine or Cree nations. They were made to comprehend the depth of the land they were surrendering, by being told, that it was the greatest distance at which a horse on the level prairie could be seen, or daylight seen under his belly between his legs. The consideration for surrender was the payment of one hundred pounds of good merchantable tobacco, to each nation annually. The treaty was signed by Lord Selkirk and by five Indian chiefs, who affixed thereto drawings of the animals after which they were named, by way of signature.... The surrender was to the Sovereign. Lord, King George the Third. The treaty was accompanied by a map which shows that the tract surrendered extended to Grand Forks in what is now United States territory. (Morris, Treaties, 15)

"Provided always that the traders hitherto established upon any part of the above-mentioned tract of land shall not be molested in the possession of these lands which they have already cultivated and improved, till his Majesty's pleasure shall be known." (Morris, 299)

Bruce Sealey and Antoine Lussier: **The Cree Indians objected to the fact that the Saulteaux Indians were grandly selling land to Selkirk when the Saulteaux were interlopers in the area. Traditionally, for perhaps 1500 years, the Cree and Assiniboine had owned the Red River area. Indeed, one reason Peguis was so helpful to the settlers was to gain allies, for at no time did the Cree or Assiniboine Indians fully accept his intrusion into the valley. It was, however, a sign of the times. The Indians slowly but surely drove the Cree and the Assiniboine out of much of southern Manitoba and Saskatchewan. The battle was still being waged when the Saulteaux rather arrogantly resold the land to the Canadian government in 1871. In selling their land to Lord Selkirk, Chief Peguis noted that he didn't recognize that the Métis had any claim to the land. (Sealey & Lussier, 43)**

R.D. Garneau: **Chief Peguis of the Ojibwa is rebuked by Bostonnais Pangman, spokesperson for the Metis, for ignoring the fact, in treaty signing, that the Metis had as much claim to the land as the Cree and Ojibwa, and implying the Metis might eradicate the Ojibwa from the region. This would be a very weak threat, as the Metis were deeply intertwined through marriage with the Ojibwa over the past two hundred years. Regardless of the shortcomings of the treaty, the real beginning of the Red River Colony should be marked from this date, and the prior colony should be referred to as the H.B.C. colony of the Red River. (Garneau)**

Missionaries at the Forks

MK: Having "solemnly promised" the appointment of a Presbyterian minister for the Scots colonists, Selkirk also undertook to secure a Roman Catholic priest for the Métis at Red River. Lieutenant Colonel Georges Fleury Dechambault, an official of the HBC in Montreal, appealed to Bishop Joseph-Octave Plessis.

G.F. Dechambault, 9 January 1818: My Lord, Permit me to repeat for Lord Selkirk the request for a priest in the spring at Red River. If he could pass the winter with the Earl, his presence could not fail to have a very favorable influence toward leading the *métis* back to religion. Lady Selkirk joins heartily in making this request to you ... My Lord, your very humble and very obedient servant, F. Dechambault.

Bishop Plessis, 23 January 1818: Sir, I beg you to present my humble respects to Lady Selkirk and to inform her, as well as milord, if you chance to be writing him, that I am heartily disposed to secure for the Red River colony all the spiritual assistance that is at my disposal, as soon as the troubles, which at this moment are dividing the two companies, leave some hope of doing so with appreciable results. Not one, but two missionaries will be sent there. I have taken steps in this direction. Events will decide the time when they will leave. I have the honor etc., J.O., Bishop of Quebec (in Nute, *Documents*, 18–9)

Adrian-Gabriel Morice, Oblate missionary and historian: Strange as it may seem, that murderous encounter had not rung the death knell of civilization in that distant land but rather proclaimed its ultimate approach; it was a catastrophe from which the salvation of the new colony would emerge. Its founder, now realizing, in effect, that no long-lasting outcome was possible without religion's soothing effect on passions unleashed by years of all-out conflict, appealed to the dedication of Monseigneur Plessis, bishop of Quebec, to send out two missionaries, the priests Norbert Provencher and Sévère Dumoulin. (Morice, *L'Ouest canadien*, 45 mk trans.)

Metis 1818–1820: The Money-Master, Fifth Earl of Selkirk, requested and financed the first Catholic priests' entry into the Red River region. This ploy was to ensure his illegal land acquisition, and it received support from the Roman Catholic Church. Some would question what part the Roman Catholic Church played in the whole infamous Selkirk affair in order to secure a toe hold in this New Metis Nation.... On July 16, the missionaries J.N. Provencher, who would become bishop, and S.G. Dumoulin arrived at Fort Douglas (St. Boniface). He settled at the forks of the Red and Assiniboine Rivers, among the Metis. Father Dumoulin, during the period 1818 to 1823, attempted to civilize the Chippewa by persuading them to live in permanent villages. This failed, as the good father could not persuade the Metis to permanently settle in villages. The Metis knew both ways of life, and the Natives said, why should the Indians do what their brothers would not do? Provencher's notion of civilization was, to the Natives, enslavement. (RootsWeb)

W.L. Morton: With them came some French Canadian families from Lower Canada to give a firm core of civilized folk to the farming settlement of the half-wild *métis*.... In 1819 the Church Missionary Society, at the request of the Committee of the Hudson's Bay Company, sent Rev. John West to the colony, and in 1820 he began his ministrations to the Indians and to such colonists as found them acceptable. From these years on the missionaries in church and school were to labour to create an oasis of civilization in Red River amid the surrounding barbarism of forest and plain. (W.L. Morton, *A History*, 56)

MK: In 1819, Reverend John West became the first HBC chaplain appointed to Rupert's Land. West noted in his journal that his orders from the company were "to reside at the Red River Settlement, and under the incouragement and aid of the Church Missionary Society . . . to seek the instruction and endeavour to meliorate the condition of the native Indians." (Willie)

Donald Gunn: In October 1820, when the Rev. Mr. West made his appearance in the settlement, nearly all the people in it were members of the Presbyterian Church. Mr West, we believe, was a pious, well-meaning man desirous of advancing the spiritual welfare of those who attended on his ministry, but he steadily adhered to the ritual of his church [Church of England] and in it the Scotch could see no spirituality, nor believe that they could receive any edification from such forms; besides, we must not forget, that the English language was to them a foreign tongue, as very few of the aged understood any but Gaelic, for which they longed vehemently. (Gunn, 213)

Metis 1818–1820: The Church of England had dispatched Chaplain John West to Red River to serve the Scottish community. His objective is to bring civilization, Christianity, education and agriculture to the west. He declared that Country marriages between a man, a woman and God were immoral and debased. This philosophy allowed the Scottish men to cast off their Country wives and to treat women as objects for temporary sexual gratification. John West represented Christian racism. He would not baptize Country Wives before they married, and would not marry them before they were baptized. He obviously considered them all heathens beyond redemption. (RootsWeb)

Rev. John West, HBC chaplain, *Journal*, 20 January 1821: From his Journal, Jan 20, 1821: We started at sunrise (at Portage) We arrived at Brandon House, the Company's provision post; and the next day, being Sunday, the servants were all assembled for divine worship at eleven o'clock: and we met again in the evening at six, where the next morning I married the officer of the post, and baptized his two children — Before I left this post, I married two of the Company's servants, and baptized 10 or 12 children. (West)

Donald Gunn: Mr. West soon perceived that his prospect of usefulness among the Scotch settlers was anything but encouraging; therefore, he extended his visits during the winter months to the trading posts in the neighbouring districts, where he met some of the native tribes and saw the poverty and deep moral depravity, which furnished him with a theme well calculated to excite the benevolence of the Christian public in behalf of the benighted savages that roam through the forests and over the plains of the western wilderness. (Gunn, 213)

Rev. John West, *Journal*, 2 June 1823: I have been adding two small houses to the Church Mission School, as separate sleeping apartments for the Indian children, who have already made most encouraging progress in reading and a few of them in writing. (in Still)

Donald Gunn: We are not prepared to say what progress was made, but this we will say, that this elementary school established by Mr. West for the instruction of a few Indian boys was the germ whence originated all the Protestant schools and colleges in Manitoba at the present time [1880]. (Gunn, 213)

Gary Still, author: West failed to win the support of the new Governor, George Simpson, who thought he was spending too much time catering to the Indians, to the neglect of the HBC retirees who also began to view him in disfavour. Early in 1824, his employment was terminated by the London committee and he would never more return to Red River. (Still)

The Coltman Commission

Electric Scotland: A Royal Proclamation was issued by the Prince Regent in Quebec in 1817 commanding all persons in the Indian territories to desist from any hostile aggression and requiring all officers and men formerly in his Majesty's service to leave the service of the Hudson's Bay Company and the North West Company within twenty-four hours after receiving knowledge of the Proclamation. The Proclamation further specially directed that no blockades should be made to prevent or interrupt the free passage of traders and their merchandise, furs and provisions throughout the North West Territories and that all persons should be free to pursue their accustomed trade without molestation. [Initially] both parties decided to ignore the Proclamation. Governor [William] Williams, who had succeeded Semple as Governor of Assiniboia, declared the Proclamation was "all damned nonsense" and that he "would drive every Nor'Wester out of the country or die in the attempt." Up in the Athabaska District Archibald Norman Macleod was equally defiant. His orders to his bullies were: "Go to it, my lads. There is no law in the Indian Territory." (Electric Scotland)

MK: As for the Commission struck to "inquire into crimes resulting from the life-and-death struggle between the Hudson's Bay Company and the North West Company for hegemony in the fur trade," Colonel William Coltman and his party set out in late spring 1817 for Red River and reached the Forks on July 5. The objective, as he saw it, was to bring the hostile parties to a truce, so that their properties would be restored and the region as a whole cleansed of violence. To make the point, Coltman read out the proclamation from the Prince Regent making public the government's "commandments."

Chester Martin: Selkirk enjoined upon the officials of the settlement the most implicit obedience to the Prince Regent's proclamation. North-West forts were to be restored, hostilities were everywhere to cease. "Truth must prevail in the end," wrote Selkirk to his lawyer, [Samuel] Gale, of Montreal; "and in the confidence that justice will ultimately be done to me, I put little importance on any wound which may be aimed at my personal feelings." (C. Martin, 132)

MK: What Selkirk was hoping for, of course, was vindication of his view that all the violence that had befallen his and the HBC's interests in Assiniboia — not to mention the deaths of settlers and Baymen at Seven Oaks — was the result of the NWC's unremitting desire to thwart them, trade and settlement alike. In a sense the NWC agreed, taking the view that none of it need have happened, had

Selkirk and the HBC not assumed they had undisputed territorial rights to build a settlement and disrupt the trade at the Forks, thus unleashing the so-called Pemmican Wars.

Since the dead of Seven Oaks could not testify, it is unsurprising that Coltman collected depositions at Red River mainly from Métis and NWC employees, who were very much about. Coltman did interview Selkirk, along with some settlers and local Cree and Saulteaux, but he appeared in no hurry to investigate the attacks on Selkirk's settlement in 1815 and 1816. While Selkirk was preoccupied with "haggling" over property and other matters he regarded as "peripheral" (in Jack Bumsted's account, *Fur Trade Wars*, 188), Coltman was dispensing immunity in return for Métis witnesses' evidence.

Roy C. Dalton, formerly professor of history, Bethel College, St Paul, Minnesota, U.S.A.: In his proceedings Coltman appears to have sought a compromise rather than a rigorous imposition of the law, which might have provoked renewed violence. A contemporary described him as "a good-natured Laugh and Grow fat sort of person who had no wish but to reconcile and tranquillize all parties." Samuel Gale, Selkirk's shrewd and able counsel from Montreal, wrote that Coltman "took it for granted that Government looked upon all parties in almost the same light . . . and like a good subject he has laboured to fulfil what he conceived to be the wishes of the Government." The Selkirk party considered this approach unjust, but could only admire the commissioner's manner of proceeding. "Such is the man's bonhomie and good nature," Lady Selkirk acknowledged in December 1817, "that none of us can quite attribute bad intentions to him." (Dalton)

MK: Coltman toured the site of the Battle of Seven Oaks but made no arrests except for Selkirk, whom he released on €6000 bail to guarantee that he would show up for court appearances in Canada. No such surety was imposed on the NWC partners. September 1, 1817, Selkirk left Red River, Commissioner Coltman two days later.

Shortly after, while everyone awaited Coltman's report, Selkirk, served with a warrant to appear in Montreal against the charges that had been brought against him by the NWC, in turn preferred 170 charges against the NWC and its partners, spending months, after a bucolic summer at Red River, in courtrooms in Montreal and York in dogged pursuit of "justice."

His biographer, Jack Bumsted, concludes that, given the bias of the courts, "entirely dominated by the NWC and their powerful friends," he hoped in vain for a verdict in his favour. Politics lay at the heart of the contest. The Nor'Westers had important political connections in political circles in the Canadas and Great Britain, and the sympathy of what Peter C. Newman called "these unyielding clusters of privilege," that "self-perpetuating oligarchy of reactionary judges, bureaucrats, politicians and theologians," aided and abetted, to be sure, by the Colonial Office in London. (Newman, 248)

Beckles Willson, historian: They addressed themselves to the Imperial Government, soliciting his Majesty's interference in order to put an end to the outrages and lawlessness, as they expressed it, of Lord Selkirk and the Hudson's Bay Company. They recalled that they had often demanded that the rights of the Company should be submitted to law, and warned the authorities that when their rivals mocked the orders of the Prince Regent, it would be impossible for themselves to confide their persons and their property to the protection of an authority with a seat so remote and exacting so reluctant an obedience. "What is to become of us," they demanded, "if we are to have no protection for our servants in these wild regions of the North?" "You have no right in these regions," was the indignant retort of the Company. "They are vested in us by Royal charter. The sooner you apprehend this truth the better for yourselves and for peace in general." Whereupon the Northmen declared that if the Hudson's Bay Company or Lord Selkirk continued to exercise illegal powers, which had for their end the destruction of their established commerce, it was inevitable that more bloodshed would follow. Such protestations had the desired effect. The Government entered into correspondence with the directors of the [HB]Company, and ordered that they should exert themselves to the utmost to prevent a repetition of lawlessness; the consequences, otherwise, must be on their own head. (Willson, *The Great Company*, 213)

Jack Bumsted, interview: The HBC in 1815, prior to sending out Governor Semple, attempted to establish courts out here [in Assiniboia] but of course when it went to the British government to ask, "What do you think?" the British government said, "Uh oh," and did not buy into the notion of courts established by the HBC out here and so it continued to be No Man's Land. This is what Commissioner Coltman says about the whole dispute: basically what it is, is a private war. And that's why Coltman refuses to lay blame on the Métis or anybody else, because this is outside of civilization. Basically, you do what you can get away with. It may be somebody else's business, but if you have more guns than they do, you win. And in the end that's exactly what happened out here.

The Coltman Report

Beckles Willson: **The commissioners made a most circumstantial report of their mission, of which both parties complained that neither had received justice, which (as Senator Masson truly observes) was a very good reason for supposing that the report was just and impartial. (Willson, 226)**

MK: **On 30 June 1818, Commissioner William Coltman submitted his report, "A General Statement and Report Relative to the Disturbances in the Indian Territories of British North America." Blame was evenly assigned — *everybody* was to blame. He found against the HBC that its attempt to enforce its Charter-given monopoly of trade in Assiniboia fell afoul of the facts on the ground, namely that the NWC and others had long been trading on this territory without interference, monopoly or no. Governor Miles Macdonell had exacerbated the situation with his Pemmican Proclamation. The Report acknowledged that the NWC, for its part, had routinely employed violence and intimidation, including the two destructions of the Selkirk colony in 1815 and 1816. But, he concluded, these were "inadvertent" explosions. As Jack Bumsted summarizes, "although he allowed that the mixed-bloods were trying to intimidate the settlers, they had not set out to murder them." (*Fur Trade Wars*, 256)**

William B. Coltman letter to Cuthbert Grant n.d.: **As for the battle itself, it is always understood that the Colony people pursued you, or came forward to meet you and fired the first shot while Boucher was speaking to them. I consider this affair, as well as other violent deeds which took place, although as serious offences against the law, yet such as may be pardoned; all except perhaps those who were the first causes and instigators. (in MacGregor, 221)**

In the Courts

Chester Martin: Five charges of robbery, six for grand larceny, nine for stealing in dwelling houses, five for rioting and pulling down houses, three for false imprisonment, one for assault and battery against the HBC. Against the NWC: 42 charges of murder or complicity, 18 of arson, nine of burglary, 16 of robbery, nine for stealing in boats on navigable waters, nine for grand larceny, seven for malicious shooting. (in Hamilton, 275)

MK: The trials arising out of the Pemmican Wars opened in 1818 in Montreal and York, in spite of Lord Selkirk's petition to London's Colonial Office, citing the impossibility of finding an impartial jury there (he preferred London). The unfolding year saw a flurry of legal activity on both sides, suits and countersuits flying through the courts, against partners, clerks and servants of the companies.

Beckles Willson: The trials which took place at Little York and at Montreal were most disastrous to the Earl. Those relating to the Semple massacre were not tried until 1818.... At the trials at York in October 1818, Sherwood, the NorthWest company's counsel, continually demanded to know why Semple was called governor. "Why," he exclaimed, with ludicrous energy, "why should this gentleman be continually dignified by the appellation of governor? The indictment charged that Robert Semple was killed and murdered; it said nothing about his being a governor. If he was a governor, then he was also an emperor. Yes, gentlemen," shrieked the counsel, working himself up to fever heat, "I repeat, an emperor, a bashaw [pasha] in that land of milk and honey, where nothing, not even a blade of corn, will ripen. Who made

THE SEVEN OAKS READER *Myrna Kostash*

him governor? Did the King? Did the Prince Regent? No; this pretended authority was an illegal assumption of power, arrogating to itself prerogatives such as are not exercised even by the King of England. I demand that Robert Semple be called Robert Semple but he was not a governor." "Come, come," cried Chief Justice Powell, "do let this trial go on. It is no matter whether he was or was not a governor, or what he was called, or called himself, he is not to be murdered, though he was not a governor." (Willson, 214)

MK: The total number of charges was impressive but "the concrete results — particularly on the criminal side — were puny," in the judgement of historian Jack Bumsted, and left unresolved the larger issues, "particularly the claims by the HBC under its charter ... by any court in either Britain or North America." (*Fur Trade Wars*, 195) Only a negligible number ever made it all the way to trial, and even then all but one ended in acquittal. Colin Robertson and four others were tried for the destruction of Fort Gibraltar and Cuthbert Grant, François Boucher and fifteen others for the murder of Governor Semple. Lord Selkirk himself was tried on charges of theft, false imprisonment and resisting arrest. (He was convicted on the charge of false imprisonment at Fort William.) Ever since, the consensus among Selkirk's biographers is that he suffered a travesty of injustice.

Peter Gagné, author: As a result of the part he [Francois Farmin Boucher] played in this "battle" and Semple's death, Boucher was put on trial in York (Toronto) at the end of October 1818. He and fellow Nor'Wester Paul Brown were charged with the murder of Governor Semple. The two were defended by Levius Peters

Sherwood, who called none other than William McGillivray, one of the partners of the North West Company, to serve as a character witness for both men. Boucher and Brown were acquitted of the charges. At that time, Boucher was young and his father was a respected landowner in Montreal. (in Barkwell, *Battle*, 15)

Heather Devine: The biased nature of the legal proceedings in favor of the North West Company at the expense of Lord Selkirk is consistent with the tenor of behavior in Loyalist Upper Canada at that time. The political and legal system of Upper Canada was dominated by Scots Loyalists, their friends, and their business associates. The virtual dismissal of charges against Nor'Westers implicated of crimes in the Selkirk controversy was predictable, given the "localist" flavor of the Upper Canadian court system, which operated to maintain the status quo rather than the impartial rule of law. In this system, the courts favored the local mercantile community and "the larger needs of St Lawrence commercialism," which included the interests of the North West Company. (Devine, "Ambition Versus Loyalty," 281, n. 89)

MK: Nevertheless, six men indicted for the murder of Robert Semple at the Battle of Seven Oaks – John Siveright, Alexander Mackenzie, Hugh McGillis, John McDonald, John McLaughlin, and Simon Fraser – were brought to trial in October 1818 in York.

Justice D'Arcy Boulton, lawyer, judge, and political figure, charge to the Jury concerning those indicted for the murder of Robert Semple: "The principal question, indeed the only one for your notice, is whether this indictment which I hold in my hand is or is not well-founded? It is an indictment for murder, charging four persons as principals and a number of others as accessories, before and after the fact, and thus embracing all the varieties which distinguish the charge of murder.... This battle did not result from the passion of the moment, there is no testimony of that nature, and the law, in a hundred instances, considers the killing of a man, though provocation may have been given, to be murder.... Therefore, if you acquit these persons, it must be on the ground that you do not believe they fired first, or that, from the conduct of Mr Semple and his party, they were justified to do so; and in either case these gentlemen are acquitted. Indeed, whichever way you look at the case against most of these gentlemen, there is, apparently, nothing that can be called evidence to prove them guilty. Some are not even sworn to as being there at all ... and if you also believe that the Hudson's Bay party fired upon the half-breeds, then nobody who is accused is guilty. But the evidence is so contradictory, that it is hard to say which to believe...."

The Jury then retired, and in about three quarters of an hour returned into Court and delivered by their Foreman a verdict of NOT GUILTY; which being recorded by the Court the Jury were discharged. (in Amos, *Reports of Trials*, 317, 332-3, 335)

MK: Sponsored by Selkirk, Andrew Amos, a British lawyer who reproduced and criticised the proceedings at some of these trials, published his book in 1820, *Reports of Trials in the Courts of Canada Relative to the Destruction of the Earl of Selkirk's Settlement on the Red River: With Observations*, denouncing the state of things as one "to which no British colony had hitherto afforded a parallel, private vengeance arrogating the functions of public law; murder justified in a British court of judicature, on the plea of exasperation commencing years before the sanguinary act; the spirit of monopoly raging in all the terrors of power, in all the force of organisation, in all the insolence of impunity." (Amos, xxiii)

As for Cuthbert Grant, the Captain of the Métis hunters on the Red River, he had turned himself in in August 1817, and had his deposition recorded by Coltman and was taken to Montreal where in the spring of 1818 a bill of indictment was found against him for theft and pillage of HBC property and for the murder of Semple and the colonists killed at Seven Oaks. Grant jumped bail and lit out for the territory — or, as Amos put it, Grant was "under the necessity of quitting Canada on account of other urgent avocations." (Amos, xvi)

Andrew Amos, lawyer: All the persons who have been tried for the part which it was alleged they had taken in the destruction of Lord Selkirk's Settlement, have been acquitted.... [These verdicts] were returned by persons who resided near two thousand miles from the scene of the offences, and from the neighbourhood of the prisoners and the witnesses. This disunion of locality and jurisdiction trenches upon the fundamental principles of English law; and the mode of trial it prescribes is not in substance a trial by jury. (Amos, viii-ix, xvi)

MK: As for the prosecutions instigated by the NWC against officers and residents of the Red River colony, Sheriff John Spencer and Governor Miles Macdonell had both been arrested at Red River in spring 1815 for breach of the peace — and later, in Montreal, in Macdonell's case, for seizure of pemmican. By February 1818, seven bills had been drawn up against Spencer, Macdonell and Colin Robertson and others for "riot" and dismantling Fort Gibraltar back in 1816. But all criminal charges in these cases were eventually "dismissed by magistrates, thrown out by grand juries or abandoned by the law officers of the Crown." (Bumsted, *Fur Trade Wars*, 215) Having spent £100,000 out of his own pocket (and another £40,000 out of the HBC's) defending himself (Newman, 248) and having been assessed £2000 for damages, Lord Selkirk left Canada in November 1818, effectively bring the lengthy litigation to an end.

Jack Bumsted: When the dust had cleared from the various trials for the murder of Robert Semple and of the trial of two settlers for stealing a cannon in 1815, all held in York in late 1818, no one had been found guilty of anything. (*Collected Letters*, LXXIII)

Denouement

Joseph Howard: But the conspiracy against [Selkirk], in which the Nor'westers had enlisted even the British Colonial Office and the courts, had its hoped-for result: Selkirk's health collapsed. Added to his discouragement and fatigue was his bitterness when it became apparent even to him that union of the warring fur companies, as desired by the Colonial Office, was the only solution. He had once been willing to consider this, but after Seven Oaks he refused to go into partnership with butchers. (Howard, 37)

Lord Selkirk, in a letter from France, April 1820: To hand over to them the sovereignty, as it may be called, of an extensive country where we had the prospect of doing so much good, is a transaction to which I cannot easily reconcile myself, and I would reckon it immoral as well as a disgrace if it were done from any view of pecuniary advantage.... I ground this resolution, not only on the principle of supporting the settlers whom I have already sent to the place, but also because I consider my character at stake upon the success of the undertaking, and upon proving that it was neither a wild nor visionary scheme nor a cloak to cover sordid plans of aggression, charges which would be left in too ambiguous a state if I were to abandon the settlement at its present stage, and above all if I were to sell it to its enemies. (in Henderson)

Beckles Willson: The health of the Earl, shattered by these anxieties as well by exposure and great physical exertion, rendered it necessary that he should seek repose in the south of France. But his ailment was mortal. He breathed his last at Pau, in the month of April 1820, surrounded by his wife and children, leaving behind him many friends and numerous admirers of the intellectual qualities and the courage of a truly great man. (Willson, 216)

Joseph Howard: In 1820 he died in the south of France, at the age of forty-nine. His twenty-year struggle to establish the colony in the face of implacable opposition even from his government had cost his personal estate one hundred thousand pounds.[3] Less than a month before, Sir Alexander Mackenzie of the North West Company had died. The two greatest figures of the fur trade were gone and union of their companies followed quickly. Their war had cost the Hudson's Bay Company forty thousand pounds in addition to Selkirk's own losses; the rival's costs were even greater.... The Hudson's Bay Company, whose name was assumed by the consolidated firm, repurchased Assiniboia in 1834

---

3 One pound in 1820 corresponds roughly to 85 pounds now (2015).

from the Selkirk estate for stock in the Company valued at fifteen thousand pounds. This repaid only a fraction of the losses of the lord of whom Sir Walter Scott, a close friend, once said: "I never knew a man of more generous distinction." (Howard, 37–8)

Beckels Willson: Whilst these various proceedings were in progress, the Red River colony was struggling against adversity. In the winter of 1817 they were forced to resort again to Pembina, owing to a scarcity of food. The next year, when a considerable area of land had been planted, and a favourable summer following, the July sky suddenly darkened, and a cloud of grasshoppers descended upon the earth. Every green thing perished before them. In greater despair and wretchedness than ever the colonists again migrated across the border. The same disaster occurred in the ensuing year, and had it not been for the bounty and care of the Company many would have starved. (Willson, 215–216)

Alexander Ross: The year 1818, which had now commenced, is an eventful one in the history of the unfortunate settlers. Food was scarce, their hitherto precarious dependence on fish, herbs, and roots became hopeless, for these all failed; … lo! just as the corn was in ear, and the barley almost ripe, a cloud of grasshoppers from the west darkened the air, and fell like a heavy shower of snow on the devoted colony.… This sudden and unexpected disaster was more than they could bear. The unfortunate emigrants, looking up towards heaven, wept. Still they laboured earnestly to establish themselves, and make this wilderness wear the aspect of a home.… Every step now was a progressive one: agricultural labour advanced, the crop looked healthy and vigorous, and promised a rich harvest. In short, hope once more revived, and everything began to put on a thriving and prosperous appearance. (Ross, 47–8)

Joseph Howard: There were to be more disasters, more hunger and bloodshed, and some would quit; but the colony survived. The earl's wards, who already had endured so much, had still to learn about drought and locusts and floods; they had to establish communication and commerce with their aggressive neighbours to the south without forfeiting their political sovereignty; they had to learn to live with the touchy new nation of the Métis. All these they managed to do, and the dream of the young Scottish lord was at last realized. (Howard, 37)

George Bryce: Thus it was that in ten years after the death of Governor Semple there were of Highlanders, De Meurons, Swiss, French voyageurs, Metis, and Orkney half-breeds, not less than fifteen hundred settlers. It certainly was a motley throng. The Rev. Mr. West the first missionary tells us that he distributed copies of the Bible in English, Gaelic, German, Danish, Italian, and French, and they were all gratefully received in this polyglot community.. . .

Wood, water and hay, were the three r's of a Red River settler's life; to cut poplar rails for his fences in spring and burn the dried rails in the following winter was quite the proper thing. There was no inducement to grow surplus grain, as each settler could only get a market for eight bushels of wheat from the Hudson's Bay Company. It could not be exported. Pemican from the plains was easy to get; the habits of the people were simple, their wants were few, and while the picture was hardly Arcadian, yet the new order of things since that time has borne pretty severely upon many, so that they feel as did the kindly old lady, "granny"

Ross, of whom we have spoken, that they were "shut in" by so many people coming to the country. The census of the whole settlement in 1849 amounted to 5,291. (Bryce, *John Black*, 63-4)

Finale

R.D. Garneau: **April 8 1820:** Thomas [Douglas] believed to the end that Selkirk Town on the Red River was a success in settling needy Europeans and in providing a haven of refuge for a great body of vagabond Scottish. Others suggest that the number of settlers in Red River as a result of Thomas Douglas was very minor when compared to those from the North West Company and to the overwhelming majority called Metis, Bois Brules, Half Breeds or just Gens Libre (Freemen). Thomas Douglas of Selkirk had attempted to establish an illegal self-sustained feudal domain but lacked the intelligence to pull it off. His colonies in P.E.I. and Upper Canada failed and he created a war at the Red River and Assiniboine Rivers. (Garneau)

MK: After Selkirk's death, probates revealed that his personal fortune now consisted of £160,000 in debts plus the struggling colony on the Red River. (Newman, 250) The HBC, the company he once controlled as majority stockholder, was sinking under the weight of £100,000 debt due to declining profits and rising costs in the fur trade. Meanwhile, the old agreement between the NWC's Montreal agents and its Wintering Partners was coming up for renewal in 1820, with a background rumbling from the Winterers that the terms of the contract needed to be renegotiated.

Beckles Willson: The death of its principal Adventurer [Sir Alexander Mac-
kenzie] strengthened, on the part of the Company, the sentiment
for peace; and by removing the chief obstacle hastened a coali-
tion of the interests of the rival traders. None then could nor can
now but perceive, if they examine the situation broadly, that the
complete annihilation of the NorthWest association was a mere
matter of time. (Willson, 217)

MK: The British Secretary of State for War and the Colonies, Henry Bathurst,
had forced their hand: in 1820 he had ordered the companies to
cease hostilities, and held out an inducement to their merger. The
new company — only the name of the Hudson's Bay Company
would be retained — would be granted exclusive trading privileges all the way from Rupert's Land to the west coast (Oregon,
Washington, and British Columbia). At the time of the merger,
the amalgamated company consisted of ninety-seven trading posts that had belonged to the NWC and seventy-six that
belonged to the HBC.

George the Fourth, by the Grace of God of the United Kingdom of Great
Britain and Ireland King, Defender of the Faith, 5 December 1821:
To all to whom these Presents shall come, greeting: ...And whereas the said Governor and Company of Adventurers of England
trading into Hudson's Bay, and certain Associations of persons
trading under the name of the "North-west Company of Montreal,"
have respectively extended the fur trade over many parts of North
America which had not been before explored: And whereas the
competition in the said trade has been found for some years past
to be productive of great inconvenience and loss, not only to the
Said Company and Associations, but to the said trade in general,

and also of great injury to the native Indians, and of other persons our subjects: And whereas the said Governor and Company of Adventurers of England trading into Hudson's Bay, and William McGillivray of Montreal, in the Province of Lower Canada, esquire, Simon McGillivray, of Suffolk-lane, in the City of London, merchant, and Edward Ellice, of Spring Gardens, in the county of Middlesex, esquire, have represented to us that they have entered into an agreement, on the 26th day of March last, for putting an end to the said competition. (in C. Martin, Appendix D, 220-1)

MK: Métis residents of Red River country had already been constrained, not to say offended, by assumptions of private property – the 116,000 sq mi the HBC granted itself as its exclusive property – by interference with their hunting and trading by the Selkirk settlement, and the regulations controlling the supply of pemmican. Now the merger of the rival companies added new complications to their situation. Posts were closed or reduced in importance, resulting in the lapse of contracts and widespread unemployment. Wages were reduced for those still in employment. With fewer employees in the enterprise, fewer provisions were required from the pemmican traders. "A golden era for the Metis had come to an end." (Pelletier, *The Skirmish at Seven Oaks*, 17)

Howard Adams, author: After the union of the two companies in 1821, the Hudson's Bay Company immediately began its revenge against the halfbreeds and Indians. Bay governors imposed even more severe restrictions and oppressive conditions on the native population than formerly. The renewed monopoly market kept many natives in perpetual debt to the Bay, psychologically as well as economically. (Adams, 49)

Jim W. Warren and Kathleen Carlisle, authors: **The merger put an end to most of the commercially inspired violence in the West, but for ordinary workers in the fur trade, the merger was not good news. When employees defied their "masters" before 1821, there was always the chance they could get a job with the competition. Now that option was gone, reducing the workers' actual power and resulting in the erosion of wage rates and working conditions. In 1824, previous profit-sharing arrangements were also abandoned.... As the nineteenth century unfolded, new groups of illegal free traders, reminiscent of the *coureurs de bois* and the merchant peddlers, arose to defy the HBC's royal monopoly and carve out modest livings trading buffalo robes, furs and pemmican. Some of the Métis sons and grandsons of voyageurs exchanged canoes for horses, oxen, and Red River carts to hunt buffalo, trade and haul freight across the plains, others established small farms. (Warren & Carlisle, *On the Side of the People*, 14-15)**

MK: But the merger also spurred a kind of migration of hundreds of Métis families — the so-called Country-Born — from the posts of the old trading system to the Red River Settlement and adjacent lands. And there they would be in contact with, even assimilated into, its institutions: churches, schools, and civil administration, "the social foundation on which a British agrarian community in harmony with the fur trade rested. Such was the plan for Red River that prevailed in the board rooms of the HBC and the Church Missionary Society in London." (Foster, "The Origins of the Mixed Bloods," 93) Some Métis officers formerly with the NWC even found themselves offered a privileged position with the new HBC.

Ron Bourgeault, interview: The HBC absorbed the NWC and gave some of their merchants access to the share-holding class in the merged HBC. They co-opted them. And the same held true for Cuthbert Grant. After the merger he and other officers of the NWC in the interior were co-opted by the HBC. It was assessed whether they would be loyal to the HBC or not. Those who were seen to be loyal were absorbed into the operation of the HBC; those who were not found to be loyal were rejected and found their way back to Quebec. So, after the merger, they merged the labour forces and you've got surplus labour all over the place. Any surplus labour not needed in the interior then became part of the colony at Red River in conjunction with the Selkirk settlers.

MK: In February 1822, the newly appointed HBC governor George Simpson made a tour by canoe of his domain, Rupert's Land, and at Fort Hibernia on the Swan River just west of Lake Winnipegosis, met the twenty-nine-year old Cuthbert Grant. They travelled together to Red River.

George Simpson of the HBC to Andrew Colvile, HBC London Committee: In the course of our Journey [May 1822] Grant opened his situation to me, but no fresh light could be thrown upon the unfortunate affair of 19th June; he denies in the most solemn manner any previous intention of Collission and assured me that the melancholy catastrophe was entirely the result of the imprudent attack made upon them by Mr. Semple's party, and once the Indian blood was raised his utmost efforts could not arrest the Savage Revenge of his Associates.... Grant is now almost 25 (sic) Years of Age, an active clean-made fellow, possessing strong natural parts and a great deal of cool determination; his manners are mild and rather pleasing than otherways. He admits he was made a tool of by A. McDonell and being a very young man at the time thought it his duty to execute or even antici- pate the wishes of his Superior whether right or wrong.... The half-breeds and Indians of this part of the Country look up to him with great respect, indeed there is not a man in the Country possesses half the influence over them.... I am there- fore of opinion that it might be policy to overlook the past and if you did not object to it he might be smuggled quietly into the Service again. (in C. Martin, f.n. 112)

MK: In due course, July 1823, Grant was made HBC clerk and special con- stable at Fort Garry [site of the former NWC post Fort Gibraltar] As his biographer George Woodcock notes, this appointment did not sit well with colonists — he was even assaulted by a group of them — who remembered the role he had played in the destruction of the settlement in 1815 and 1816. Grant took a strategic retirement from the HBC in 1824 but was encouraged to settle near the colony and was granted land at White Horse Plain on the Assiniboine River. There, with about a hundred Métis families, he founded the village of Grantown (St François Xavier) in the spring of 1824. To supplement their food sup- ply they were encouraged to farm. A church, a boys' school, a blacksmith shop, a mill, and a trading store consolidated the settlement. By 1827 Grant had thirty-four acres under cultiva- tion and looked upon himself as *seigneur* of White Horse Plain, or, as he would later be known, "Chief of the half-breeds and warden of the Plains" when the HBC authorized him to pre- vent the "illicit" (unlicensed) trade in furs within the district. The irony is stark.

George Woodcock: Here Grant, as warden of the plains, magistrate, and sheriff, was on the side of the company. When Pierre-Guillaume Sayer was tried for illicit trading in 1849, Grant was on the bench as one of the magistrates. With a large body of armed Métis vociferously supporting Sayer in the court-room and proclaiming [free trader James] Sinclair as their leader, Sayer was found guilty of trading furs but went unpunished. The verdict was heralded in the colony as the end of the HBC monopoly. (Woodcock, "Grant")

MK: "He had transferred his loyalties to the new masters," writes Woodcock, "and his value was recognized. He was still sufficiently respected by the Métis to be elected captain of the annual buffalo hunts." (Woodcock, "Grant") But in what did Grant's "loyalty" to the HBC really consist? A leader of his Métis people, he had set out, from the NWC's post on the Qu'Appelle, as Captain-General with his troop of horsemen to confront the traditional rival at the Bay's Fort Douglas and its settlement and wrest back control for the NWC. It has been suggested that, eventually, he realized he had been manipulated, "duped," by the NWC, who had never had his or his people's interests at heart. In his panoramic history of the Métis, Marcel Giraud relates an encounter between the HBC trader, Peter Fidler, and Cuthbert Grant, who travelled together from Fidler's Brandon House to Red River to meet with Commissioner William Coltman in 1817. Giraud asserts that a "firm friendship and confidence" had been established between them by the time they arrived at Red River. Grant had spoken confidentially of his profound disappointment, even bitterness, in the collapse of the "national ideal" of the Métis nation.

Marcel Giraud: Accusing the North West Company of having incited him to the violences he had committed, he offered to betray the interests of the partners between whose hands he had been nothing but a tool. [According to Fidler's *Journal* of Brandon House for August 1817] he denied the idea he had once passionately defended, he renounced the role of leader of the Métis nation which he had so recently assumed with vigor, he even offered to serve the British company that had been represented as the usurper of the land over which, by right of birth, the Bois-Brûlés claimed sovereign rights of property. (Giraud, 475)

MK: Margaret A. Macleod and W.L. Morton, authors of *Cuthbert Grant of Grantown; Warden of the Plains of Red River*, conclude that, although the Métis understood and accepted that the "bloodshed" at Seven Oaks had been an "accident," an unintended collision of armed groups, later it was also understood within their community that "ultimate responsibility" for the violence and death lay with the NWC at Qu'Appelle who had urged on Grant and his men, flag flying. It was this knowledge of their deception that made it possible, they argue, for the Métis and Red River colonists to reconcile. "In it lay the possibility that Cuthbert Grant would in the long run be remembered not as the destroyer but as the guardian of the Red River colony." (Macleod & Morton, 68)

Grant died on July 15, 1854, his role as "guardian" of his people on the plains already in decline. Coming to prominence was the St-Boniface farmer and miller, Louis Riel Sr.

"A halfcast [Métis] and his two wives."
Painted by Peter Rindisbacher circa 1825.
(Library and Archives Canada, MIKAN no: 2835810)

EIGHT: THE HISTORIANS

Chester Martin: Selkirk's name in Canada, however, is inseparably connected with the West. The Red River Settlement, it has been seen, relapsed for half a century into an obscure frontier colony, at once thrifty, primitive, and self-reliant. Probably no part of the British self-governing dominions has had a stranger history: founded by an individual proprietor, twice destroyed by men of kindred race, overwhelmed during its early years by almost unparalleled disaster, developed for two decades under the protection of a private family, relapsing into the ownership of a monopolistic trading company which was accused by its enemies, justly or unjustly, of having 'locked the door upon the settlement and put the key in its pocket'; and finally, after an ignoble insurrection in 1869, taking its place as one of the most promising provinces of the Dominion. It was half a century after Selkirk's death before the British Government began to see promise in the West. (C. Martin, 179)

MK: The land "claimed" by the settlers who eventually homesteaded in southern Manitoba — not necessarily direct descendents of the Selkirk colonists of the early 1800s — was land that came to represent a sense of community forged by a pioneer generation of utopians, a "race" of exceptional Britons who did not know themselves as such but would be created by the historians who came after.

Parks Canada Historian Lyle Dick has reviewed the work of several generations of historians of the Battle of Seven Oaks. He has a particular interest in the amateur or "grass-roots" historians who wrote when there were still living witnesses to 1816 and who, in effect, wrote in collaboration with oral history. Charles Napier Bell, for example, was a professional white collar worker in Winnipeg. He was Secretary of the Board of Trade, a prominent person in the business community.

Lyle Dick, interview: So he interviewed old-timers who included a few surviving witnesses to Seven Oaks. I think they were just children at the time, but in any event there is that direct connection to the grass roots, to that first-hand perspective, to these important historical events.

Charles Bell: [Peguis and other Saulteaux] went out the morning after the engagement and brought in the bodies of the killed, or as many as could then be found, for a small number, I am informed by eye-witnesses, were concealed in the heavy brush in the vicinity, as wounded men had crawled into thickets and there died. Mrs Kaufman, who yet lives in Kildonan east (since died, 1892), informs me that she saw the Indians bring in the dead bodies to Fort Douglas with carts, and that Governor Semple and the doctor were buried in board coffins, and the others wrapped up in blankets, the whole number being interred in a grove of trees on the south side of the creek southwest of the fort, and quite near the spot whereon now stands the residence of ex-Mayor Logan.... Donald Murray states positively that all these bodies were removed some years after to St John's Church graveyard, but he is not now able to locate the site of their re-interment. (in Blanchard, 83)

Lyle Dick, interview: George Bryce on the other hand was also from Ontario but he was a pioneer in academic approaches to history that stressed the importance of detachment, of removal of the practitioner from the evidence – he didn't want to be influenced unduly by first-hand accounts or oral history. So he stressed written sources. The problem though for Bryce was that the written sources he relied upon were not sources that would represent a balanced treatment of Seven Oaks. So these are the two main traditions: the vernacular or amateur tradition, the outgoing tradition, superseded, pushed aside, by the academic tradition, represented by Bryce, which stressed the use of written sources – letters, documents, journals – rather than oral testimony.

In constructing a historical role for his ethnic group and class, no other historian matched the contribution of George Bryce.... [In the conclusions to Mr. Bryce's books] the collective hero, for whom the Selkirk settlers were earlier stand-ins, was revealed as the Anglo-Canadian group to which the author belonged.

George Bryce: Three years from now will be the hundredth year since the landing on the banks of Red River of the first band of Selkirk Colonists. It was as we have seen a struggle of an extraordinarily bitter type. To us it seems that no other American Colony ever had such a continuous distressing and terrific struggle for existence as had these Scottish Settlers....

We say that had it not been for the Selkirk Colonists we would have stood to lose our Canadian West. It was a settlement nearly a hundred years ago of families of men and women, and children that gave us the firm claim to what is now the three great provinces of Manitoba, Saskatchewan and Alberta. Was it not worth while? Was it not worth ten, yes, worth a hundred times more suffering and discouragement than even the first settlers of Red River endured to preserve our British connection which the Hudson's Bay Company, loyal as it was, with its Union Jack floating on every fort, could not have preserved to us any more than it did in Oregon and Washington. It was the Red River Settlement that held it for us. We are beginning to see to-day that Canada could not have become a great and powerful sister nation in the Empire had the West not been saved to her.

...And, if so, we owe it to Lord Selkirk and to Selkirk Settlers, who stood true to their flag and nationality. (*The Romantic Settlement*, 318–19)

MK: This very partisan, anglocentric view of events was challenged by only one of Bryce's contemporaries, Charles Napier Bell, who presented to his readers very contrary views from both sides of the conflict.

Lyle Dick: Thereafter, alternative perspectives on Seven Oaks survived only in the French language, in twentieth-century works by Louis-Arthur Prud'homme and Auguste-Henri de Trémaudan. Within the new Anglo-Canadian tradition, these works, as well as Bell's pluralistic account, were quickly forgotten, while Bryce's representation of a massacre was endorsed and reproduced by numerous professional and popular historians and novelists of his own period and since. (*Historical Writing*, 68)

MK: The historians Dick reviews were not unaware of the challenge they faced in narrating and analyzing conflicting "histories" of Red River, but would overcome them by stringent loyalty to the "facts."

Alexander Ross: A colony thus forming itself, by a kind of extemporary process, in the face of many opposing interests, and in the midst of warring elements, may be supposed to exhibit certain aspects, social or material, on which great difference of opinion must of necessity exist. These points of interest have been a source of continually recurring difficulty to the writer, who has guarded himself, as far as possible, by endeavouring to ground his conclusions, not on opinion, but on facts.... His statements, it is confidently hoped, will shed a not doubtful light on the past and present condition of the different races, savage and civilized, now inhabiting these lands; and thus will afford materials of the highest importance to the future historian. (Ross, vi-vii)

MK: And so it turned out to be. Alexander Ross was a retired sheriff and councillor when he wrote his books in the 1850s. Appraising his approach to western history a century later for an American edition of *The Red River Settlement*, a Minneapolis journalist wrote admiringly of Ross as a "fair and candid reporter."

Jay Edgerton, staff writer, *Minneapolis Star*: There is none of the smug superiority that often characterized whites on the frontier; nor is there the other extreme, the mawkish sentimentality that persisted in seeing all red men as "noble savages," the facts to the contrary notwithstanding. In reading "The Red River Settlement" it is well to keep in mind that its author brought to his task many assumptions that we may look upon today as archaic or, at least, "quaint." The people of whom he writes functioned from these same assumptions. We will get the most out of Ross' book if we try to read it in the context of his time. (Edgerton, unpaginated)

MK: However, another half century later, in the view of Andrew den Otter, Professor Emeritus in the Department of History at Memorial University of Newfoundland, writers such as Ross, Morton, and Giraud (translated by George Woodcock) are precisely the problem: Ross, who had a Native-born wife and thirteen Mixed-blood children, believed Red River to be a "mere speck, an isolated spot in the midst of a benighted wilderness," (Ross, 157–8) and accordingly wrote a history that "recounts the drama of planting an agricultural, British, and Christian culture in an undeveloped and primitive landscape." (den Otter, 273) The Métis themselves he dismissed as a people who "take no delight in cultivating the soil. Their thoughts, their ideas, their energies, are all limited to buffalo-hunting, fiddling and horse-racing." (Ross, 126) Marcel Giraud, a Francophone scholar, writing in the 1940s, took two authoritative volumes to describe the origins of the Métis people and their inevitable "decline" back into the wilderness, and the "regressive" influence of their aboriginal ancestry, away from the civilizing forces of the European element. While W.L. Morton, writing in the 1950s and 1960s, "vehemently" rejected the characterization of the Métis as savages, nevertheless, in den Otter's view, he "still clung to the civilization-wilderness theme. 'Red River was not a frontier,' he maintained, 'but an island of civilization in the wilderness.'" As for Giraud's translator, he speaks for himself:

George Woodcock: The Métis were a people given a sense of historical mission by those outsiders — the bourgeois of the North West Company — who invented the concept of a "Métis nation." Yet they recorded no history of their own, an anomaly largely due to the fact that during the period when they played a notable role in western Canada they were mostly illiterate.... Writing the history of such a people presents its special problems, since the historian in such a situation is really involved in a kind of elaborate mirror play. He has to trace their record by reflection, in the way other people saw them, and he will find this kind of record has its intermittencies, when facts have to be supported by conjecture. More than that, there are the problems of point of view. A missionary's or a fur trader's perception of a Métis hunter is invariably conditioned by his own calculations. ... So we have our accounts of the Métis seen from the outside, but — since this was a people lacking in those forms of artistic self-expression that are languages of the spirit — we have little tangible record of their inner lives. (in Giraud, xi-xii)

MK: The Francophone point of view on the history of Red River, with its affinity with "la francophonie" and the Roman Catholic church, such also as the work of Abbé Georges Dugas, a missionary in Manitoba 1866-1888 and writing in the early 1900s, was sometimes and pointedly in opposition to the Anglophilism of George Bryce and others.

Georges Dugas: [The French Métis] were the most numerous population and one has to admit that, without being perfect, they had excellent qualities. Cheerful and open with their own people, strictly honest and without a care for the future, hospitable toward strangers and generous to a fault, they spent their adventurous life fishing, as guides for horse-drawn caravans or on the buffalo hunt. On the other hand, they are by nature religious and respectful of authority. Spread out along the rivers, their little houses comprised a single room for a generally large family, enclosed by paltry fencing which sheltered half a tiny field in which they grew oats and barley for their race horses and the needs of the household rather than grow wheat, a glut of which was produced in the Scottish part of the colony. (Dugas, 45–6 mk trans)

MK: The crucial tension between the "savage" wilderness or plain of the hunt and the civilized farm of agriculture lay at the heart of so much early historiography of Red River, even in a writer as sympathetic to the Métis as Dugas.

Georges Dugas: Agriculture and the sedentary life did not attract them. They despised the state of dependence to which the Scottish farmers, whom they called "gardeners," had subjected themselves, and much preferred the freedom and great outdoors and the excitement of the buffalo hunt. (Dugas, 46 mk trans)

MK: Even as recently as 2012, even after the ultimate success of the "gardeners" has been corrected to include non-Anglo-Saxon settlers, the triumph of agriculture was evoked in a celebratory mood.

Red River 200: Why is the Selkirk Settlement important, and why should we be marking the Bicentenary? There are two reasons why the Selkirk Settlement at Red River was so important. First, by planting here a colony of British subjects, Lord Selkirk made it unlikely that the expansionist United States would simply continue north and west, and annex all of what is now western Canada. Second, the Settlement began the shift of western Canada from a hunter-gathering to a farm economy, based on grain growing, which can support a large population. After Confederation, this made it possible for dense settlement by immigrants from eastern Canada and Europe. Thus the Settlement was the beginning of one of the most important movements in Canadian history and the establishment of the farming system of the Prairie Provinces, with the wealth and opportunities that it offered to hundreds of thousands of immigrants.

MK: But, unsurprisingly, given its violence, the Battle of Seven Oaks has served as the sensational focus of much of the historical and journalistic interest in Red River.

Lyle Dick, interview: What prompted my interest in the Battle of Seven Oaks was the second volume of Peter C Newman's *Company of Adventurers*, his history of the HBC. I had written an extended review article of the first volume entitled "Company of Adventurers," and I had an expectation that Seven Oaks might be particularly dramatized in his second volume and I found that, sure enough, that was the case. There was a fairly lurid or graphic treatment of the violence at Seven Oaks and I really wanted to know where this fit in to the overall historiography of Seven Oaks. Was it an accurate depiction? Was it a fair depiction?

Peter C. Newman: Cuthbert Grant pulled the trigger, wounding Semple in the thigh, and that shot set off the slaughter. . . . When the Métis threw themselves on the ground to reload, the Semple survivors thought they had all been felled and with a cheer threw their hats in the air. Before those hats had landed, another multiple blast resounded. Roger, the Royal Engineer, charged the Métis with his bayonet and was halted in his tracks, dying on his knees. (Newman, 230)

Lyle Dick, interview: The term "massacre" as it refers to this military confrontation dates from immediately following the battle and to allegations on the Selkirk side that the majority of settlers killed were massacred by the Métis. That was not the conclusion of Coltman and his co-commissioner Fletcher when they undertook their comprehensive analysis of Seven Oaks which was published in 1819. They concluded it was not a massacre ["an inadvertent explosion rather than a deliberate action"]. And it seemed a very well-considered conclusion.

Jack Bumsted, interview: At the time [1816-17], Selkirk and his people claimed it was a massacre. The NWC and their people saw it as a legitimate defense of Aboriginal rights or whatever. Later on in the nineteenth century of course and in the early years of the twentieth century, it was seen as a nasty encounter.

Plaque text

BATTLE OF SEVEN OAKS

Here at the Frog Plain, on June 19, 1816, Robert Semple, Governor of the Red River Settlement, and about 26 men confronted a North West Company brigade from the Assiniboine River, led by the young Métis clerk, Cuthbert Grant. The Métis saw the Settlement as a threat to their way of life; Semple, brave but obstinate, was prepared to insist on his authority as Governor. Tempers flared, a shot was fired, and Semple and twenty of his men were cut down. Regardless of what Grant's plan had originally been, he was now committed to action, and went on to capture Fort Douglas, headquarters of the Settlement.

BATAILLE DE SEVEN OAKS

Le 19 juin 1816, dans la Grenouillère, le gouverneur de la colonie de la rivière Rouge, Robert Semple, avec vingt-six hommes, affronta une brigade de la Compagnie du Nord-Ouest, commandée par Cuthbert Grant. Les Métis considéraient la colonie comme une menace pour leur mode de vie et Semple, brave mais têtu, tenait à faire respecter son autorité. La querelle s'enflamma. Semple et vingt de ses compagnons furent tués. Modifiant son plan initial, Grant devait dès lors passer à l'action: il captura le centre de la colonie, fort Douglas. (Goldsborough)

MK: What alternatives to the word "massacre" present themselves for what happened at Seven Oaks? Dick suggests "incident."

Lyle Dick: I consulted *Webster's New International Dictionary* (1971 edition) to see what alternative definitions of the term "incident" might apply to Seven Oaks, as I am choosing to deal with it. I'll give just a few of these: "Occurring merely by chance or without intention or calculation"; "An uncommon happening"; "A military situation marked by fighting without formally declared war"; "Something arising or resulting from something else of greater or principal importance"; "A happening or related group of happenings subordinate to a main narrow plot. e.g. "The Melodrama and the Romance must be made up of swift successions of startling incidents." (Dick, *Historical Writing*, 65-6)

Joseph E. Martin, management consultant and historian: When I spoke to the Manitoba Historical Society twenty-five years ago [in 1940] the term "battle" was used. I vividly remember giving the lecture at the annual meeting of the Society, recognizing that there were a lot of sensitivities in the room, and being as careful as I've ever been in a public address. I thought I'd done a marvellous job of being absolutely neutral. I received very good, polite applause but at the end of the evening Anne Henderson, President of the Lord Selkirk Society, came up to me, eyes blazing, and said: "How could you Joe?" I said: "How could I what ...?" She said: "You know it wasn't a battle ... you know it was a massacre ... how could you have called it a battle?" (J. Martin, "Conflict at Red River")

Lyle Dick, interview: Yes, indeed, the majority of persons killed or wounded were on the Selkirk side but they were very inexperienced in battle and they had also initiated the shooting, which was established by the eye-witness accounts. In the period of Red River you don't see the term massacre coming up, I think, because Red River for all intents and purposes was an aboriginal society; the majority of people living there had native blood, whether Anglophone or Francophone. I don't think there was an enduring resentment or feeling that Seven Oaks was a dark stain on the history of the colony. It was regarded as an unfortunate incident.

But that changed in 1870 when Rupert's Land was handed over to Canada and this Anglo-Canadian settlement group wanted to rewrite the history of the Battle of Seven Oaks to put forward their own versions of history and their own imperatives relating to how the west should be developed and under whose tutelage. And that's when you find this preoccupation with the so-called massacre. It appears prominently in the work of George Bryce. Bryce wrote no less than six accounts of Seven Oaks. He regarded it as the most important event in western Canadian history. And the interpretation of a massacre at Seven Oaks continues right through the writings of W.L. Morton right up to about 1970.

MK: It would be the task of historians writing after 1970 to go beyond the "civilized-primitive debate," historians such as Jennifer Brown and Sylvia van Kirk who introduced the history of women and children in the fur trade, or Gerhard Ens, who, like sociologist Ron Bourgeault, argues for a Métis identity "not defined by biology, blood, or religion, but rather by the economic and social niche they carved out for themselves within the fur trade" [cited in den Otter 291] or Emma LaRocque who has challenged historians to "demythologize this myth" of the dichotomy of civilization/savagery by exposing how actively involved the Red River Métis were in commerce, transportation, food supplies, and linguistics [den Otter 294] or Lyle Dick's comprehensive review of how the historians have written about the Battle of Seven Oaks in particular.

Lyle Dick, interview: The Battle of Seven Oaks as a *massacre* serves the foundational myth of Anglo-Canadians in the west because it offers an opportunity to present the Métis as violent, lacking in self-control, unruly, lawless. All of those things which could be used to discredit their claim to western lands. This is the period when western lands are being surveyed, parcelled off and granted to homesteaders, sold by the CPR to settlers. So this was a period when land was very much an issue of contention. Why indeed did we have two resistances led by the Métis in western Canada in 1870 and 1885? Land was a central component of both those armed conflicts and I think it's important to remind ourselves of that.

MK: In his seminal essay published in 1991, "The Seven Oaks Incident and the Construction of a Historical Tradition, 1816 to 1970," Dick analyzed categories of text ranging from contemporary primary accounts, the Coltman Report, histories written in the first period of the Red River settlement – written mainly by amateurs, what Dick has called "vernacular" historians, not professionally trained but interested as individuals in history and who included their own reflections – and those after Manitoba's entry in Confederation in 1870, when the historians were professionals, following academic discipline. His revisionist account of the *historiography* of Seven Oaks that all these texts represent has been picked up by Métis activists such as the Métis Nation of Ontario, Region 4 and their website.

Métis Nation of Ontario, Region 4: The "Battle of Seven Oaks" marks the birth of the Métis Nation. Historians have chosen to interpret this particular battle in a negative light, showing the Métis as the aggressors contrary to the evidence. Historians of the past have chosen to show the Métis as savages, and therefore as the ones who fired the first shot and afterwards mutilating the bodies....

Parks Canada historian, Lyle Dick, in a recent article on the Battle of Seven Oaks, reviewed Coltman's report and stated that first, the first shot was fired by Selkirk Settlers, second, that the Hudson's Bay Company and settlers had a high attrition rate because they were "standing together in a crowd, unaccustomed to the use of fire-arms or any of the practices of irregular warfare," while the Métis were "all excellent marksmen, advantageously posted in superior numbers around their opponents, and accustomed as huntsmen, and from the habits of Indian warfare, to every device that could tend to their own preservation, or the destruction of their enemy" and third, in respect to the mutilation of the bodies afterward, Coltman concluded that the individuals responsible were a French Canadian and his three sons.

Many people today still believe that the Métis "massacred" the settlers in a savage manner and that ultimately the battle was the fault of the Métis because they fired the first shot even when there is evidence to the contrary. We as Métis people need to start writing our own history and reviewing past historical writings to ensure the truth is put forward. By understanding our past we can become stronger in the future. (Métis Info. Series)

MK: An example of this new understanding "put forward" is the online publication of essays such as "Battle of Seven Oaks 1816" (no author indicated) posted by the Critical Thinking Consortium at the University of British Columba and reposted on her website by teacher Marcia Lalonde.

Marcia Lalonde, educator: As far as the Metis were concerned, the battle of Seven Oaks confirmed their suspicions that British settlement, hostile to both Native and French Canadian Catholic culture, would interfere with their traditional economy and society. Their economy was based on trapping, provisioning fur traders, hunting buffalo as well as farming. Unlike the British settlers, the Metis did not participate in agriculture as a full-time occupation. The buffalo, not agriculture, provided most of their livelihood, from clothing to food. And buffalo in these years took up most of the space that settlers would, in the years to come, want to devote to farming, just as the farms would interfere with the grazing areas of the buffalo. . . . As the settlers in Alberta would discover decades later, farming was just not compatible with the unfenced grazing of large animals. The competition between the settlers and the Metis was not just a dispute about civilization versus savagery, but a competition between two political economies. The Battle of Seven Oaks made all these differences clear for the first time: that the Metis were a coherent group with particular goals, values and economy, and these were in conflict with agricultural settlement. If Seven Oaks was the first battle in their fight to preserve the Metis way of life, that last was fought seventy years later under Louis Riel. (Lalonde, 120)

Lyle Dick, interview: Some of these important events relating to the history of western Canada and particularly relating to the Métis community such as Seven Oaks in 1816, the Northwest resistance of 1870, and the second Northwest Resistance of 1885 are not over and done with. They may have happened in the past but they have not yet been concluded in terms of the issues revealed: in these economic justice and opportunities to participate fully in western Canadian and Canadian society in general. For Anglo western Canadians the issues that resonate would include communities' desire to get more in touch with their past. If people realize that some of our foundations of our understanding of the past are built on myth, I like to think they would want to get a bit closer to their history so that they're not dealing so much with myths as they're dealing with concrete realities. And I think that would be better for everyone.

Summing Up

MK: European no less than British-Canadian historians and ethnographers failed to notice the emergence of a new nation on the Canadian plains – whether as "too marginal" to be perceived or, as German scholar of Native and Minority Studies, Hartmut Lutz, has argued, "too unsettling for European racist ideologies against miscegenation? Or, would a recognition of the economic importance and territorial claims of the Métis have been too challenging for the construction of a new Canadian nation?"

Hartmut Lutz: The emergence of a new people in the borderlands between First Nations and Europeans, the "Métis" or "Halfbreeds," were the living proof that a colonial ethnogenesis had taken place in North America, for which the European perception was unprepared. No preconceived iconography or narrative conventions could accommodate this new nation in Canada. So, the Métis were seen and not seen at the same time, sketched and painted but not recognized as generically distinct, described in words as individuals, or defined as members of certain occupational groups, perhaps, but not identified as members of a nation. (Lutz, "'Inventing' Canada's Aboriginal Peoples," 209–210)

Duke Redbird, Métis poet, journalist, and activist: Most white historians have assumed that possessiveness is a primary motivator, the territorial imperative, if you will. Land, to the white man, was to be possessed.... The Metis had developed a way of life that was co-operative rather than competitive ... In other words, dissolution of conflict – not dominance in conflict – was the goal ... A basic idea of this book [We Are Metis] is that the Metis were indeed civilized and that that civilization was undermined, both

consciously and otherwise by both Europeans and Canadians. . . .
This is the challenge to white-biased history, that there was a civilization of Metis people that has not been destroyed, but rather
exists today, not only among the Metis but in the mind of every
Canadian whose ancestors were in North America when Riel first
said, "We are Metis." (Redbird, 6–7)

Jack Bumsted, interview: I am a historian. I write history and I try to base
my history on evidence, particularly documentary evidence, and
moreover I try to look at all sides of a controversy and try to
see things in their broadest possible context. The trouble is that
I'm losing ... I'm losing to a popular groundswell of support for
Aboriginals and Métis and I don't see myself as *against* those people. I don't feel that the story can be told, at this point in time, from
their perspective because there isn't enough evidence to go on. It's
all on the Internet, quotations from people whose names I don't
recognize, who make absurdist statements of one kind or another.

And one of the problems, it seems to me, is that there is an
enormous amount of ignorance surrounding not just this episode
but the entire early history of western Canada. It's ignorance that
comes from the fact that not many people are asking questions
about sovereignty or about rights. Some are. And there's been
some interesting work done on that whole matter but for the
most part what you read in the popular press is just that.

Lyle Dick, interview: I think history in general needs to get more in touch with
its grass roots. And we had that in the 19ᵗʰ century. We as a discipline have become more removed from the grassroots than I think
is healthy. Oral history is one antidote to the reifications of written
texts and written historiography. And another way to reconnect is

to get in touch with communities, the way they write their history. In the 21st century we see some important work being produced by the Métis community, and examples of that are the studies that are produced by the Gabriel Dumont Institute and by the Métis historiography and mechif culture heritage and folkways.

I like the notion that we don't necessarily agree on all the issues of history, I don't see how that is possible in fact, because you have very many perspectives. I'm not seeking agreement personally so much as I want to see dialogue on an equal basis between people who hold different viewpoints or interpretations of history. Let's have more discussion. Let people consider the evidence, debate among themselves and hopefully that will lead us to if not an improved, a better understanding of each other's position in the future. To me that would be healthy for history.

Alfred Silver: Listing all the details and decisions involved in the layering on of flesh over the scraps of old bones would fill another couple of books. In the places where there were no traces left at all, I simply made it up, although I'm pleasantly surprised on looking back that a high percentage of the personal histories are based on verifiable evidence. It's amazing what you can find out about people from parish records and third parties' diaries.... I can't claim I've read every book or parish record or crumbling-paged journal or scrutinized every microfiche and every gravesite.... After all my grumbling about misinformation in supposedly factual history books, it would be remiss of me not to point out that there was also a good deal of very solid and painstaking work done before I came along, without which it would not have been possible for me even to consider writing a book such as this. I have my own prejudices and preferences, but for what it's worth, I thank them all. (Silver, 556)

The Métis flag. The blue colour represents
the Métis historical association with the
North West Company.

NINE: LEGACIES

Settler

George Bryce: No element, however, did so much for Red River of old as the intelligent and high-spirited officers of the Hudson's Bay Company, of whom many settled in the country. There was among them also a strong Highland and Orkney strain. In few countries is the speech of the people generally so correct as it was in the Red River settlement. This undoubtedly arose from the influence of the educated Hudson's Bay Company officers. At their distant posts on the long nights they read useful books and kept their journals. Numbers of them collected specimens of natural history, Indian curiosities, took meteorological observations and the like. Though all may not have been the pink of perfection, yet very few bodies of men retained as a whole so upright a character as these. I have but to mention such names as Pruden, Bird, Bunn, Stewart, Lillie, Campbell, Christie, Kennedy, Heron, Ross, Murray, Mackenzie, Hardistv, Graham, McTavish, Bannatyne, Cowan, Rowand, Sinclair, Sutherland, Finlayson, Smith, Balsillie, and Hargrave and others, who have settled on the Red River to command, I know, your assent to my assertion. (Bryce, "Worthies")

MK: As George Bryce himself acknowledged in that same address to the Manitoba Historical Society in 1896, as early as 1816 there was already a people who called themselves the New Nation on the Red River, led by the "Scoto-French half-breed, Cuthbert Grant," and who "having tasted blood in the death of Governor Semple," were turbulent ever after.

No amount of heroic genealogy of the HBC could disguise the reality of a colony of flesh and blood that had been established in trauma and whose "founding myth" evolved from the obvious tenacity of colonists to survive and overcome the "unhallowed triumph of the murderers," in the phrase of Alexander Ross. For Ross, the Red River fur trader and historian, "Western Canadian history began with the granting of the Hudson's Bay Company charter in 1670, while he hailed the 'real object' of Selkirk's scheme as 'the pious and philanthropic desire of introducing civilization into the wilderness'," according to Lyle Dick. "It was a sustained effort by Ross to privilege his own European ethnicity in opposition to the posited savagery of all Native peoples within the Red River settlement, including persons of mixed race." (in *Making Western Canada*, 10]

Even after its re-establishment in 1816 and the merger of the competing fur trading companies in 1821, the settlement continued to be assailed by privations and encumbered by grievances as the decades rolled on — plagues of grasshoppers, drought, poor hunting, marauding Sioux to the south. It was from such material the settler myth-making would have to be constructed. In July 1822 a meeting of "the Scotch settlers" complained of the high cost of goods, their crop losses, and indebtedness. They were also still waiting for the promised clergy "of their own tenets, and [to] preach in their own language." The structure of Fort Douglas, that once-formidable bastion of HBC power on the Red, was described in melancholic detail by Andrew Bulger, a British officer and newly-appointed governor of Assiniboia.

A. Bulger, writing 4 August 1822: As to what is styled "Fort Douglas." It is well situated, though there is a better position for a fort about 200 yards higher up, upon the land which Mr. Pritchard gave up. But as to the fort itself it is, as Mr. Halkett [Lord Selkirk's executor] can tell you, the most filthy miserable place imaginable. It is, by at least 25 feet, too small, and the stockades are for the most part rotten and tumbling down. The buildings, except one, are mere log huts, very old and so full of holes as to be perfectly unsuitable. The only one that is of any value is what is called the new house, but even this is nothing more than the shell of a badly built log house, being nowhere boarded outside, and having but two rooms finished inside and so badly have these been done that the light may be seen through the walls in many places. (in "Original Letters")

MK: And, by 1826, that very killing ground of the Battle of Seven Oaks known as the Frog Plains was the site of a half-yearly fair and market.

Alexander Ross: The Scotch settlers, meanwhile, not so easily chilled by disappointments, promptly decided on the course they were to take; without a moment's hesitation, or loss of time, they resumed work on their cheerless farms, which were then bare and naked as on the first day they came to the country. This was the fourth time the Scotch settlers had commenced the world anew in Red River, all the fruits of their former labours having disappeared, like the morning dew. The advanced state of the season held out but little hope of their labours being crowned with success; yet barley, potatoes, and even a little wheat sowed as late as the 22nd of June [1826], came to maturity. In such a latitude as Hudson's Bay, this would appear almost incredible; but such was the effect of the short warm summer of those regions. The patience and perseverance of the Scotch were amply rewarded from this time, for we are now brought to the year 1827, which commences a new era in the settlement. Several causes contributed to this result. The dross had been purged away from our community, so that we were now one people in thought, word, and deed. Before the year 1830 had passed, the colony was completely re-established, and more promising and thriving than ever. (Ross, 109, Hurtig reprint)

MK: The HBC, "for the guidance of the settlers," drew up a list of rules, dated about 1830, that would be construed retrospectively to have had a "civilizing" effect on the settlers as worthy "ancestors" of the Anglo-Canadian population of the 1880s.

"Great mischief arises to the young timber and to the crops from the improper practices of allowing unringed pigs to roam at large. It is therefore directed that every individual finding these animals trespassing on his lands do seize the same for his own benefits; and the constables are further empowered and ordered to seize all unringed pigs which they may find straying in any part of the Settlement for their own use as a perquisite of office."

"Another highly improper practice is that of catching horses belonging to other people and riding or driving them to a distance, which if continued must be severely punished. Many settlers have been robbed of their horses by Indians; this arises in a great measure from their own cowardice, every man being equally justified in pursuing and firing upon a horse-thief as upon robbers entering his house by force."

"Some indolent persons it is observed very improperly throw out the manure from their stables upon the river during the winter season, thereby not only impoverishing their own land but driving away the sturgeon and other fish from the river; such highly reprehensible conduct shall be severely visited whenever it is repeated.

"The heathenish and blasphemous practices of conjuring over sick persons it is to be lamented still manifests itself from time to time in the settlement. It is therefore notified that any settlers who will hereafter dare to admit such devilish rites into their houses shall be banished from the colony and the pretending conjurors tried for their lives." ("Original Letters")

In the same vein, John MacBeth, lawyer and politician, and direct descendent of a settler who had arrived in the contingent of 1815, addressed the historical society in 1893 on "social customs and amusements of the early days in Red River Settlement and Rupert's Land."

John MacBeth: *Old Time Unions*: In these early days people were "married and given in marriage," and I believe the custom prevails even in our times of greater advancement and enlightenment; but O, what a different affair a wedding in the old times was to those of the present day!... A wedding in the olden times in the Red River settlement was not the tame affair of the present day. It did not consist in orange blossoms, ushers, a wedding breakfast, congratulatory speeches, wedding presents and last but not least, the orthodox honeymoon trip. A wedding breakfast they certainly had, and several of them for that matter, and dinners and suppers galore.

... These festivities have been known to go on with unabated vigor and joyous hilarity for three days and three nights. It is true they were rather hard on moccasins.... when I use the word "dancing" I mean "dancing": not the dances of modern days; no, instead of pianos and orchestras we had the good old fashioned fiddle, and always plenty of able and willing hands to play it. Instead of the effeminate, easy going and dreamy waltz, we had the always exciting and lively "Red River jig," which required not only skill to dance but lots of endurance as well; instead of the modern cotillion and quadrille we danced the ever reliable old Scotch reel or reel of four. (J. MacBeth)

Vera Kelsey: In the beginning, Red River Settlement was used as a synonym for the colony's changing names. Gradually, it became an inclusive title, synonymous with Assiniboia. When the settlement at the forks of the Red and Assiniboine Rivers reorganized and rebuilt after the Great Flood [1826], the British Protestant community on the west bank took back the name for its own use; the east bank settlement retained its parish name of St. Boniface. To clarify confusion, the following series of the original colony's changing names may be helpful: 1812, Point Douglas; 1813, Colony Gardens; 1817, Kildonan [described by the Free Press 1894 as "a rifle shot or so north of the Winnipeg City Limits"] 1826, Red River; 1858, Fort Garry — or Garry for short; 1873, Winnipeg. (Kelsey, 79)

MK: By 1885, Manitoba historian George Bryce, addressing the Manitoba Historical Society, could look back on seventy years of the settlement's broadly civilizing mission.

George Bryce: The old Red River life has gone never to return; a new Kildonan has spread itself out into Springfield, Sunnyside, Millbrook, Grassmore, Brant, Argyle, and elsewhere; a Boisbrule overflow has taken place to St. Albert, Batoche, Qu'Appelle, and to many a lonely lake and river in our North-west plains; the English halfbreed has hurried west to Edmonton, Prince Albert, and Battleford, to find a home like that on his old Red River. It will never be quite appreciated by those from abroad of later years what the Red River settlement did for us who succeed it. It marked the slow but sure process of an influence of Christianization and civilization of many of our Indians; it gave the introduction from a barbarous and wandering life to habits of order and settled work; it furnished a valuable pioneering and trading agency for the fur trade, for surveying our plains, and for our Canadian exploration; it gave us the nucleus of our present educational and religious organizations; it made the H.B. Co. not only a trading company, but a company helping forward in different lines the improvement of the Indians, and made them the friends of education and religion, and if I read the story of its history aright it saved to Britain and Canada, the vast Northwest which would otherwise not unlikely have met the fate of Oregon. (Bryce, "Old Settlers")

MK: In 1869, the Canadian government had purchased Rupert's Land from the Hudson's Bay Company. Métis uncertainty about securing title to their farmland, as well as fear of their marginalization, as

French-speaking Roman Catholic Mixed-bloods amid increasing immigration from Canada and the United States, had lain behind the so-called Red River Rebellion or Resistance of 1869–1870 under the leadership of Métis Louis Riel. In 1891, a mere twenty-one years after the ouster of Riel's provisional government and on the 75th anniversary of the Battle of Seven Oaks, a monument commemorating the battle, and now barely legible, was finally erected in Winnipeg (the oldest historic marker in Western Canada) at the intersection of Main Street and Rupert's Land Boulevard, approximately near the location of the battle, now a leafy neighbourhood north of the Forks.

Manitoba Historical Society, Annual Report for the Year 1889: The society has had under consideration the desirability of erecting, upon the site of that engagement, a monument to commemorate the battle of Seven Oaks. Arrangements for a plot of land upon the battlefield were made early in the year. Designs for the monument were invited, and it was ultimately decided to erect a plain stone shaft, to cost about $150. (Manitoba Historical Society)

George Bryce and Charles Bell: The monument is of native Selkirk stone, and the workmanship a credit to the designer, Mr. S. Hooper. It stands nine feet six inches in height, and its size is four feet at the base. On the top is carved a wreath of flowers. The inscription is on the west side, facing Main street. On the upper portion are carved the words, "Seven Oaks," and beneath is the inscription: "Erected in 1891 by the Manitoba Historical Society, through the generosity of the Countess of Selkirk, on the Site of Seven Oaks, where fell Governor Robert Semple and twenty of his officers and men, June 19th, 1816." (Bryce & Bell, in Blanchard, 89–90)

MK: Even if those who gathered to honour the occasion were not themselves direct descendents of the families of Red River in 1816 — many were English-speaking Protestants from Ontario, an immigration hostile to Catholicism and oblivious of Métis culture and history — they evoked that lineage in order to supersede it as "Canadians all," a solvent in which past differences would dissolve. (Lt-Gov John Schultz had played a leading role in opposing Riel's government.)

Lieutenant-Governor John Schultz: Mr. President and members of the Historical Society, Ladies and Gentlemen.... I see all around me here worthy children of such worthy sires, the descendents of those pioneer Selkirk settlers whose tale of sorrow, suffering and danger always evokes sympathy and wonder. Mr. President, we are, if I mistake not, near the place where the first plow turned the first furrow — presage of peace, plenty and prosperity — on the eastern verge of that vast prairie which extends to the Rocky Mountains; and having suitably marked the scene of battle, let us bury with the foundation of this monument the feuds, jealousies and strifes of the past which it recalls.... We are Canadians all, from the Atlantic to the Pacific, and we may look forward with that hope which is justified by the immensity and value of our resources, by the law-abiding, moral and religious character of our people (in Bryce & Bell; in Blanchard, 88-89)

Lyle Dick, interview: The dominant narrative which survived in the history books was the narrative of the Anglo-Canadian settlement group which arrived after 1870 who had no roots in western Canada. But because of the contested character of western Canadian lands, I believe it was necessary for this group of newcomers to establish a kind of bloodline, to legitimize their position in the west; and they looked back to the Selkirk settlers as their imagined ancestors. They wanted to set up their own dominance in western Canada, socially, economically, culturally, politically and so to me the Selkirk settlers were a passport to legitimacy as their adopted forbears.

MK: Winnipeg has sprouted various monuments that together amount to a commemoration in stone and text of settler history as it has been recalled from one generation to the next. The oldest Anglican parish west of the Great Lake, now St John's Cathedral, founded in 1820 on a site chosen by Lord Selkirk himself in 1817, has a graveyard adjacent that dates back to the first group of settlers in 1812.

On August 10, 1967, the Lord Selkirk Association of Rupert's Land, which "serves as a link to bind together the descendants of the hardy men and women who first settled on the banks of the Red River in the early 1800s, and to perpetuate the memory and preserve the spirit, traditions, and history of those first agricultural settlers," erected a monument on Winnipeg's Anderson Avenue to commemorate the Earl's meeting, near its location and 150 years after the event to the day, with his settlers "who had remained loyal during the troubled years of 1812–1817. In his memory and theirs this cairn is raised." (Goldsborough)

In 1987, the Association dedicated a cairn located in Joseph Zuken Heritage Park to the first planting of wheat – the bushel and a half of seed which Miles Macdonell had brought from Scotland – in the Selkirk Settlement, "recognized as the first European agricultural colony in the Western Interior of North America." (Goldsborough) In 2009, the descendents proved no less plucky than their forebears. From the Association's website: "I was thinking perhaps the 2 of us (great great, and great, great, great grand-daughters [of original settlers]) might somehow do some commemorative march on snowshoes? Anyone else interested in this idea? Say April 2012, from Churchill Creek to York Factory?"

On the 175th anniversary of the arrival of the Selkirk settlers, in 1993, another monument, located near the Alexander Docks, depicts a stylized Scots thistle, "the floral emblem of Scotland since ancient times," and is dedicated to Thomas Douglas, Fifth Earl of Selkirk, and marks the historical origins of Manitoba "as a European settled territory." (Goldsborough)

As for the man himself, Lord Selkirk Fifth Earl of Douglas, a monument was unveiled in October 1955. "In 1962, the city spruced up the triangle of land with 16 linden trees, a flagpole, benches and a cobblestone base.... Unfortunately, the Lord Selkirk monument has become so obscure now, the Winnipeg Arts Council asked if it could be moved to allow for a public art program. A civic committee denied the request." (Cassidy)

And what of the memory among today's Scots of Selkirk's accomplishment, namely the emigration to Red River of so many of the countrymen and countrywomen devastated by the Clearances? I looked for a commemoration in Scotland itself. In Kirkcudbright, the charming artists' colony across from Selkirk's birth place at Saint Mary's Isle on the southwest coast of Scotland, his family is principally recalled by the name of the Selkirk Arms Hotel, but he has his own modest plinth, placed near the Selkirk Memorial for a later Earl, James Dunbar, that stands at the corner of St Mary's and St Cuthbert's street in the big-treed park by the Kirk. It was erected in 1978 not by a local council but by the assiduous Historic Sites Advisory Board of Manitoba:

"This plaque erected in the memory of one of Kirkcud-bright's greatest sons Thomas Douglas 5th Earl of Selkirk. Born 1771 in St Mary's Isle. Lord Selkirk's attempts to settle land-less Scots overseas led to the founding of colonies in the present Canadian provinces of PEI, Ontario and Manitoba. In 1820 in the midst of legal disputes concerning his Red River settlement, Lord Selkirk died. Today, the centre of the original Red River settlement founded in 1812 forms part of Winnipeg. *Jamais arriere* [never back] *Firmior quo paratior* [the stronger the better prepared]."

In the Museum of the Isles in Armedale, Skye, I learn that "in North America the early settlers were faced with endless forest. Not for nothing did they call Canada 'Tir nach craobh' ('the land of the tree') and 'An Talamh fhuar' ('the cold land') and that emigrants to Canada made for Glengarry, Ontario; Pictou, Antigonish, and Cape Breton in Nova Scotia; and even Selkirk settlers to Prince Edward Island, but not a word of Red River. When Canadian writer Don Gillmor, with ancestral roots in the Highlands, rented a car and went in search of their home ground, he found a great vacancy.

Don Gillmor, author: A few kilometers down the road, at Ardlochy, there was the site of a settlement that had been razed during the Clearances. A large map indicated where the buildings had been. From the perspective of the map I looked down onto grass, toward hills — there was no rubble or unrestored remains, none of the usual historical evidence. The site had the framework of a tourist attraction — road signs, listings in books, historical plaques — but there was nothing, in effect, to see, just the negative space of what had vanished.... It seemed like the perfect memorial to emigration, the blankness a fitting monument. (Gillmor, 91)

MK: Not quite, as it happens. There is a memorial to emigration, a proper one, in Helmsdale, Sutherlandshire, unveiled in 2007 ("commissioned by Dennis MacLeod, who was born and brought up in Helmsdale before making his fortune in gold mining in South Africa"). The inscription on the monument, in Gaelic and English, reads, in the boilerplate prose of emigrant mythologizing everywhere: "The Emigrants commemorates the people of the Highlands and Islands of Scotland who, in the face of great adversity, sought freedom, hope and justice beyond these shores. They and their descendants went forth and explored continents, built great countries and cities and gave their enterprise and culture to the world. This is their legacy. Their voices will echo forever thro the empty straths and glens of their homeland."

In September 2008, a matching statue, known as the Selkirk Settlers Monument, was unveiled in Winnipeg. It depicts four figures, the very gendered nuclear family of settlement: the kilted man is looking ahead into an unknown future, while beside him a boy is looking up to him for guidance or reassurance. The woman, wrapped in a shawl, is holding a baby and is looking back towards the home they have been forced to leave. The monument, a project of the St Andrew's Society of Winnipeg ("the oldest continuing Scottish Society in Western Canada, founded in 1871"), "reflects the bravery, effort and sacrifice these peoples made in establishing Winnipeg, [and] will be placed upon the same river bank these people arrived at those many years ago. We trust you share in our feelings of admiration for such an accomplishment." (St. Andrew's Society)

Others of their descendants, as noted in the museum on Skye, expelled from the Red River settlement after the attacks of June 1815, had sunk new roots in Ontario. (Unmentioned are those Mixed-bloods of Scottish descent who made their way west from Red River, to establish settlements around Edmonton and on the Saskatchewan River.) Aberdeen writer David Craig, in *On the Crofters' Trail: In Search of the Clearance Highlanders*, "followed the grapevine," travelling from one informant to the next, relying as much on oral as documented history.

David Craig: The hundred and twenty people who left the Forks on June 15th, 1815 came east along what is now the Minnesota border, canoed by Lake Superior, "St Mary's River," and Lake Huron to Georgian Bay, landed at Penetanguishene, canoed down Lake Simcoe, and came ashore for good near Hollands Landing, fifteen miles from Mrs Reynolds's home. Her farmhouse is elegant and white among shade-trees; its land has been sold off for turf farms and dust now streams in dirt-coloured clouds from flayed fields. Mrs Reynolds's great-great-grandfather Robert Sutherland of Borobol in Strath Kildonan was married to Isabella Bannerman of Dirible by the first governor of the Red River settlement, Miles MacDonnell, at the Forks in January 1815. . . . Mrs Reynolds, tall and straight-backed in a gown of brown and black and cream, showed me her great-grandfather's plain silver communion cup, gave me tea in her great-grandmother's cup and saucer with handpainted flower design, and directed us to the West Gwillimbury graveyard where they were buried. . . . Beside a brick church with narrow shoulders, guarded against animals by a split-cedar fence, many 'Natives of Sutherlandshire' lay under marble stones the colour of old snow. (Craig, 231, 232)

MK: In recovering a "bloodline" in the Selkirk colony, one could go backward to the emptied-out village of the Highlands — or forward to the prodigious fertility of prairie wheat farms. In spite of HBC Governor (1820-1860) George Simpson's bluster that "there was no future in agriculture before the Canadian West," by 1915 the output of grain from the Canadian West was estimated at more than 500,000,000 bushels. (C. Martin, 181) "It may be said with a measure of truth that Selkirk in this respect builded better than he knew." (C. Martin, 183)

Grant MacEwan: If Canadian agriculture, through which the nation made its finest contribution to world needs, were to choose a Patron Saint or Founding Father, what candidate would have an equal claim upon the high honor? It would seem to belong to Thomas Douglas, 5th Earl of Selkirk.... What emerged at Red River was a gigantic pilot plant or experimental farm.... If the agricultural colony had the character of an experimental farm, Lord Selkirk was like the director of research, and was the author of nearly every facet of the experimental program.... Without him and his ambitious undertaking in settlement, the country would have remained in the selfish embrace of the fur trade much longer. (MacEwan, *Cornerstone Colony*, 5-6)

Jack Bumsted, interview: Lord Selkirk, *yes,* had a vision of agricultural colonization for crofters and Highlanders in North America. Did he have a vision for the vast fields of wheat in western Canada, the answer to that is probably not. He did have a vision of an agricultural colony in Red River — he had done the research, he knew the soil was good. He also, interestingly enough, knew that if he planted a colony at The Forks of the Red River, that the Americans were not likely to be able to move in and claim this territory. This was one of the reasons for the *size* of the grant that he had received.

And Selkirk was also very political and very cross with the British government. Selkirk was an imperialist in the worst/best sense of the word, whichever you want. And he was very cross with the British government for its failure really to appreciate that it had to be *doing* something in this vast expanse of wilderness. But, in any case, he didn't have a vision for waving fields of wheat but at the same time that vision got built into the story by those who write the history of the west and particularly of Manitoba at the end of the 19th century and the beginning of the 20th century. The guys who wrote this history were essentially white, Anglo-Saxon Protestant imperialists from eastern Canada and men like George Bryce told the story in ways which made Lord Selkirk out to be much more of a visionary than he was.

George Bryce: Lord Selkirk's scheme is dazzling almost beyond belief. A territory is his, purchased out and out, from the Hudson's Bay Company, about four times the area of Scotland, his native land, and the greater part of it fertile, with the finest natural soil in the world, waiting for the farmer to give a return in a single year after his arrival. A territory, not possessed by a foreign people, but under the British flag! A country yet to be the home of millions! It is worth living to be able to plant such a tree, which will shelter and bless future generations of mankind. (Bryce, *Romantic Settlement*, 43)

Celebrating 200 Years of Farming Experience: The farm lots were long and narrow, each with a river frontage of about 400 feet (six surveyor's chains), and all on the west side of the Red River. They extended about two miles into the prairie. The lots began at a line just south of the present Bannerman Avenue, and then were laid out, side by side, north to the place where the old Kildonan stone church was later built [near Frog Plain where Cuthbert Grant's party camped after the Battle], and then beyond to the present boundary of the City of Winnipeg. The lines of the streets in this part of Winnipeg, running slightly north of west, preserve the layout of the lots as they were surveyed by Peter Fidler, the Hudson's Bay Company surveyor, in 1817. (Red River 200)

MK: Two hundred years after the first implanting of the Scottish colonists, the mixed bloodline of Scotsmen and Aboriginal women that produced those other "visionaries" of the Red River, Métis such as James Isbister (Orkney father, Métis mother), James McKay (Scottish father, Métis mother), the myriad descendants of Peter Fidler, or indeed Cuthbert Grant, were no longer evoked. On his genealogical tour of the Highlands, Canadian writer Don Gillmor, chatting with a pub patron, found a new context for the bloodline.

Don Gillmor: We argued pleasantly for an hour about politics, television and global weather systems. He said it was a shame the way Canadians treated their natives. I pointed out that it was the Scots settlers who had first displaced the plains tribes from their land. Ironically, the Assembly of First Nations had recently toured the Highlands, meeting with the Scottish Crofters Union to compare their suffering and their shared sense of self-determination. The crofters apologized on behalf of the Scottish settlers who had left in the nineteenth century and appropriated native land. (Gillmor, 86)

Rev. R.G. MacBeth: **My father, who entered the colony in 1815, and never abandoned it or ceased being active in its life till that day when, at the age of ninety years, he passed away.... I can see him yet, a powerfully-built figure, in the old wooden armchair which is now one of my prized possessions. He would bring down his strong hand on the arm of the chair, as he told his story with Highland passion. I can hear the story flow on till he felt the inadequacy of language as recollections rushed upon him ... but there can be no two opinions as to the difficulties these colonists triumphantly battled with, and if you seek their monument, look around you on the religious and educational, as well as the material, greatness of the North-West. (R.G. MacBeth, 51–2)**

Métis Nation

Paul Savoie, poet, musician, editor: **Métis**

> **stands before each thing**
> **reconsiders**
> **mixed blood stirred**
> **stirred becomes one**
> **new blood**
> **métis looks**
> **métis breathes**
> **a dual stance**
> **suspended**
> **midway**
> **between le nouveau monde**
> **and the ancient promise**
> **(Savoie, trans. © Pierrette Requier)**

MK: The events surrounding the Fur Trade Wars, the Selkirk Settlement and
the Battle of Seven Oaks have long receded from living memory, but they have produced a rich legacy of *meaning* among the
communities who lay claim to historical memory – the Métis,
the descendants of European settlers, and, as we have seen, the
historians.

In the early days of contact between Indigenous peoples and
European fur traders, both groups saw advantages in the co-
habitation of Indigenous women and European men, namely the
development of relations with the women's tribal group and the
consolidation of commercial and trading transactions, on the one
hand; on the other, access to trade goods, language skills, and
familiarity with Euro-Canadian practices. (Devine, *The People*, 106)
As far back as the early days of the French regime in New France,
church-sanctioned intermarriage between the Europeans and the
Indigenous people had been actively promoted, as a non-violent
approach to conquest and occupation of foreign territory by the
creation of "one people." (Devine, *The People*, 35) As a result, by
1700 in the territory of New France there was already a mixed-
blood population, mainly adopted into Huron and Algonquin
groups, and known by the Algonquins as "wissakodewinmi,"
meaning "burned stick" or, in French, "bois-brûlé." (Purich, 16–18)

Fred Shore and Lawrence Barkwell write that the process by
which the *Métis* came into existence had to wait until French
voyageurs and coureurs de bois reached the area of the Great
Lakes. (Shore & Barkwell, 3) It is part of the history of western Canada that, as the fur trade expanded ever westward, these
mixed-blood people developed a distinct and territorial identity
as they formed communities on the open hunting and trading
grounds of Rupert's Land, notably around the Red and Assiniboine

River valleys, with their close family and economic ties with the North-West Company fur trade depots. But this identity had many stages to go through. Métis historian Heather Devine posits initial "proto-Métis" family groups, apart from the aboriginal parent band, but who "continued to cultivate aboriginal values, attitudes, and modes of behaviour." (Devine, *The People*, 107)

John Macdonnell of the NWC may have believed, contrary to all experience and observation, that "Red River is thinly inhabited, overrun by some rascally savages, and some Canadian Freemen and Half Breeds," (in J. Brown, 172) but he himself had a Métis country wife, Magdeleine Poitras, with whom he raised six children and moved with them and Magdeleine to a farm in Upper Canada upon his retirement. As historian Jennifer Brown points out, because of such intimate connections, the NWC could and did make the case that, at the time of violent conflict in the Red River, for all their ties of work and kinship with the fur traders, Cuthbert Grant and his troop "were defending an identity and interest of their own." In a letter of 14 March 1818, Nor'Wester William McGillivray wrote that "they one and all look upon themselves as members of an independent tribe of natives, entitled to a property in the soil, to a flag of their own, and to protection from the British government." (in J. Brown)

Fred Shore and Lawrence J. Barkwell: By 1810 the Métis were being referred to as the "New Nation" and the Wars were a direct cause of a growing Métis realization that they were, in effect, a Nation. During these pivotal years, the need to wage war, to defend their homes and to organize politically to protect their investment in the fur trade, radically increased the rate of Métis nation-building. (Shore & Barkwell, 4)

MK: The very early history of the Métis people in the Red River basin and the decades of competitive struggle between the HBC and the NWC for dominance in the fur trade in Rupert's Land meant that, in the evolution of Métis identity, Red River would represent a primordial homeland.

Rita Schilling, author: It was by instinct that Indians were drawn into the great basin of the Red River. It was by design that white men followed them. Here on this vast plain, covered with rich soil, grew hardy and succulent grasses for millions of buffalo. And here, where three great river basins, the Nelson, the St Lawrence and the Mississippi, joined, there grew a new people. ... The Metis population regarded themselves as "gens libres," Free Canadians, and because of their dark skins they were called the Bois Brules. They were muscular, active, excitable, imaginative, ambitious, passionate, restless, pleasure-loving and devout. They were equally skillful with horse, gun and paddle, masters of the art of trapping, and in the pursuit of buffalo they were "Prince of the Plains." (Schilling, 1, 2)

Adrian Hope, author: *Ode to the Métis*

The stalwart men of Scotland,
France and England too;
Adventure, fortune seeking
In this land so new.
The faint of heart never ventured;
The weak ones did not go,
The brave, the strong who entered,
Made this country grow.
They married Indian maidens,

The best ones they could find,
And built for them log cabins
And to them they were kind.
Their progeny, the Métis
Or Half-Breed if you will,
Had access to both cultures
And a special job to fill.
They had a happy, carefree life
Of living off the land.
And they had friends among the Whites
And every Indian band.
Red River, Manitoba
Became their native home
As hunters, traders, trappers
Throughout the west they'd roam.
They started a new nation
With equality for all . . .
The challenge now is different,
But whatever it might be,
We know that we will conquer.
We are the Great Métis. (Hope, 5)

MK: And, if the Red River valley was the heartland of the emerging Nation, the Battle of Seven Oaks, the climactic event of the struggle with the HBC and the Selkirk Colony, provided it its foundational "myth" of origin. As historian George F.G. Stanley asserted with all the confidence of a Euro-Canadian perspective, with the shots exchanged at Seven Oaks, "the métis became a people with a history." It was not a history or even story of a "miserable massacre" but of a "glorious victory" against a British occupation that would resound down the generations. (Stanley, 13) But it can also be argued, from the perspective of some Métis commentators, that "the Metis culture consisting of unique values, concepts, attitudes, behavior are but transitional stages as the Metis adopted what they conceded the best from their Indian, French and English cultures. This culture was evolving long before the Battle of Seven Oaks and continues to this very day." (Garneau)

A Métis priest's prayer: "Our Metis culture God is like the sash. The lives of the Metis have been woven together from a variety of cultures, traditions and beliefs.... For example, God, we are the descendants of the English, of the French, of the Indian-Cree and Ojibway and Scots to name a few. We speak a variety of languages: English, Canadian French, Michif French, Michif Cree and Mashkegon. Look at the sash: it is a composite. It is a mixture. It is Metis. It is made of a variety of elements, like the lives of the Metis. Look at its pattern, its fabric, its colors. Nonetheless, these disparate elements form an integrated whole. Similarly, the different ethnic backgrounds and different languages to the Metis blend into one another to form a rich tapestry like the lives and culture of the Metis." ("Métis Culture")

MK: Another potent symbol of *métissage* is the Métis flag, typically described as a banner of blue (associated with Métis employees of the NWC) or red (associated with those of the HBC) superimposed by a white infinity symbol that represents the notion of the unity of two cultures that will live on forever in its uniqueness. (According to Wikipedia, "the symbol is drawn from the mark made by Catholic and other missionaries in birth and baptismal church records, beginning in the 1600s, to denote a parent who was Indian.")

Maqtewekpaqtism: It is the oldest Canadian patriotic flag indigenous to Canada. The Union Jack and the Royal Standard of New France bearing the fleur-de-lis are older, but these flags were first flown in Europe. As a symbol of nationhood, the Métis flag predates Canada's Maple Leaf flag by about 150 years!

MK: It was the Métis riding with Captain Cuthbert Grant against the HBC who were first presented this flag in 1815 by NWC partner Alexander Greenfield Macdonell — according to University of Manitoba Archives and Special Collections, it was red — and so it remains fixed also as an icon of Seven Oaks.

Joseph Howard: The Nor'westers ... had done their work well. The new nation had been born, and like all infants it had quickly adapted itself to the pattern of its elders' thoughts. It had learned that land and water, the resources by which men lived, could be privately owned. And it had learned about race and color. (Howard, 37)

MK: Much has been made of the relationship between the Métis and their employers or associates, the NWC, in the development of "national consciousness" — that the Nor'Westers goaded the Métis into open conflict with the Selkirk settlement by insinuating their prior claim to the land of the Red River region through their mothers, that they militarized them (naming Cuthbert Grant "Captain-General of all the Half-Breeds" of an irregular Métis cavalry (Woodcock, "Grant") and even created a flag for them, and that, duped, the Métis served as" little more than the private army of the Northwesters." (Woodcock, Dumont, 29) The Métis are thus patronized as a people "captivated" by the simplicity of the sketchy argument for a national idea (Giraud, 408) and whose enthusiasm for it "was always ready to flicker or even to go out … without the artificial sustenance of external stimuli," such as the Nor'Westers' promise of loot from the settlement. (Giraud, 475) This perspective on the formation of their national identity has been much revised to account for Métis agency.

Fred Shore: In conclusion, it appears that the Métis were in fact slowly coming to national stature when they were rapidly and successfully stimulated to realize their potential and to accept the title and practice of nationhood. The suggestion may have come from certain NWC bourgeois but it fell on fertile ground and woke the people to the realization of who and what they were. (Shore, 81)

MK: As historian Heather Devine reminds us, when the Canadian government assumed control over Rupert's Land in 1870, the quite distinct populations of First Nations and Métis had to be enumerated and land claims settled, whether in the form of treaties with the Indian bands or "scrip" (title to individual plots of land) to the Métis population who had taken simple possession of land without legal title. (In any case, even after 1821, the HBC did not sell land to locals, only provided leases for 999 years.) More to the point, the settlement of land claims was meant to consolidate relations between the authorities in Ottawa and the Métis communities after the "rebellion" of Louis Riel's provisional government. The Manitoba Act of 1870 provided for a land deal in which 5,565 square kilometers of land were to be set aside for seven thousand children of the Red River Métis.

A mere seven years later in 1877, on the occasion of his visit to Manitoba, Frederick Temple Hamilton-Temple-Blackwood, 1st Earl of Dufferin, esteemd by Alexander Morris, Treaty

Commissioner, to have a "keen appreciation of men and facts," was pleased to observe that "there is no doubt that a great deal of the good feeling thus subsisting between the red men and ourselves is due to the influence and interposition of that invaluable class of men, the Half-breed settlers and pioneers of Manitoba, who, combining as they do the hardihood, the endurance and love of enterprise generated by the strain of Indian blood within their veins with the civilization, the instruction, and the intellectual power derived from their fathers, have preached the Gospel of peace and good will, and mutual respect, with equally beneficent results to the Indian chieftain in his lodge and to the British settler in the shanty." (in Morris, 293-4)

But it was not until the twenty-first century, generations removed from the Battle of Seven Oaks, that in 2013 the Supreme Court of Canada found that the federal government had failed, decade after decade, to follow through on the promised land settlement even though, in the view of the Court, "a timely implementation of land grants was crucial, given the imminent arrival of waves of North American and European settlers into Manitoba."

Gregory Scofield, poet:

> If I pull from this bag of rattling bones
> the fiddle, the bow bone,
> if I go down the lazy Red,
> lay singing in the grass
> will the faces of our ancestors
> take shape in the clouds
> and will the clouds name themselves,
> each river-lot stolen? (Scofield, 10)

CBC News: "Section 31 conferred land rights on yet-to-be-identified individuals – the Métis children," the ruling says. "Yet the record leaves no doubt that it was a promise made to the Métis people collectively, in recognition of their distinct community. The honour of the Crown is thus engaged here."

Manitoba Métis Federation President David Chartrand said he had been fielding emotional phone calls all morning. "Such pride at home right now, and tears are being shed. They're crying and they're phoning," Chartrand said. "They can't even talk on the phone properly because there's so much joy at home right now.... Our country did not give us any kind of credence and respect and felt they just could take whatever they wanted, and today our justice system is saying, 'No, you can't. You were wrong. Now fix it,'" said Chartrand. ("Métis celebrate")

Métis National Anthem: **Proud to be Métis**
We are proud to be Métis, watch our Nation rise again.
Never more forgotten people, we're the true Canadian.
From across the plain they traveled, from Red River to the Peace.
Looking for their homeland, that would help them to replace
All the land that had been taken, and the dreams that had been dashed.

Their brave heroes now called traitors, and courageous deeds now past.
But their spirit was not broken, and their dreams never died.

Their determination strengthened even while the people cried,
As they waited for the battle, that would end their years of pain.
And the final bloodless battle, when the Nation rose again.
("Metis Culture")

MK: As for legal *identity* as a people, in Canada's *Constitution Act* of 1982, under
section 35, Métis were included as one of the Aboriginal peoples of
Canada: 35 (2) *in this Act, the aboriginal peoples of Canada includes the
Indian, Inuit and Métis peoples of Canada*. This went some way to clear
up the ambiguities left after the Treaty negotiations in the 1870s
with First Nations in the North-West Territory but where, west of
Manitoba, no special enumeration of Métis communities had been
made of people who were no longer eligible for Manitoba scrip.

Alexander Morris, the Commissioner who had negotiated
those treaties on behalf of the Crown, wrote in 1880 of the "Half-
breeds" that they belonged to three "classes": those who have
farms and homes; those who are "entirely identified with the
Indians," living with them and speaking their language; those
whom he called the "wandering Half-breeds of the plains," chiefly
of French descent who live by the hunt of the (dwindling) buffalo
and have no settled homes. (Morris, 295)

But it would be the work of the Métis people themselves to
apply Section 35 of the Constitution Act to their communities.
In 2002, the Métis National Council invited those who qualify
to "register" as Métis.

In 2003, the Supreme Court of Canada confirmed that Métis
are a rights-bearing Aboriginal people and set out the compo-
nents of a Métis definition for the purpose of claiming Aboriginal
rights under section 35 of the *Constitution Act*, 1982. These are:
• Self-identification as a member of a Métis community.
• Ancestral connection to the historic Métis community whose
practices ground the right in question
• Acceptance by the modern community with continuity to the
historic Métis community. ("Citizenship")
But is it so clear cut? To register or not to register?

Tara Gereaux, author: Was I Métis because a plastic card said I was? I ignored the doubt at first, but it burrowed in. Got stuck. Then I learned from census statistics that the fastest-growing population in Saskatchewan is the Métis population — it doubled between 1996 and 2006. This growth has been attributed in part to people discovering their Métis heritage after a time in which it had been buried or forgotten, when racism and assimilation efforts made it shameful, and even dangerous, to self-identify.

I will never know exactly why and when my own family's Métis history was buried; I only know that it was. ... I thought about these census statistics, about all the people like me who had just discovered their history. Then I thought about all the people who have lived their entire lives as Métis. What do they think of people like me? ... But I began to realize that my own confusion and uneasiness regarding the Métis citizenship card in my possession stemmed from the fact that I didn't know anything about the group of people I was now supposed to belong to. I started to attend Métis cultural events and social gatherings. ...

During these past two years, I've gained knowledge about our country's history and my own history, I've become involved in the Métis community, and, most importantly, I've developed new relationships. These are the things helping me to discover my Métis-ness. Not the card. ... I know this is contradictory, and it's hard to reconcile. But personally, I have to honour my citizenship card because there's a journey behind it. A journey I'm still on. One that's leading me to a new way of being in the world. (Gereaux)

EPILOGUE

Don Freed, songwriter: "Bittersweet Oaks "
Oh my God!
Bitter-sweet oaks!
What's happened here today?
Such emotions!
Pray that time will take this taste away.

We were brave and we were angry
We were not in wrong.
Jubilations ... song of glory ... sing it
Loud and strong!

Comrades we have won the day
These intruders had to pay
We met their force and shot them down
It's quiet now ... there's not a sound
They lie in pieces on the ground
Pieces!

Oh my God!
Bitter-sweet oaks!
What's happened here today?
Such emotions!
Pray that time will take this taste away.
                    (Freed)

269

CHRONOLOGY

1670   Charter of the Hudson's Bay Company.

c. 1775   The Red River des Métis Settlement at The Forks of the Red and Assiniboine.

1783–84   Official organization of the North West Company in Montreal.

1805   Selkirk writes Observation on the Present State of the Highlands of Scotland.

1809   The NWC builds Fort Gibraltar at The Forks.

1811   Lord Selkirk acquires Grant of Assiniboia from the Hudson's Bay Company.

JULY 26   The Edward and Ann with working party sails for Hudson Bay from Stornoway, Lewis Island, Outer Hebrides.

1812

MAY   Cuthbert Grant leaves Montreal for Assiniboia.

JUNE   American troops en route to attack Montreal cut Nor'West's supply line.

271

JUNE 24   The Robert Taylor with first party of colonists sails for Hudson Bay from Sligo, Ireland

AUGUST 30   Stornoway workmen reach The Forks.

SEPTEMBER 4   Governor Miles Macdonell formally proclaims Point Douglas site of Red River settlement.

MID-OCTOBER   Sligo colonists reach The Forks.

NOVEMBER   All colonists and Macdonell winter over at Fort Daer, Pembina country.

1813   The Hudson's Bay Company builds Fort Douglas at The Forks.

MAY   Colonists return from Fort Daer to Point Douglas.

JUNE 28   The Prince of Wales with second party of colonists sails for Hudson Bay from Stromness, Orkney Island, Scotland.

1814

JANUARY 8   Gov. Macdonell issues Pemmican Proclamation, unleashes so-called Pemmican Wars.

JUNE-AUGUST   Stromness colonists arrive at The Forks.

JUNE 18   A temporary truce is negotiated between NWC and HBC.

JUNE 19   Chief Grandes Oreilles of the Saulteaux addresses NWC partners and servants at The Forks.

JULY 14   Macdonell announces a prohibition on the running of buffalo with horses near the settlement.

JULY 17   The Hadlow sails to Hudson Bay with the third party of colonists, mainly from Kildonan.

JULY   The NWC's annual general meeting at Fort William discusses strategy vis-à-vis the Selkirk colony.

AUGUST   Duncan Cameron and Alexander Greenfield Macdonell arrive at Fort Gibraltar.

FALL 1814   NWC factor Duncan Cameron at Fort Gibraltar appoints Cuthbert Grant and three others "captains of the Métis."

OCTOBER   Duncan Cameron repudiates the June compromise; Macdonell orders the Nor'Westers to quit Fort Gibraltar within six months.

1815

SPRING	Cuthbert Grant at Fort Gibraltar rallies the Métis.
MAY 19	Peter Fidler from Brandon House reports Selkirk colony horses shot.
JUNE	Duncan Cameron sends for Métis and freemen to attack colony.
JUNE 11	Colony is destroyed, Gov. Macdonell surrenders, and a large party of colonists leave for Upper Canada.
JUNE 25	Articles of Agreement entered into between the Métis and the Hudson's Bay Company re: dispersal of colony.
AUGUST 19	35 settlers return to the colony accompanied by Colin Robertson of the HBC.
OCTOBER 13	Chief Peguis visits settlement.
OCTOBER 15	Colin Robertson apprehends then releases Duncan Cameron.
NOVEMBER 3	Governor Robert Semple arrives at Fort Douglas with the party of Kildonan settlers.
NOVEMBER 15	Lord Selkirk arrives in North America.

1816

MARCH	Duncan Cameron names Cuthbert Grant "Captain-General of all the Half-Breeds."
MARCH 17	Colin Robertson seizes Fort Gibraltar.
APRIL	Settlers return from Fort Daer; Métis gather at Fort Qu'Appelle under Grant's command.
MAY 8	Grant's party ambushes boats of the HBC and seizes cargo.
JUNE 1	Grant and company capture Brandon House and its stores of pemmican.
JUNE 11	Semple destroys Fort Gibraltar.
JUNE 16	Métis forces reach Portage la Prairie.
JUNE 17	Semple learns that "histile force" is moving toward Fort Douglas.
JUNE 18	Grant's party moves to Frog Plain.
JUNE 19	Battle of Seven Oaks.
JUNE 20	Surviving settlers abandon colony for Jack River; Selkirk receives news of its destruction.
AUGUST 13	Lord Selkirk arrests Nor'Westers at Fort William.

1817

JUNE 21   Selkirk arrives at The Forks; settlers return from Jack River.

JULY 1   Selkirk with five Saulteaux and Cree chiefs including Peguis sign treaty.

JULY 5   Commissioner Wm. Coltman and party reach The Forks.

SEPTEMBER 1   Selkirk leaves Red River.

1818

JUNE 30   Commissioner Coltman submits his report.

OCTOBER   Trials relating to charges against both Lord Selkirk and the NWC open in Montreal and York.

NOVEMBER   Lord Selkirk leaves Canada.

1820

MARCH 12   Death of Sir Alexander Mackenzie.

APRIL 8   Death of Lord Selkirk.

1821

MARCH 26   Merger of HBC and NWC.

JULY   Cuthbert Grant is made HBC clerk and special constable at Fort Garry.

1854

JULY 15   Death of Cuthbert Grant

1869–70   The Hudson's Bay Company surrenders Rupert's Land back to the Crown.

BIOGRAPHIES OF CITED WRITERS

Howard Adams (1921–2001): **Saskatchewan-born Métis scholar and activist;
his great-grandfather stood with Louis Riel and Gabriel Dumont
during the Northwest Rebellion. Author of *Prison of Grass* and
A Tortured People.**

Amos, Andrew (1791–1860): **Lawyer and professor of law in England, published many works on legal, constitutional, and literary subjects,
including *Report of Trials in the Courts of Canada Relative to the
Destruction of the Earl of Selkirk's Settlement on the Red River*.**

Barkwell, Lawrence J. (1943–): **Author, lecturer, historical researcher. Editor and
co-editor of multiple collections on Métis history. Coordinator of
Metis Heritage and History Research for the Louis Riel Institute,
Winnipeg, and sits on the Board of Directors of the Friends of
Upper Fort Garry.**

Alexander Begg (1839–1897): **Born in Quebec City, moved west for business
reasons to the Red River settlement in 1867. Vigorous advocate for representative government for the people and was at first**

supportive of both the Métis and Hudson's Bay Company; later, editor of the *Victoria Daily News*.

Charles Napier Bell (1854–1936): Historian, author, co-founder of the Manitoba Historical and Scientific Society. Came to Manitoba in 1870 with the Wolseley Expedition, and kept a notebook entitled "Notes on the Red River Expedition, etc." Bell is credited with having introduced figure skating into western Canada; he once skated from Winnipeg to Selkirk on the Red River.

Ron Bourgeault (1943–): Professor of Sociology at the University of Regina; editor of *1492-1992: Five Centuries of Imperialism and Resistance*.

Jennifer Brown (1940–): Professor Emerita of History from the University of Winnipeg; Canada Research Chair, Aboriginal Peoples and Histories from 2004-2011; editor of such books as *Telling our Stories: Omushkego Lessons and Histories from Hudson Bay*, author of *Strangers in Blood: Fur Trade Company Families in Indian Country*.

George Bryce (1844–1931): Historian, educator, cleric. Co-founder of University of Manitoba, co-founder and President of Manitoba Historical and Scientific Society, President of Royal Society of Canada, and prolific writer on many subjects, including the history of the Selkirk Settlement.

A.H. Reginald Buller (1874–1944): Born in Birmingham, educated in London and Germany; moved to Manitoba in 1904 for a professorship. One of the University of Manitoba's first science professors; a botanist ironically plagued by asthma; also a writer of poetry and author of *Essays on Wheat*.

J (Jack). M. Bumsted (1938–): Historian of the fur trade in Canada; professor of history at Tufts University, Simon Fraser University, and University of Manitoba. Fellow of the Royal Society of Canada in 2003 twice awarded the J.W. Dafoe Book Prize. Lives with his wife in Winnipeg, where they own a bookstore.

Marjorie Wilkins Campbell (1901–1986): Author and editor. Recipient of two Governor General's Literary Awards for her books *The Nor'Westers: The Fight for the Fur Trade* and *The Saskatchewan.* Worked as consultant to the Ontario government on the restoration of Fort William.

David Craig (1981–): Author; Professor of creative writing, Lancaster University, England.

Andrew A. Den Otter (1941–2014): Professor Emeritus of History at Memorial University, conducted research on irrigation, coal mining, and railways in western Canada; his published works include *Civilizing the Wilderness: Culture and Nature in Pre-Confederation Canada and Rupert's Land.*

Heather Devine (1955–): Historian specializing in Canadian native history, American Indian policy, and western-Canadian ethnic history at the University of Calgary; author of *The People Who Own Themselves: Aboriginal Ethnogenesis in a Canadian Family, 1660–1900.*

Lyle Dick (1951–): Historian and author of over 100 publications on topics in Canadian and American history, historiography, and Arctic history; worked for Parks Canada for 35 years, and currently serves on advisory committees for the Canadian Museum of History and the National Capital Commission in Ottawa.

L'abbé (Georges) Dugas (1833–1928): Writer of western Canadian history, including the Riel rebellion, from a French Canadian perspective. Born in Lower Canada, Dugas travelled to Red River as a missionary in 1866, and offered a counter-perspective to Anglo-Canadian historians such as George Bryce.

Jay Edgerton (?): Staff writer for the *Minneapolis Star* in the 1950s.

Edward Ellice, Mercator (1783–1863): Born in England; a supplier for the North West Company; unsuccessfully tried to purchase the Hudson's Bay Company in 1804. Later played an active role in merging the rival companies in 1821, and his political connections were of great use to the new HBC.

Don Freed (1949–): Canadian singer-songwriter of Métis descent, best known for his music about life on the western Canadian prairies. His albums include *The Valley of Green and Blue*, which celebrates his heritage and Métis independence.

R.D. (Richard Dick) Garneau (1937–2015): Historian, and researcher; of Métis, American Indian, and European roots. Sought to trace the genealogy of his Métis clan of Garneau back to the first settlement in Canada. Made his research and writings public on his website in 1999, following the Metis tradition of "caring and sharing."

Rev. Alfred Campbell Garrioch (1848–1934): Anglican priest of mixed-blood roots, born at Kildonan, MB. Published translations into the

Beaver language and an English-Beaver and Cree dictionary. In retirement wrote *First Furrows* and *The Correction Line*.

Tara Gereaux (1975–): First novel, *Size of a Fist*, published in 2015. Her writing has won several non-fiction and screenwriting awards, including Event's 14th Annual Creative Non-Fiction Competition. From the Qu'Appelle Valley in Saskatchewan but currently resides in Regina.

Don Gillmor (1959–): Author, journalist, and writer of children's books. Wrote *Canada: A People's History*, which was also made into a documentary television series by CBC; he lives in Toronto.

Marcel Giraud (1900–1994): Professor and French colonial historian born in Nice, France. Hailed for his extensive and groundbreaking work on the French in Louisiana and the Métis in western Canada. Author of *The Métis in the Canadian West*.

Gordon Goldsborough (1959–): Environmental scientist, educator, historian, and active contributor of articles and databases for the Manitoba Historical Society.

John Morgan Gray (1907–1978): Publisher, author, soldier, professional hockey player, early biographer of Lord Selkirk; was president of Macmillan Company and worked to support authors of Canadian literature.

Donald Gunn (1797–1878): Left Scotland at age sixteen as an employee of the Hudson's Bay Company. After the HBC-NWC merger, settled in Red River, played a significant role in the community as a scientist, educator, and politician, and librarian of the only public collection of books in Red River.

James Joseph Hargrave (1841–1894): HBC trader, journalist, author; born at York Factory into upper class fur trading society, nephew of William Mactavish, governor of HBC and Assiniboia. Educated in Scotland, returned to Canada as a HBC employee to the Red River settlement in 1861.

Anne Matheson Gordon Henderson (1896–1985): Historian, active member of the Manitoba Historical Society, descendant of Red River settlers.

Douglas Hill (1935–2007): Writer and editor of books on fiction, non-fiction, science, and folklore, best known for his works of science-fiction and fantasy. Author of *The Opening of the Canadian West*.

Joseph Kinsey Howard (1906–1951): Renowned for historical and geographical writings about Montana, wrote landmark biography *Strange Empire: Louis Riel and the Métis People*.

Vera Kelsey (1891–1961): Born in Winnipeg, moved to North Dakota in 1900. Travelled extensively, drawing inspiration from many different areas of the world in her works of fiction, non-fiction, and mystery.

Howard Angus Kennedy (1861–1938): Journalist and writer; moved to Canada in 1881 to become a farmer, instead became a newspaperman and writer; worked in both Britain and Canada, and covered the Riel Rebellion for *Montreal Witness*.

Margaret Laurence (1926–1987): **Novelist, Companion of the Order of Canada. Born in Neepawa, educated in Winnipeg, lived and worked in Somalia and Ghana, which inspired her works of African fiction. Won two Governor General's Awards for her novels *A Jest of God* and *The Diviners*.**

Antoine S. Lussier (1947–): **Educator and historian; taught at the RCMP Academy in Regina and Brandon University, where he was Chairman of the Native Studies Department. Co-editor of several books with Bruce Sealey, including *The Métis: Canada's Forgotten People*.**

R.G. (Roderick George) MacBeth (1858–1934): **Presbyterian minister, historian, author, and lecturer. Born Red River settlement to Scottish immigrants who arrived alongside Lord Selkirk. Wrote accounts of social history at Red River as well as histories of the Canadian Pacific Railway and the RCMP.**

Grant MacEwan (1902–2000): **Lieutenant Governor of Alberta; also an agriculturalist and historian, and editor and contributor to several agricultural journals. Wrote *Grant MacEwan's West: Sketches from the Past, Cornerstone Colony: Selkirk's Contribution to the Canadian West*, and *Métis Makers of History*.**

James G. MacGregor (1905–1989): **Author and historian of Western Canada; Past-President of the Canadian Authors' Association, Member of Order of Canada; author of *Vilni Zemli: Free Lands — The Ukrainian Settlement of Alberta* and *Peter Fidler: Canada's Forgotten Explorer*.**

Hugh MacLennan (1907–1990): Novelist, essayist, Rhodes Scholar, professor of English at McGill University, three-time recipient of Governor General's Literary Award for fiction. Author of *Two Solitudes* and *The Watch That Ends the Night*.

Margaret Arnett Macleod (1877–1966): Historian and collector; first woman elected to the Council of the Champlain Society; first collector of indigenous Manitoba songs, which included the discovery of Pierre Falcon's ballad commemorating the Battle of Seven Oaks.

Chester Martin (1882–1958): Historian, professor; educated at Oxford University. Returned to Canada and worked in Public Archives, assembling *Lord Selkirk's Work in Canada*. Head of the History department at University of Toronto until his retirement in 1953.

Donald George McLean (1932–2012): Veteran, educator, historian, writer; worked for the Gabriel Dumont Institute, through which he published three books on Métis history, including *Home From the Hill: A History of the Métis in Western Canada*.

Donald McLeod (1779–1879): First wrote to the *Edinburgh Weekly Chronicle* in 1840–41 on the subject of the Highland Clearances, which displaced McLeod and his family from the Country of Sutherland. Eventually settled in Woodstock, Ontario, and published *Gloomy Memories in the Highlands of Scotland*.

Martin McLeod (1813–1860): From the Montreal area; traveled to Red River alongside James Dickson, who planned to recruit an army of Métis in the Texans' struggle against Mexico. His journal provides insights into winter living at the Red River settlement.

Kent McNeil (1945–): **Professor of Property Law, First Nations and the Law, and Trusts at Osgoode Hall Law School, York University; special research interests in indigenous rights, including land rights, treaty, and sovereignty; author of** *Emerging Justice? Essays on Indigenous Rights in Canada and Australia.*

A.G. (Adrien Gabriel) Morice (1859–1938): **French-born Oblate missionary, clergyman-historian, ethnographer. Recognized as Person of National Historical Significance for creating a writing system for the Dakelh language of the Dakelh (Carrier), a First Nations people of Northern B.C.**

A.S. (Arthur Silver) Morton (1870–1945): **Historian, lecturer, archivist. Arrived at the University of Saskatchewan in 1914, where he turned to western Canadian history, focused on the fur trade and the settlement of the prairies, best known for** *A History of the Canadian West to 1870-71.*

W.L. (William Lewis) Morton (1908–1980): **Historian, especially of Manitoba; head of History department at University of Manitoba, served on national committees and councils, including the Champlain Society and the Board of Directors for CBC; edited Alexander Begg's** *Red River Journal.*

Peter C. Newman (1929–): **Writer, journalist, biographer, Companion of the Order of Canada. Editor of** *Toronto Star* **and** *Maclean's,* **wrote biography of Prime Minister John Diefenbaker and a two-volume history of the Hudson's Bay Company,** *Company of Adventurers* **and** *Caesars of the Wilderness.*

John Perry Pritchett (1902–1981): **American historian, author of several books, including *The Red River Valley, 1811–1849: A Regional Study* and *Black Robe and Buckskin: The Story of Catholic Pioneering in Northern North America*.**

Alexander Ross (1783–1856): **Scots-born fur trader, schoolmaster, politician, author. After 1825, took on administrative roles within the Red River colony, married an Indigenous woman, with whom he had at least thirteen known children who were raised in Assiniboia. A prolific writer of the Northwest.**

E.S. (Edgar Stanford) Russenholt (1890–1991): **Author of *The Heart of the Continent: Being the history of Assiniboia — the truly typical Canadian community*, as well as successful children's texts, and articles for the Manitoba Historical Society. Also a historian, television personality, soldier, and homesteader.**

Paul Savoie (1946–): **French-Ontarian poet, musician, and editor born in Saint Boniface, now based in Toronto.**

Gregory Scofield (1966–): **Métis, poet, playwright, teacher, social worker; past writer-in-residence at Memorial University and University of Winnipeg, author of *The Gathering: Stones for the Medicine Wheel* and *Singing Home the Bones*.**

D. Bruce Sealey (1929–?): **Author of children's books and Métis history, including *Jerry Potts*, *Cuthbert Grant and the Métis (We Built Canada)*, *Statutory Land Rights of the Manitoba Métis*. Fluent in Cree, coauthored *The Métis: Canada's Forgotten People* with Antoine Lussier.**

Fred Shore (?): Educator, specializes in Métis history and political issues of the Inuit, First Nations and Métis peoples. Long-time advocate for Aboriginal affairs; worked for the Manitoba Métis Federation, currently teaches and the Department of Native Studies at the University of Manitoba.

Maggie Siggins (1942–): Author, film producer, journalist. Recipient of the 1992 Governor General's Award for her non-fiction work, *Revenge of the Land: A Century of Greed, Tragedy and Murder on a Saskatchewan Farm*. Author of the controversial biography, *Riel: A Life of Revolution*.

Alfred Silver (1951–): Canadian novelist, playwright, and songwriter who grew up in the prairies; primary publications include *Acadia, A Place Out of Time*, and *Red River Story* – part of his Red River Trilogy. He now lives in a farmhouse in Nova Scotia, where he continues to write historical novels.

George F.G. Stanley (1907–2002): Historian, author, soldier, teacher, public servant, and designer of the Canadian flag. Companion of the Order of Canada. Wrote *The Birth of Western Canada: A History of The Riel Rebellions* and *Toil And Trouble: Military Expeditions To Red River*.

Joseph Tassé (1848–1895): Writer, journalist, translator, historical researcher, politician; born at Laval, QC, later founding member of the Royal Society of Canada, appointed to the Senate in 1891.

Auguste-Henri de Trémaudan (1874–1929): **Resident of France, Saskatchewan, and Manitoba; collected numerous writings, rare documents, and oral testimonies about the history of the Métis.**

Samuel Hull Wilcocke (1766–1833): **Author, journalist; publicist for the North West Company during the Red River conflict with the H BC; his relationship with the N WC later changed; he was accused, imprisoned, and acquitted for suspicions of forgery and grand larceny against the Company.**

Beckles Willson (1869–1942): **Born in Montreal, international journalist, soldier, writer. Published works on Anglo-American relations and Canadian history include *Ypres* and *The Great Company: … Hudson's Bay.***

Louis Aubrey Wood (1883–1955): **Professor of Economics at University of Western Ontario and University of Oregon, author of *The Red River Colony: A Chronicle of the Beginnings of Manitoba*.**

WORKS CITED

Adams, Howard. *Prison of Grass: Canada From the Native Point of View*. Toronto: New Press, 1975.

Amos, Andrew, ed. *Report of Trials in the Courts of Canada, relative to the destruction of the Earl of Selkirk's settlement on the Red River: With observations*. London: John Murray, 1820.

Anderson, Grant. "The Buffalo Hunt." In *Métis Legacy: Michif Culture, Heritage and Folkways*. Eds. Lawrence J. Barkwell, Leah M. Dorion and Audreen Hourie. Saskatoon, SK: Gabriel Dumont Institute and Pemmican Publications, 2006. 208–212.

Barkwell, Lawrence J., ed. *The Battle of Seven Oaks: a Metis Perspective*. Winnipeg, MB: The Louis Riel Institute, 2014.

Barkwell, Lawrence J., Leah Dorion, and Darren R. Préfontaine. Eds. *Métis Legacy: A Metis Historiography and Annotated Bibliography*. Winnipeg, MB: Pemmican Publications, 2001.

"Battle of Seven Oaks National Historic Site of Canada." Parks Canada. Available at http://www.pc.gc.ca/apps/dfhd/page_nhs_eng.aspx?id=149

Begg, Alexander. "Early History of the Selkirk Settlement." In *Historical Essays on the Prairie Provinces*. Ed. Donald Swainson. Toronto: McLelland & Stewart, 1970. 1–17.

——— . *History of the North-West*. Vol. I. Toronto: Hunter, Rose & Co., 1894.

Blanchard, Jim, ed. *A Thousand Miles of Prairie: the Manitoba Historical Society and the History of Western Canada*. Winnipeg, MB: University of Manitoba Press, 2007.

Brown, Alice E. "A Brief Chronology of Events Relative to Lord Selkirk's Settlement at Red River–1811–1815." *Manitoba Pageant*, April 1962, Vol. 7, No. 3. Available at www.mhs.mb.ca/docs/pageant/07/selkirkchronology.shtml

Brown, Jennifer S.H. "Métis." The Canadian Encyclopedia. Historica Canada, 2009. Available at www.thecanadianencyclopedia.com

Bryce, George. *John Black: The Apostle of Red River.* Toronto: William Biggs, 1898.

——. "The Old Settlers of Red River." *MHS Transactions*, Series 1, No. 19, 1885. Available at www.mhs.mb.ca/docs/transactions/1/settlers.shtml

——. "Worthies of Old Red River." *MHS Transactions*, Series 1, No. 48, 1896. Available at www.mhs.mb.ca/docs/transactions/1/redriverworthies.shtml

——. *The Romantic Settlement of Lord Selkirk's Colonists.* Winnipeg, MB: Clark Bros & Co., 1909. Bryce, George, and Charles Bell. "Seven Oaks." In *A Thousand Miles of Prairie: the Manitoba Historical Society and the History of Western Canada.* Ed. Jim Blanchard. Winnipeg, MB: University of Manitoba Press, 2007. 64–93.

Bryce, George & Bell, Charles, eds "Original Letters and other Documents relating to the Selkirk Settlement.: In *MHS Transactions*, Series 1, No. 33, 1889. Available at www.mhs.mb.ca/docs/transaction/1/selkirkletters.html

Buller, Reginald. *Essays on Wheat.* In "From a single seed–Tracing the Marquis wheat success story in Canada to its roots in the Ukraine." Agriculture and Agri-Food Canada. Government of Canada: 2007. Available at www4.agr.gc.ca/AAFC-AAC/display-afficher.do?id=1181305178350&lang=eng

Bumsted, J. (Jack) M. "Sovereignty." Unpublished paper, 2007.

——. *Lord Selkirk: A Life.* Winnipeg, MB: University of Manitoba Press, 2008.

——. *Fur Trade Wars: The Founding of Western Canada.* Winnipeg, MB: Great Plains Publications, 1999.

——, ed. The Collected Writings of Lord Selkirk 1810–1820. Vol. II. Manitoba Record Society, 1988.

Campbell, Marjorie Wilkins. *The Nor'Westers: The Fight for the Fur Trade.* Toronto: Macmillan, 1962.

Cassidy, Christian. "Monument easy to miss: Tribute to our founder hidden away." *WinnipegFreePress.com.* Republished from the *Winnipeg Free Press* print edition: March 4, 2012 A1. Available at www.winnipegfreepress.com/local/monument-easy-to-miss-141343243.html

"Citizenship." Métis National Council. Available at www.metisnation.ca/index.php/who-are-the-metis/citizenship

Coltman, William B. *Papers Relating to the Red River Settlement.* Ottawa: House of Commons, July 12, 1819. Available at www.mocavo.com/Papers-Relating-to-the-Red-River-Settlement-Microform/151352/201#200

Craig, David. Letter to the Editor, *London Review of Books*, Vol. 33, No. 21. November 3, 2011. Available at www.lrb.co.uk/v33/n21/letters

——. *On the Crofters' Trail: In Search of the Clearance Highlanders.* London: Jonathan Cape, 1990.

Dalton, Roy C. in collaboration with. "Coltman, William Bacheler," in *Dictionary of Canadian Biography*. Vol. 6. University of Toronto/Université Laval. Available at www.biographi.ca/en/bio/coltman_william_bacheler_6E.html

De Chateaubriand, François-René. *Mémoires d'Outre-tombe*. Orig. trans. 1848. Book VII: Chapter 10: DIGRESSIONS. Available at poetryintranslation.com/PITBR/ Chateaubriand/ChateaubriandMemoirsBookVII.htm#_Toc116903535

Den Otter, Andrew A. *Civilizing the Wilderness: Culture and Nature in Pre-Confeder-ation Canada and Rupert's Land*. Edmonton, AB: University of Alberta Press, 2012.

Devine, Heather. "Ambition versus Loyalty: Miles Macdonell and the Decline of the North West Company." *New Faces of the Fur Trade – Selected Papers of the Seventh North American Fur Trade Conference-Halifax, Nova Scotia, 1995*. Eds. Jo-Anne Fiske, Susan Sleeper Smith, and William Wicken. East Lansing, Michigan: Michigan State University Press, 1998: 247–281.

———.*The People Who Own Themselves: Aboriginal Ethnogenesis in a Canadian Family, 1660 – 1990*. Calgary, AB: University of Calgary Press, 2004.

Dick, Lyle. "Historical Writing on 'Seven Oaks': The Assertion of Anglo-Canadian Cultural Dominance in the West," in Robert Coutts and Richard Stuart, eds. *The Forks and the Battle of Seven Oaks in Manitoba History*. Winnipeg, MB: Manitoba Historical Society, 1994.

———. "The Seven Oaks Incident and the Construction of a Historical Tradition, 1816 to 1970," *Journal of the Canadian Historical Association / Revue de la Société historique du Canada* 1991, New Series, Vol. 2, 1991. 91–113.

———. "The Seven Oaks Incident and the Construction of a Historical Tradition, 1816 to 1970," in: Catherine Cavanaugh and Jeremy Mouat, eds. *Making Western Canada: Essays on European Colonization and Settlement*. Toronto: Garamond Press, 1996, 1–30.

———. "The Seven Oaks Incident and the Construction of a Historical Tradition, 1816 to 1970," in Margaret Conrad and Alvin Finkel, eds. *Foundations: Readings in Pre-Confederation Canadian History*. Toronto: Pearson Longman, 2004, 254–72.

Dugas, l'Abbé G. *Histoire de l'Ouest canadien de 1822 à 1869: époque des troubles*. Montréal: *Librairie Beauchemin*, 1906.

Edgerton, Jay. "Introduction." *The Red River Settlement: Its Rise, Progress and Present State*. Minneapolis: Ross & Haines, 1957. Unpaginated.

Education Scotland. *"Red River Colony." Available at* www.educationscotland.gov.uk/ scotsandcanada/redrivercolony/index.asp

Electric Scotland. *Alberta, Past and Present, Historical and Biographical*. Vol 1. Ch. III. Available at www.electricscotland.com/history/canada/alberta/ vol1chap3.htm

Ellice, Edward. *The Communications of Mercator Upon the Contest Between the Earl of Selkirk and the Hudson's Bay Company, on One Side, and the North West Company on the Other*. Montreal: Printed by William Gray, 1817.

Foster, John E. "The Origins of the Mixed Bloods in the Canadian West." In *The Prairie West*. Eds. R. Douglas Francis and Howard Palmer. Edmonton, AB: Pica Pica Press, 1985. 86–99.

Freed, Don. "Bittersweet Oaks." Available at www.metismuseum.ca/resource.php/05243

Garneau, Richard (Dick). "Métis CULTURE 1812–1814; 1816–1817." *Canadian History: A Distinct Viewpoint*. Available at metis-history.info/metis-d.shtml

Garrioch, Rev. Alfred Campbell. *First Furrows: A History of the Early Settlement of the Red River Country*. Winnipeg, MB: Stovel Co. Ltd., 1924.

Gereaux, Tara. "Defining who is Métis: The Métis registry and politics of state recognition." In *Briarpatch Magazine*. January 1, 2013. Available at briarpatchmagazine.com/articles/view/defining-who-is-metis

Gillmor, Don. *The Desire of Every Living Thing: A Search for Home*. Toronto: Random House, 1999.

Giraud, Marcel. *The Métis in the Canadian West*. Vol 1. Trans. George Woodcock. Edmonton, AB: U of Alberta Press, 1986. Orig. 1945.

Goldsborough, Gordon. "Historic Sites of Manitoba." Manitoba Historical Society. Available at www.mhs.mb.ca/docs/sites/index.shtml

Gray, John Morgan. *Lord Selkirk of Red River*. East Lansing: Michigan State U Press, 1964.

Groome, Francis H., ed. "Parish of Kildonan." In *Ordnance Gazetteer of Scotland: A Survey of Scottish Topography, Statistical, Biographical and Historical*. Orig. published in parts by Thomas C. Jack, Grange Publishing Works, Edinburgh: 1882–1885. Available at www.scottish-places.info/parishes/parhistory121.html

Gunn, Donald. *A History of Manitoba from the Earliest Settlement to 1835*. Ottawa: MacLean, Roger, & Co., 1880.

Halkett, John. *Statement Respecting the Earl of Selkirk's Settlement Upon the Red River*. London, 1817. Reprint by Coles, 1974.

Hamilton, Gwain. *In the Beginning*. Steinbach, MB: Derkson Printers Ltd., n.d.

Hargrave, James Joseph. *Red River*. London: Stationers' Hall, 1871.

Henderson, Anne Matheson. "The Lord Selkirk Settlement at Red River." Parts 1–3. *Manitoba Pageant*, Autumn 1967–Spring 1968, Vol. 13, No. 1–3. Available at www.mhs.mb.ca/docs/pageant/13/selkirksettlement1.shtml

Hill, Douglas. *The Opening of the Canadian West*. London: Heinemann, 1967.

Hope, Adrian. "Ode to the Métis." October 1968. Reprinted with permission of Margaret Gross (Hope) in Mackay AB. In *Métis Legacy*. Vol. I. Eds. Lawrence J. Barkwell, et al. Winnipeg: Pemmican Publications, 2001.

Howard, Joseph. *Strange Empire: Louis Riel and the Métis People*. Toronto: James Lorimer & Co., 1974; Orig. 195.

Hunter, James. *Last of the Free: A History of the Highlands and Islands of Scotland*. Edinburgh: Mainstream Publishing, 1999. 2003 reprint.

Kelsey, Vera. *Red River Runs North!*. NY: Harper & Bros, 1951.

Kennedy, Howard Angus. *The Book of the West*. Toronto: Ryerson Press, 1935.

Lalonde, Marcia. "Battle of Seven Oaks: 1816." *Snapshots of 19th Century Canada*. The Critical Thinking Consortium, n.d. Available at marcialalonde.weebly.com/uploads/9/3/8/2/9382401/7_oaks.pdf

Laurence, Margaret. *The Diviners*. Toronto: McClelland & Stewart, 1974.

Lutz, Hartmut. "'Inventing' Canada's Aboriginal Peoples: Metis Moving From Invisibility to International Interaction." In *Contemporary Achievements: Contextualizing Canadian Aboriginal Literatures*. SALC Vol. 6 (Studies in Anglophone Literatures and Cultures), ed. Martin Kuester. Augsburg, Germany: Wissner-Verlag, 2015.

MacBeth, John. "Social Customs and Amusements of The Early Days in Red River Settlement and Rupert's Land." *MHS Transactions*, Series 1, No. 44, January 1893. Available at www.mhs.mb.ca/docs/transactions/1/socialcustoms.shtml

MacBeth, Roderick George. *The Selkirk Settlers in Real Life*. Toronto: W. Briggs, 1897.

MacEwan, Grant. *Grant MacEwan's West: Sketches from the Past*. Saskatoon, SK: Western Producer Prairie Books, 1990.

———. *Cornerstone Colony: Selkirk's Contribution to the Canadian West*. Saskatoon, SK: Western Producer Prairie Books, 1977.

MacGregor, James G. *Peter Fidler: Canada's Forgotten Explorer*. Calgary, AB: Fifth House, 1998.

Mackenzie, Alexander. *Voyages from Montreal ... in the Years 1789 – 1793*. Ed. Charles W. Colby. Toronto: Radisson Society of Canada, 1927.

MacLennan, Hugh. *Each Man's Son*. Toronto: Laurentian Library, Macmillan of Canada, 1972. Orig.1951.

Macleod, Margaret Arnett. *Songs of Old Manitoba*. Toronto: Ryerson Press, 1960.

Macleod, Margaret Arnett and William L. Morton. *Cuthbert Grant of Grantown: Warden of the Plains of Red River*. Toronto: McClelland & Stewart, 1963.

Manitoba. Historic Resources Branch. "First Farmers in the Red River Valley." Winnipeg, MB: Manitoba Tourism, Culture, Heritage, Sport and Consumer Protection, 1994.

Manitoba Historical Society. "MHA: Annual Report for the Year 1889." Available at www.mhs.mb.ca/docs/annual/1889.shtml

Maqtewekpaqtism. "Métis Nation (Canada)." CRW Flags Inc. www.crwflags.com/fotw/flags/ca_metis.html

Martin, Chester. *Lord Selkirk's Work in Canada. Oxford Historical and Literary Studies*. Vol. 7. Oxford: Clarendon Press, 1916.

Martin, Joseph E. "Conflict at Red River: Collision at Seven Oaks." In *The Forks and the Battle of Seven Oaks in Manitoba History*. Eds. Coutts, Robert, and Richard Stuart. Winnipeg MB: Manitoba Historical Society, 1994. Available at www.mhs.mb.ca/docs/forkssevenoaks/sevenoakscollision.shtml

———. "The 150th Anniversary of Seven Oaks," *MHS Transactions*, Series 3, No. 22, 1965–66. Available at www.mhs.mb.ca/docs/transactions/3/sevenoaks.shtml

Mays, Herbert J. "Macdonell, Miles," in *Dictionary of Canadian Biography*. Vol. 6. University of Toronto/Université Laval. Available at www.biographi.ca/en/bio/macdonell_miles_6E.html.

McLean, Donald George. *Home From the Hill: A History of the Métis in Western Canada*. Regina, SK: Gabriel Dumont Institute, 1987.

McLeod, Donald. *Gloomy memories in the Highlands of Scotland: versus Mrs. Harriet Beecher Stowe's Sunny memories in (England) a foreign land, or, A faithful picture of the extirpation of the Celtic race from the Highlands of Scotland.* Glasgow: A. Sinclair. 1892. Available at archive.org/details/donaldmcleodsglooomcleuoft

McLeod, Martin. "Buffalo Hunting in the West, from Martin McLeod's Journal." *Manitoba Pageant,* January 1957. Available at www.mhs.mb.ca/docs/pageant/02/buffalohunting.shtml

———. "The diary of Martin McLeod." St Paul, *Minnesota:* Minnesota *History Bulletin,* Vol. 4, 1921 – 22. 351 – 439.

McNeil, Kent. "Sovereignty and the Aboriginal Nations of Rupert's Land." *Manitoba History,* No. 37, Spring/Summer 1999. Available at www.mhs.mb.ca/docs/mb_history/37/aboriginalsovereignty.shtml

"Métis celebrate historic Supreme Court land ruling." *CBC News.* CBC/Radio-Canada: March 8, 2013. Available at www.cbc.ca/news/canada/story/2013/03/08/pol-metis-supreme-court-land-dispute.html

"Métis Culture: Métis Flag." French River Métis Tribe. Available at www.frenchrivermetistribe.ca/mtisculture.htm

"Métis Info. Series: The Battle of Seven Oaks." Métis Nation of Ontario, Region 4. Available at www.members.shaw.ca/mno-ssm/metis-info/seven-oaks.htm

Morice, Fr. Adrian-Gabriel. *L'Ouest canadien: Esquisse Géographique, Ethnographique, Historique Et Démographique.* Neuchâtel: P. Attinger, Société neuchâteloise de géographie, 1929.

Morris, Alexander. *The Treaties of Canada with the Indians of Manitoba and the North-West Territories.* Calgary, AB: Fifth House, 1991. Orig. 1880.

Morton, Arthur S. *A History of the Canadian West to 1870 – 71.* London: Thomas Nelson, 1937.

Morton, William L. *Manitoba: A History.* Toronto: University of Toronto Press, 1957. Reprinted with additions, 1970.

Newman, Peter C. *Caesars of the Wilderness.* Vol. II of *Company of Adventurers.* Viking Penguin, 1987.

Nute, Grace Lee, ed. *Documents Relating to Northwest Missions 1815 – 1827.* St Paul, Minnesota: Clarence Walworth Alvord Memorial Commission, 1942.

Oliver, Edmund H. ed. *The Canadian North-West, Its Early Development and Legislative Records.* Ottawa: Government Printing Bureau, 1914.

Payne, Michael. *The Fur Trade in Canada: An Illustrated History.* Toronto: James Lorimer & Co., 2004.

Peguis. "A Reply to the Selkirk Settlers' Call for Help." In *Manitowapow: Aboriginal Writings From the Land of Water.* Eds. James Sinclair Niigaanwewidam and Warren Cariou. Winnipeg, MB: HighWater Press, 2011.

Pelletier, Joanne. *The Skirmish at Seven Oaks.* Regina, SK: Gabriel Dumont Institute, 1985. www.metismuseum.ca/resource.php/03153

Pritchett, John Perry. *The Red River Valley 1811 – 1849: A Regional Study.* New Haven: Yale University Press, 1942.

Public Archives of Canada. *Red River Settlement: Papers in the Canadian Archives Relating to the Pioneers*. 1910. Reprint. London: Forgotten Books, 2013.

Purich, Donald. *The Métis*. Toronto: James Lorimer & Co., 1988.

Redbird, Duke. *We are Métis: A Métis View of the Development of a Native Canadian People*. Willowdale, ON: Ontario Métis and Non Status Indian Association, 1980.

Red River 200. www.redriver200.ca. Inactive link. Accessed January 28, 2015.

Robertson, Colin. "Excerpts from the journal of Colin Robertson." Ed. Alice E. Brown. *Manitoba Pageant*, September 1962, Vol. 8, No. 1. Available at www.mhs.mb.ca/docs/pageant/08/robertsonjournal.shtml

Robinson, Henry Martin. *The Great Fur Land: Or Sketches of Life in the Hudson's Bay Territory*. New York: Putnam's Sons, 1879.

RootsWeb Ancestry. "Métis 1818–1820." n.d. Available at www.rootsweb.ancestry.com/~mnrrvn/Metis-1818–1820.html

Ross, Alexander. *The Red River Settlement: Its Rise, Progress and Present State*. Minneapolis: Ross & Haines, 1957; orig. 1856.

Russenholt, Edgar S. *The Heart of the Continent: Being the history of Assiniboia – the truly typical Canadian community*. Winnipeg, MB: MacFarlane Communication Services, 1968.

Savoie, Paul. *Bois Brûlé*. Montreal: Editions du Noroît, 1989.

Schilling, Rita. *Gabriel's Children*. Saskatoon Métis Society, 1983.

Scofield, Gregory. "Women Who Forgot the Taste of Limes." *Singing Home the Bones*. Vancouver: Polestar, 2005.

Sealey, Bruce, and Antoine Lussier. *The Métis: Canada's Forgotten People*. Winnipeg, MB: Pemmican Publications, 1975.

Selkirk, Thomas Douglas, Fifth Earl of. *Observation on the Present State of the Highlands of Scotland*. London: Longman, Hurst, Rees and Orme, 1805.

———. *On the civilization of the Indians in British America*. London: Printed by J. Brettell, 1816. Available at peel.library.ualberta.ca/index.html

———. *The Memorial of Thomas Earl of Selkirk*. Montreal: Printed by Nahum Mower, 1819.

Shore, Fred J. "The Origins of Métis Nationalism and the Pemmican Wars, 1780–1821," in *The Forks and the Battle of Seven Oaks in Manitoba History*. Eds. Robert Coutts and Richard Stuart. Winnipeg: Manitoba Historical Society, 1994.

Shore, Fred J., and Lawrence Barkwell. *Past Reflects the Present: The Métis Elders' Conference*. Winnipeg, MB: Manitoba Métis Federation, 1997.

Siggins, Maggie. *Marie-Anne: The Extraordinary Story of Louis Riel's Grandmother*. Toronto: McClelland & Stewart, 2008.

Silver, Alfred. *Red River Story*. New York: Ballantine, 1990.

St. Andrew's Society of Winnipeg. "Selkirk Settlers: An Introduction to the Selkirk Settlers." 2011. Available at standrews-wpg.ca/history/selkirk-settlers.cfm

Stanley, George F.G. *Manitoba 1870: a Métis Achievement*. Winnipeg, MB: University of Winnipeg Press, 1972.

Still, Gary. "The First Red River Churches and Schools St Boniface And Kildonan, 1812–1823," in *Red River Ancestry.ca*. Available at www.redriverancestry.ca/

Strachan, John. "A letter to the Right Honourable the Earl of Selkirk, on his settlement at the Red River, near Hudson's Bay." London: Printed for Longman, Hurst, Rees, Orme & Brown etc., 1816. Available at peel.library.ualberta.ca/index.html

Swainson, Donald, ed. *Historical Essays on the Prairie Provinces*. Toronto: McLelland & Stewart, 1970.

Tassé, Joseph. *Les Canadiens de l'ouest*. Montréal: Cie. de l'Imprimerie canadienne, 1878.

Trémaudan, Auguste Henri de. *Histoire de la nation métisse dans l'ouest canadien*. Montréal: Editions Albert Lévesque, 1935.

Thompson, Arthur N. Rev. *The Expansion of the Church of England in Rupert's Land From 1820 to 1839 under the Hudson's Bay Company and the Church Missionary Society*, Thesis, University of Cambridge 1962.

Warren, Jim, and Kathleen Carlisle. *On the Side of the People: A History of Labour in Saskatchewan*. Regina, SK: Coteau Books, 2005.

West, John. *A Journal of the Reverend John West*. In Gary Still, "The First Red River Churches and Schools St Boniface And Kildonan, 1812–1823." Available at www.redriverancestry.ca/

Wilcocke, Samuel Hull. *A Narrative of Occurrences in the Indian Countries of North America Since the Connexion of the Right Hon. The Earl of Selkirk with the Hudson's Bay Company ... and Subsequent Proceedings at Fort William, in Upper Canada*. London, 1817; rep. SR Publishers, 1968.

——. *Report of the Proceedings Connected with the Disputes Between the Earl of Selkirk and the North-West Company, at the Assizes Held in York in Upper Canada, October 1818: from minutes taken in court*. Montreal: Printed by James Lane & Nahum Mower 1819. Available at peel.library.ualberta.ca/index.html

Willie, Richard A. "WEST, JOHN." In *Dictionary of Canadian Biography*. Vol. 7. University of Toronto/Université Laval. Available at www.biographi.ca/en/bio/west_john_7E.html

Willson, Beckles. *The Great Company: being a history of the Honourable Company of Merchants-Adventurers Trading Into Hudson's Bay*. Toronto: Copp, Clark, 1899. Available at www.forgottenbooks.com/readbook_text/The_Great_Company_1667–1871_v2_1000188524/235

Wood, Louis Aubrey. *The Red River Colony: A Chronicle of the Beginnings of Manitoba*. Toronto: Brook & Co., 1915. Available at canadiangenealogy.net/chronicles_canada.htm

Woodcock, George. *Gabriel Dumont: The Métis Chief and his Lost World*. Edmonton: Hurtig Publishers, 1976.

——. "Grant, Cuthbert (d. 1854)." In *Dictionary of Canadian Biography*. Vol. 8. Toronto: University of Toronto/Université Laval. Available at www.biographi.ca/en/bio/grant_cuthbert_1854_8E.html

——. "Translator's Introduction," in Marcel Giraud, *The Métis in the Canadian West* vol 1. Trans. George Woodcock. Edmonton, AB: University of Alberta Press, 1986. Orig. 1945.

FURTHER READING

Anonymous. "The Canadian Boat Song." Electric Scotland. Available at www.
    electricscotland.com/poetry/canadian_boatsong.htm
Archives of Manitoba. Province of Manitoba, 2015. Available at www.gov.mb.ca/chc/
    archives/
Barkwell, Lawrence J., ed. *The Battle of Seven Oaks: a Metis Perspective*. Winnipeg,
    MB: The Louis Riel Institute, 2009.
Barkwell, Lawrence J., Leah M. Dorion, and Audreen Hourie. Eds. *Metis Legacy*.
    Vol. II: *Michif Culture, Heritage and Folkways*. Saskatoon, SK: Gabriel Dumont
    Institute and Pemmican Publications, 2006.
Barron, Frank L. *Victimizing His Lordship: Lord Selkirk and the Upper Canadian
    Courts*. Manitoba History, Number 7, Spring 1984. Available at www.mhs.
    mb.ca/docs/mb_history/07/victimizinglordship.shtml
Begg, Alexander. In *Alexander Begg's Red River Journal, and Other Papers Relative to
    the Red River Resistance 1869 – 70*, edited by W.L. Morton. Toronto: Champlain
    Society, 1956.
Bell, Charles Napier. *The Earliest Fur Traders on the Upper Red River and Red Lake,
    Minn. (1783 – 1810)*. Winnipeg, MB: Saults & Pollard Ltd., 1926.
Bourgeault, Ron G. 1492 – 1992—*Five Centuries of Imperialism and Resistance*.
    Winnipeg, MB: Society for Socialist Studies. Halifax, N.S.: Fernwood, 1992.
Brown, Jennifer S.H. *Strangers in Blood: Fur Trade Company Families in Indian
    Country*. Vancouver: University of British Columbia Press, 1980.
———. "North West Company." *The Canadian Encyclopedia*. Historica Foundation,
    2007. www.thecanadianencyclopedia.ca
Bryce, George. *Manitoba Its Infancy, Growth and Present Condition*. London:
    Sampson, Low & Searle, 1882.

Bumsted, J (Jack). M. "Another Look at the Founder: Lord Selkirk as Political
Economist." In *Thomas Scott's Body: And Other Essays on Early Manitoba
History*. Winnipeg, MB: University of Manitoba Press, 2000. 37–56.
——— . *Dictionary of Canadian Biography*. Winnipeg, MB: University of Manitoba,
1999.
——— . *The People's Clearance: Highland Emigration to British North America,
1770 – 1815*.
——— . *Trials and Tribulations: The Red River Settlement and the Emergence of
Manitoba 1811 – 1870*. Winnipeg, MB: Great Plains Publications, 2003.
——— . "Trying to Describe the Buffalo: An Historiographic Essay on the Red River
Settlement." In *Thomas Scott's Body: And Other Essays on Early Manitoba
History*. Winnipeg, MB: University of Manitoba Press, 2000. 11–36.
Dictionary of Canadian Biography. University of Toronto/Université Laval, 2003–
2013. www.biographi.ca/
Dugas, l'Abbé G. Trans. J.M. Morice. *The First Canadian Woman in the Northwest*.
Winnipeg, MB: Historical and Scientific Society of Manitoba, 1902.
Ens, Gerhard J. *Homeland to Hinterland: The Changing Worlds of the Red River Métis
in the Nineteenth Century*. Toronto: University of Toronto Press, 1996.
Francis, Daniel. *Battle for the West: Fur Traders and the Birth of Western Canada*.
Edmonton: Hurtig Publishers, 1982.
Friesen, Gerald. *The Canadian Prairies: A History*. Toronto: University of Toronto
Press, 1987.
——— ."'Justice Systems' and Manitoba's Aboriginal People." *River Road: Essays on
Manitoba and Prairie History*. Winnipeg, MB: University of Manitoba Press,
1996.
Gagné, Peter J. *French-Canadians of the West: a biographical dictionary of French-
Canadians and French Métis of the western United States and Canada*. Paw
Tucket, Rhode Island: Quintin Publications, 2000.
Garry, Nicholas. *Diary of Nicholas Garry, Deputy-Governor of the Hudson's Bay
Company from 1822 – 1835: a detailed narrative of his travels in the Northwest
Territories of British North America in 1821*. Originally published in 1900 in the
transactions of the Royal Society of Canada. Available at peel.library.ualberta.
ca/bibliography/142.html
Gordon, Irene. *The Battle of Seven Oaks*. Canmore, AB: Altitude Publishing, 2005.
Gutteridge, Don. *Riel, a Poem for Voices*. Fredericton: Fiddlehead Poetry Books,
1968.
Harmon, Daniel Williams. *A Journal of Voyages and Travel in the Interior of North
America*. Orig. 1820.
Healy, William J. *Women of Red River: Being a book written from the recollections of
women surviving from the Red River era*. Winnipeg, MB: Peguis Publishers, 1970.
Orig. 1923.

Henderson, Anne Matheson. "The Lord Selkirk Association of Rupert's Land." *Manitoba Pageant*, April 1962, Vol. 7, No. 3. Available at www.mhs.mb.ca/docs/pageant/07/selkirkassociation.shtml

Hill, Robert B. *Manitoba: History of Its early Settlement, Development and Resources.* Toronto: W. Briggs, 1890.

Historica Canada. The Canadian Encyclopedia. Historica, 2015. Available at www.thecanadianencyclopedia.com

Huck, Barbara, ed. *Crossroads of the Continent: A History of The Forks of the Red and Assiniboine Rivers.* Winnipeg, MB: Heartland Associates, n.d.

Hutchison, Bruce. *The Unknown Country: Canada and Her People.* Toronto: Longman, Green and Co., 1946.

Innis, Harold. *The Fur Trade in Canada.* Toronto: University of Toronto Press, 1956.

Jackson, James A. "The Pemmican War." *The Centennial History of Manitoba.* Winnipeg, MB: Manitoba Historical Society, 1970. 49–54.

Jackson, John C. *Jemmy Jock Bird: marginal man on the Blackfoot frontier.* Calgary: University of Calgary Press, 2003.

Klinck, Carl F. "Wilcocke, Samuel Hull," in *Dictionary of Canadian Biography*, vol. 6, University of Toronto/Université Laval. Available at www.biographi.ca/en/bio/wilcocke_samuel_hull_6E.html.

Kroll, Charlene. "The man after whom Chief Peguis trail is named." Canstar Community News. Online ed. February 2, 2013. Available at www.winnipegfreepress.com/our-communities/herald/correspondent/The-man-after-whom-Chief-Peguis-trail-is-named-190895051.html

Kuester, Martin, ed. *Contemporary Achievements: Contextualizing Canadian Aboriginal Literatures.* SALC Vol. 6 (Studies in Anglophone Literatures and Cultures). Augsburg, Germany: Wissner-Verlag, 2015.

"La chanson des Bois-Brûlés." Societé historique de St-Boniface, 2010. Available at shsb.mb.ca/node/374

Ladd, George van der Goes. *Shall We Gather at the River? Toronto: United Church of Canada,* 1986.

Lee, Mary Madeline. *The New Nation – Christ's Chosen People.* 1987. Publisher unknown.

Lord Selkirk Association of Rupert's Land. *Selkirk Settlers of Red River and Their Descendants* 1812 – 1997. Winnipeg, MB: Lord Selkirk Association of Rupert's Land, 1997.

Macdonald, Sharon. "The Gaelic Renaissance and Scotland's Identities." *Scottish Affairs.* No. 26, Winter 1999. Available at scottishaffairs.org/backiss/pdfs/sa26/sa26_Macdonald.pdf

MacKinnon, Iain. "Crofters: Indigenous People of the Highlands and Islands." Scottish Crofting Foundation, 2008. Available at www.crofting.org/uploads/news/crofters-indigenous-peoples.pdf

MacLennan, Hugh. "The Red." *The Seven Rivers of Canada.* Toronto: Macmillan, 1961.

Macleod, Margaret Arnett. "Legend of White Horse Plain." *Manitoba Pageant*, Vol. 3, No. 2, January 1958.

——."Life in the Early West." *MHS Transactions*, Series 3, 1947–48 Season. Available at www.mhs.mb.ca/docs/transactions/3/earlywestlife.shtml

Manitoba Historical Society. *Memorable Manitobans*. MHS, 2015. Available at www. mhs.mb.ca/docs/people/index.shtml

"Map of 1817, showing Lord Selkirk's Grant of 116,000 square miles, known as Assiniboia, including The Forks." Image. Wikipedia Commons, 2015. Available at en.wikipedia.org/wiki/File:Selkirks_land_grant_(Assiniboia).jpg

Matheson, Rev. Samuel P. "Introduction." In Roderick G. MacBeth. *The Romance of Western Canada* Toronto: Ryerson Press, 1920.

Mathews, Robin. *Selkirk*. Toronto: Steel Rail Educational Publishing, 1977.

McDonald, Archibald. *Reply to the Letter, Lately Addressed to the Earl of Selkirk, by the Hon. And Rev. John Strachan*. London: W. Gray, 1816.

McGillivray, Simon. Edited by Jean Morrison. *The Northwest Company in Rebellion: Simon McGillvray's Fort William Notebooks, 1815*. Thunder Bay, ON: Thunder Bay Historical Museum Society, 1988.

McGoogan, Ken. *Ancient Mariner*. Toronto: HarperCanada, 2003.

——. *How the Scots Invented Canada*. Toronto: HarperCollins, 2010.

"Métis people (Canada)." Wikipedia, 2015. Available at en.wikipedia.org/ wiki/M%C3%A9tis_people_(Canada)

Morice, Fr. Adrian-Gabriel. *Histoire abrégée de l'ouest canadien: Manitoba, Saskatchewan, Alberta et Grand-Nord*. St-Boniface, MB: the author, 1914.

Owram, Doug. *Promise of Eden: The Canadian Expansionist Movement and the Idea of the West, 1856 – 1900*. Toronto: 1980. See pages 85, 92, 192–216.

Pannekoek, Frits. "The Historiography of the Red River Settlement." *Prairie Forum*, Vol. 6, No. 1, 1981. 75–85.

——. *A Snug Little Flock: The Social Origins of the Riel Resistance of 1869 – 70*. Winnipeg, MB: Watson & Dwyer, 1991.

Payment, Diane. *"The free people – Otipemisiwak," Batoche, Saskatchewan, 1870 – 1930*. Ottawa: National Historic Parks and Sites, Parks Service, Environment Canada, 1990.

Peers, Laura. "The Ojibwa, Red River and The Forks 1770–1870." In *The Forks and the Battle of Seven Oaks in Manitoba History*. Eds. Robert Coutts and Richard Stuart. Winnipeg, MB: Manitoba Historical Society, 1994.

Peter Fidler. Winnipeg, MB: Historic Resources Branch, 1984.

Pierre Falcon. Winnipeg, MB: Historic Resources Branch, 1984.

Prud'homme, Louis Arthur. *L'Engagement des Sept Chênes: Mémoires de la Société Royale du Canada*. Ottawa: Printed for the Royal Society of Canada, 1918.

Racette, Calvin. *Flags of the Métis*. Regina, SK: Gabriel Dumont Institute, 1987.

Rasky, Frank. *The Taming of the Canadian West*. Toronto: McClelland & Stewart, 1967.

"Red River Colony." Wikipedia, 2015. en.wikipedia.org/wiki/Red_River_Colony

"Red River: First Farmers." Canadian Geographic Education, 2015. Adapted from *First Farmers in the Red River Valley*, Historic Resources Branch, Manitoba Culture, Heritage and Citizenship, 1994. Available at www.cgeducation.ca/resources/rivers_of_canada/red_river/first_farmers.asp

"Red River Settlement: The Selkirk Settlers." *Canada: A People's History*. CBC, 2001. Available at www.cbc.ca/history/EPCONTENTSE1EP6CH5PA2LE.html

Redbird, Duke. "I am a Canadian." Presented at Queen Elizabeth's Silver Jubilee, 1977. Available at hrsbstaff.ednet.ns.ca/mdejong/i_am_a_canadian%20poem.htm

Ross, Eric. *Beyond the River and the Bay by "Alexander Bell Robertson, the imaginary writer of this book."* Toronto: University of Toronto Press, 1970.

"The Royal Charter for incorporating the Hudson's Bay Company, A.D. 1670." Posted by William F. Maton, 1997. The Solon Law Archive. Available at www.solon.org/Constitutions/Canada/English/PreConfederation/hbc_charter_1670.html

Sangster, Charles. "The Red Men–A Sonnet." In *The Penguin Treasury of Popular Canadian Poems and Songs*. Ed. John Robert Colombo. Toronto: Penguin, 2002.

Schmidt, Louis, "Preparation of pemmican/taureau," cited in *Pemmican*. www.saskschools.ca/~mandelassash/newsite/metisfacts

Schofield, Frank Howard. *The Story of Manitoba*. Winnipeg, MB: The S.J. Clarke Publishing Company, 1913.

Sealey, Bruce. *Statutory Land Rights of the Manitoba Metis*. Winnipeg, MB: Manitoba Metis Federation Press, 1975.

———. ed. *Stories of the Métis*. Winnipeg, MB: Manitoba Metis Federation Press, 1975.

Selkirk, Thomas Douglas, Fifth Earl of. *A Sketch of the British Fur Trade of North America*. London: James Ridgeway, 1816. Available at www.canadiana.org/view/21028/9

Shore, Fred J. "Developing Métis Law, 1700–1868," in *Past Reflects the Present: The Metis Elders' Conference*. Winnipeg, MB: Manitoba Métis Foundation, 1997.

———. "The Origins of Métis Nationalism and the Pemmican Wars, 1780–1821." In *The Forks and the Battle of Seven Oaks in Manitoba History*. Eds. Robert Coutts and Richard Stuart. Winnipeg, MB: Manitoba Historical Society, 1994.

"Speech of His Honor Lieutenant-Governor Schultz on the Occasion of his Unveiling the Monument Erected by the Manitoba Historical Society, near the Old King's Highway, to Commemorate the Battle of Seven Oaks, 19th June 1891." Pamphlet. Winnipeg, MB: Manitoba Free Press Print, 1894.

Spragge, George Warburton, ed. *The John Strachan letter book: 1812 – 1834*. Toronto: The Ontario Historical Society, 1946.

The Project Gutenberg eBook, The Romantic Settlement of Lord Selkirk's Colonists, by George Bryce. Project Gutenberg, 2005. Available at www.gutenberg.org/files/17358/17358-h/17358-h.htm

Thompson, David. *David Thompson's Narrative of His Explorations in Western America 1784–1812*. Ed. J. B. Tyrrell. A Facsimile Edition. New York: Greenwood Press 1968. Originally published as Champlain Society Publication XII, Toronto, 1916.

Thompson, John Herd. *Forging the Prairie West*. Oxford: Oxford University Press, 1998.

Tuttle, Charles R. "Life of Hon. Donald Gunn." In Donald Gunn, *A History of Manitoba from the Earliest Settlement to* 1835. Ottawa: Maclean, Roger & Co., 1880. ix-xvii.

Vandiveer, Clarence A. *The Fur Trade and Early Western Exploration*. New York: Cooper Square Publishers, 1971.

Waterson, Elizabeth. "John Galt and 'The Lone Shieling'." N.d. Available at canadianpoetry.org/volumes/vol6/waterston.html

Wiebe, Rudy. *The Scorched-Wood People*. Toronto: McClelland & Stewart, 1977.

PERMISSIONS

Excerpts from Heather Devine's "Ambition versus Loyalty: Miles Macdonell and the
Decline of the North West Company" and *The People Who Own Themselves:
Aboriginal Ethnogenesis in a Canadian Family, 1660 – 1990* are reprinted with
kind permission from Heather Devine.

Excerpts from Lyle Dick's "Historical Writing on 'Seven Oaks': The Assertion of
Anglo-Canadian Cultural Dominance in the West" and "The Seven Oaks
Incident and the Construction of a Historical Tradition, 1816 to 1970" are
reprinted with kind permission from Lyle Dick.

Within are excerpts from "First Farmers in the Red River Valley," reprinted by
permission of Historic Resources Branch, Manitoba.

Lyrics of Don Freed's *Bittersweet Oaks* were reprinted with kind permission from
Don Freed.

Excerpts from Tara Gereaux's "Defining who is Métis: The Métis registry and politics
of state recognition" are reprinted with kind permission from Tara Gereaux.

Excerpts from Don Gillmor's *The Desire of Every Living Thing: A Search for Home* are
reprinted with kind permission from Don Gillmor.

Excerpts from Marcia Lalonde's "Battle of Seven Oaks: 1816" are reprinted by
permission of The Critical Thinking Consortium.

Excerpts from Margaret Laurence's *The Diviners* are reprinted by permission of
Penguin Random House Canada.

Excerpts from Hartmut Lutz's "Inventing' Canada's Aboriginal Peoples: Metis
Moving From Invisibility to International Interaction" are reprinted with kind
permission from Helmut Lutz.

Excerpts from J.G. MacGregor's *Peter Fidler: Canada's Forgotten Explorer* are
reprinted by permission of the publisher.

Excerpts from Hugh MacLennan's *Each Man's Son* are reprinted with kind
permission from Sharon Ellis.

Excerpts from Kent McNeil's "Sovereignty and the Aboriginal Nations of Rupert's Land" are reprinted with kind permission from Kent McNeil.

Excerpts from Peter Newman's *Caesars of the Wilderness* were reprinted with permission from Penguin Random House Canada.

Within are excerpts from *Ordnance Gazeteer for Scotland*, reprinted by permission of Bruce M. Gittings, Editor.

Excerpts from Duke Redbird's *We are Métis: A Métis View of the Development of a Native Canadian People* are reprinted by kind permission of Duke Redbird.

Excerpts from Bruce Sealey's and Antoine Lussier's *The Métis: Canada's Forgotten People* are reprinted with permission from Pemmican Publications.

Excerpts from Fred Shore's "The Origins of Métis Nationalism and the Pemmican Wars, 1780–1821" are reprinted with permission from the Manitoba Historical Society.

Excerpts from Alfred Silver's *Red River Story* are reprinted with kind permission from Alfred Silver.

Excerpts from Jim Warren's and Kathleen Carlisle's *On the Side of the People: A History of Labour in Saskatchewan* are reprinted with kind permission from Jim Warren.

IMAGE CREDITS

Chapter One: "Thomas Douglas, 5th Earl of Selkirk, 1771–1820." Source: Glenbow Museum, Call Number: NA-2247-1

Chapter Two: "Colonists on the Red River in North America, ca. 1822" Source: Library and Archives Canada/Peter Rindisbacher collection/c001937

Chapter Three: "Old Fort Douglas, Red River 1815" Source: Library and Archives Canada/c-018184

Chapter Four: "Buffalo Hunting in the Summer, ca. 1822" Source: Library and Archives Canada/David Ives Bushnell collection of Canadiana/c-114472

Chapter Five: "Winter fishing on ice of Assynoibain & Red River, 1821" Source: Library and Archives Canada/Peter Rindisbacher collection/e011161354

Chapter Six: "The Fight at Seven Oaks, 1816" Source: Library and Archives Canada/ Charles William Jefferys fonds/e010999518

Chapter Seven: "Cuthbert Grant" Source: Archives of Manitoba, Kerr, John 5 (N12762)

Chapter Eight: "A halfcast [Métis] and his two wives" Source: Library and Archives Canada/Peter Rindisbacher collection/c-046498

Chapter Nine: Métis flag is public domain.

INDEX

Page numbers in italics refer to illustrations.

land title
  formal possession of Assiniobioa by HBC (1812), 42–44, 51
  HBC assumption of private property, 211
  HBC land grant to Selkirk, 24, 51
  HBC land title under Charter, 25–26
  historiography of Métis, 231–32
  Indigenous traditional territory, 189
  Métis inclusion/exclusion from, 114, 189, 231–32, 245–46, 263–65
  Peguis on, 106
  river lot system, 186–87
  Selkirk land treaty (1817), 187–89, 274
  territorial imperative, 235
  See also law and legal issues
languages, 43, 85, 86, 192, 208
LaRocque, Emma, 231
Latour, J. Baptiste, 169
Laurence, Margaret
  biographical notes, 281
  excerpts from The Diviners, 20, 33, 63, 170–71
law and legal issues
  co-existence of Indigenous and European law, 7–8
  early views on idea of law, 70, 198
  HBC Charter, 4, 25–26, 201
  illegal free fur trade, 212, 215
  lack of courts in Assiniboia, 198
  lawsuits for/against HBC and NWC (1817), 197–98
  Métis "laws" of the hunt, 14–15
  monopoly rights of HBC, 4
  NWC and British legal authority, 70–71, 74, 82–83, 107, 177
  political background in Upper Canada, 197, 202–4
  river lot system, 186–87
  See also Charter, HBC; land title; trials
Letendre, Joseph, 156
Lockport archaeological site, 16–17
Lord Selkirk Association, 248
Lussier, Antoine S., 5, 138, 156, 189, 281, 284
Lutz, Hartmut, 235

MacBeth, John, xix, 187, 243–44
McBeth, Robert, 150
MacBeth, Roderick George
  biographical notes, 117, 281
  excerpts by, 14–15, 25–26, 117, 187, 256
McDermott, Andrew, 47
Macdonald, Alexander, 162
Mcdonald, Archibald, xix, 60
McDonald, John, xix, 73–74, 82, 177, 202–3
Macdonell, Alexander Greenfield (NWC)
  biographical notes, xix, 41, 83
  ambush of HBC boats (1816), 135–36
  burning of colony, 106–7, 114–15
  capture of Fort Douglas, 145
  excerpts by, 83–84, 128, 129, 133, 137, 145
  Indian relationships, 97

  invitation to Saulteaux to attack colony (1816), 137–38
  with Métis forces, 144
  Métis national identity, 75–77, 96, 128, 262
  NWC loyalty, 41
  Pemmican War, 83–84, 84–85, 199
  personal traits, 84–85
Macdonell, Allan, 177
Macdonell, Anthony, 155
Macdonell, John, xix, 34, 83, 258
Macdonell, Miles (HBC)
  biographical notes, xix, 33, 83
  accompanies first colonists (workmen), 37–47
  arrest by NWC (1815), 81, 82, 100, 111, 204
  authority of, 70–71, 74, 82–83
  Coltman Report on, 199
  criminal charges against, 204–5
  emigration agent, 33–37
  excerpts by, 40, 42, 45–46, 48, 62–64, 66, 71, 82, 104
  food shortages and supplies, 62–64, 70–71
  formal possession of RR, 42–44
  governor of Assiniboia, 88–89, 104
  mental stress, 82–83, 88
  Métis relations, 71–72, 75–76, 114
  military power, 71, 88, 96
  in Pembina area, 45–46
  Pemmican Proclamation, 65–66
  personal traits, 33–34, 37, 39, 74, 82, 123
  surrender to NWC (June 1815), 100
  See also Pemmican War
MacEwan, Grant, 45, 61–62, 141, 161, 253, 281
McGillis, Hugh, 177, 202–3
McGillivray, Simon, xx, 35, 104, 107, 211
McGillivray, William (NWC)
  biographical notes, xx
  Cuthbert Grant's guardian, 78
  excerpts by, 101, 258
  merger of NWC and HBC, 211
  Pemmican War, 83–84
  repossession of Fort William (1817), 184
  Selkirk's arrest of (1816), 176–78
  views on Métis, 258
  witness at trial for murder of Semple, 202
MacGregor, James G., 38, 96–97, 101–2, 108, 281
Machicabou (Stepping Ahead or Starts to Stand), Chief, 136, 153–54
MacKay, Elizabeth, 97
McKay, James, 255
MacKay, John, 97, 119
McKay, Thomas, 135–36
M'Kay, Daniel, 155
Mackenzie, Sir Alexander (NWC)
  biographical notes, xix
  death of, 206, 210
  defender of Nor'Westers, 25
  influence on Selkirk, 18–19
  plan to buy HBC, 22

Born and raised in Edmonton, Alberta, award-winning non-fiction writer Myrna Kostash is the author of ten books, including *All of Baba's Children* and *The Doomed Bridegroom: A Memoir.* In addition to contributing articles to magazines such as *Geist, Canadian Geographic,* and *Literary Review of Canada,* Kostash has written radio documentaries and theatre playscripts. Her creative non-fiction has appeared in numerous Canadian and international anthologies, such as *The Thinking Heart: Best Canadian Essays, Slice Me Some Truth: An Anthology of Canadian Creative Nonfiction, Desire: Women Write About Wanting, Literatura na S'wiecie* (Warsaw), and *Mostovi* (Belgrade).

A founder of the Creative Nonfiction Collective, Kostash has also served as president of the Writers' Guild of Alberta and as chair of the Writers' Union of Canada. In 2008 the Writers Guild of Alberta presented her with the Golden Pen Award for lifetime achievement, and in 2009 she was inducted into the City of Edmonton's Arts and Culture Hall of Fame. In 2010 she received the Writers' Trust of Canada Matt Cohen Award. Her latest book, *Prodigal Daughter: A Journey into Byzantium,* was released in 2010 by the University of Alberta Press. She is at work on a public family history about her grandparents.